OUTDOOR LIFE
THE SPORTSMAN'S AUTHORITY SINCE 1898

ON THE EDGE

TRUE TALES OF
HIGH ADVENTURE FROM
Outdoor Life's
BEST STORYTELLERS

CREATIVE
PUBLISHING
international

MINNETONKA, MINNESOTA

Creative Publishing international, Inc.
5900 Green Oak Drive
Minnetonka, MN 55343
1-800-328-3895

CREATIVE
PUBLISHING
international

Chairman: Iain Macfarlane
President/CEO: David D. Murphy
Vice President/Retail Sales & Marketing: James Knapp
Director, Creative Development: Lisa Rosenthal

ON THE EDGE
Executive Editor, Outdoor Group: Don Oster
Senior Editor & Project Leader: David R. Maas
Managing Editor: Jill Anderson
Associate Creative Director: Brad Springer
Copy Editors: Janice Cauley, Hazel Jensen
Mac Designers: Joe Fahey, Patricia Goar
Production Services Manager: Kim Gerber

Printed on American paper by: R. R. Donnelley & Sons Co.
10 9 8 7 6 5 4 3 2 1

The Library of Congress Cataloging-in-Publication Data

On the edge : true tales of high adventure from Outdoor life's
    best storytellers.
      p.   cm.
    ISBN 0-86573-105-5
      1. Hunting Anecdotes. 2. Hunting stories. 3. Fishing Anecdotes.
    4. Fishing stories. I. Creative Publishing International.
    II. Outdoor life (Denver, Colo.)
    SK33.05 1999
    799--dc21   99-32155

Outdoor Life is a Registered Trademark of Times Mirror Magazines, Inc., used under
license by Creative Publishing international, Inc.

Table of Contents

Introduction

*L*ike most old outdoorsmen, I survived my share of close calls and narrow escapes. I fell over cliffs, came within a breath of drowning and dodged the bullets of a too-excited hunter. And what could have been more dramatic than lying sprawled—as I did—within a few yards of a tremendous and suspicious Kodiak grizzly that padded almost up to where I lay face down at the rim of an Alaska island. I can only thank my Guardian Angel that the huge bear had approached from the downwind side and that it moved on in the same direction.

That's the stuff suspense is made of.

I sold my first story to *Outdoor Life* in 1935. From that date I was a continuous contributor to the magazine on a free-lance basis, until I was employed full time as one of its Field Editors. This was in 1950 and, though I retired as an active employee in 1973, I continue to be on the staff as a regular contributor. During those early years, my assignments, either proposed by the editors or at my suggestion, carried me from one end of the western hemisphere to the other. I hunted or fished in all of the states and provinces and many of the South American countries and islands on my side of the world. Fortunately, I always came back to my Georgia home in one piece and was able to sit down to my old manual typewriter and recount one or two experiences from each adventure.

Whatever period of life we are in, whether our creative days are just beginning or close to the end, many of us (me included!) would give whatever chance we have for peaceful eternity for the privilege of stepping back into the past to share in the magnificent adventures recounted here by some of the colorful outdoorsmen in the early years of the century. We are blessed to have many of those eloquent years recorded in the pages of *Outdoor Life*.

I am convinced that the editors of Creative Publishing international have here created a treasury of the world's most classic adventure stories on hunting, fishing and the outdoors. Those skilled in literary gems have predicted that *On the Edge* will stand high in the titles of America's most thrilling pieces of literature.

Charles Elliott

Danger in the Field

A TITLE WITH wonderful double meaning, "Brave Was My Dog" appeared in the February 1962 issue of *Outdoor Life*. "Brave" was the author's dog. And the dog was brave. Bravery granted the hound a life; bravery took it away. And because of Brave, Steve Matthes lived to tell the tale.

Matthes was a full-time professional lion hunter for the California Department of Fish and Game when Brave was born to Matthes'

A Brave REMEMBRANCE

by Larry Mueller

bitch, Belle. In a litter of 11 other red pups, Brave had peculiar dun hair that was somewhere between rough and smooth. Because he knew that no "bad blood" could have gotten into the line, Matthes picked up the pup, thinking that it would have to be destroyed. At the last moment, however, he was diverted by Belle's pleading eyes.

That evening Matthes was called to eliminate a sheep-killing lion 500 miles away on the eastern slope of the Sierra Nevada. When he returned several weeks later, the odd pup had grown odder still. The pup was all legs and eyes. One ear lay like a hound's; the other tried to stand up. Matthes' wife, Vera, and son, Eddie, had become fascinated with the "funny little dog," as they called him, but Matthes didn't share their enthusiasm.

Early the next morning, Matthes walked to the kennel for one last look before the inevitable. The alert "funny pup" boiled out of the box to greet him with luminous, penetrating dark eyes that seemed to convey almost human intelligence. Suddenly, from that small throat came the loudest bawl Matthes had ever heard from a pup. In disbelief, he made a quick step toward the pup to evoke another response. Instead of jumping back and barking like a normal pup, this strange little fellow held his ground, bristled a bit, and bellowed again.

Matthes opened the gate. The whole litter, led by the precocious pup, raced 100 yards to the cage housing Matthes' pet mountain lion, Cleo. In seconds the pup located Cleo on her ledge and began baying. When the other pups joined in half-heartedly, Cleo charged the tiny pack. All of the pups, save the peculiar one, scattered like quail. The odd pup held his ground, tail between his legs and hair bristling, yet trying to bite Cleo through the wire. Angered, Cleo tried to bite back, caught her teeth in the mesh, and was bitten in the nose by the young hound. Matthes broke up the fight and carried the pup back to the kennel, with his opinions and intentions completely reversed.

Matthes had started in hounds with a bitch that traced back to Ben Lilly's lion and bear pack. To her genes—and those of her descendants—he had added the blood of hounds from the famous lion packs of Carl Hurt, Jay Bruce, Wiley Carroll, Jack Butler, the Lee brothers, Smokie Emmett and Gus Landergen. He had bred only lion dogs to lion dogs. In the mid-1940s, he'd intensified his line with an inbreeding program designed to produce natural lion hounds— hounds with an affinity for lions, the kind of affinity that bird dogs have for birds and beagles for rabbits. In this weird little pup, it appeared that he had accomplished that aim. Matthes left the kennel wondering about a name. Nothing seemed to fit.

At breakfast, Eddie asked how to go about naming something that looked like the pup. Vera, picking up dishes, said, "Well, the funny little thing surely is brave."

"That's it," Eddie exclaimed. "That's his name—Brave!"

STEVE MATTHES BRED LION DOGS to lion dogs in an effort to produce a line of hounds that had a natural affinity for chasing cougars.

At 5 ½ months, Brave was in the pack on a three-day lion chase. The older hounds' pads were cut and worn by shale, so Matthes called a halt, welcoming a rest himself. Instead, he was jerked awake by Brave's almost hysterical bawling at something in the dark. Throughout the night Brave would quiet briefly, only to resume baying.

Exhausted from lack of sleep, but curious, Matthes untied Brave and his sire, Red, soon after dawn. It was a lion that Brave had smelled down in the gorge. The pair treed the cat out of hearing behind a ridge. Two hours later, Matthes found them and shot the lion. When the skinning was finished, Matthes ordered the dogs to come along, and started for camp. Brave struggled to his feet and collapsed, leaving Matthes to carry a lion hide and a 25-pound hound through thick brush and 110° heat.

Brave went on to enjoy a long career as Matthes' all-time best lion dog. When other hounds' feet would give out after several days on a lion they couldn't jump or tree, Brave would have two or three days of running left. He could move a two-day old track as if it were eight hours old. His early mad courage later became tempered with caution. Speed and alertness made him outstanding on lions that would not tree. He'd dart in, bite and leave an empty hole in the air before the lion could spin around. Brave was indeed a natural lion dog.

I was anxious to see the descendants of this brave hound. It was 1990. We couldn't chase California's protected lions, but Matthes, now well into his 70s, had invited me along on a bear hunt. Mostly, however, I wanted to meet the man. I had read the book he wrote, also called Brave, and the more I'd read, the more fascinated I'd become.

Matthes had wonderfully exciting stories to write, but they weren't just tales. Matthes is an extremely intelligent, deep feeling, courageous and especially perceptive houndsman. He learns from his experiences.

While trailing a cat into what he calls Medicine Flat, for example, Matthes began to notice an unusual number of old scats. They all contained great amounts of the wire grass prevalent in the area. Also prevalent in those scats were large numbers of dead tapeworms.

Matthes had plenty of time to watch as his hounds old-trailed through the low valley—a strange place for a cat to go. Lions love the rocky high places. Sure enough, Matthes found fresh scats from the lion that his hounds were chasing. These scats, too, contained wire grass and tapeworms. After the lion was jumped, treed and dispatched, Matthes made a careful examimation of its intestines. Only a few short tape worm segments remained attached. This explained why every lion he'd killed had had several tapeworms, but none had suffered the great infestations noticed in domestic cats. The lions knew how to cure themselves. Our dogs probably eat grass for similar reasons.

I tried to catch Matthes on my way to Oregon. He wasn't home. On my way back, he was in San Bernardino. A month later I caught up with Matthes in Arizona. California had gotten too crowded for his brother Jack, so Jack had bought a place near Camp Verde. Steve was there to help him unpack.

My wife and I arrived just ahead of the movers, who dumped everything on the ground and left. Matthes has one leg shorter than the other—plus constant pain—due to a wreck with a dog, a horse and a bear. He says that it makes the hills steeper. On that day, though, he grabbed one end of a piece of furniture, so I grabbed the other. With all of us working, we hauled everything inside before the predicted rain. And thus began the interview of a lion, jaguar and bear hunter who has spent a lifetime being hard to catch at any one spot.

We didn't get to hunt. I didn't get to meet Matthes' three remaining hounds. But for three days my recorder and I were privy to the experiences of a man who has truly enjoyed life, who is clever and clear-minded enough to have been anything he desired, but who chose an adventurous life above monetary wealth. The older we grow, the more we realize that success has been in the living experiences, not in the counting of numbers in a ledger. And nothing focuses so clearly on what is genuine than a confrontation that threatens to steal what really counts.

This happened to Matthes in the rugged California coastal range between Santa Barbara and Ventura. With Brave and the rest of his pack, Matthes was cold-trailing the biggest lion of his career. As he was fighting his way through the thick, semitropical brush, he suddenly heard Brave break over the main ridge, hot behind the jumped cat. Matthes stopped. The chase was coming straight down the ridge toward him.

Matthes heard feet in the leaves, and the gigantic lion came into view. It stopped in a small, 20-foot clearing, breathing too heavily to go on. And there wasn't a tree tall enough to climb within a half-mile. Matthes was struck with fear. If he didn't get that lion first, it could easily kill his entire pack.

Matthes arrived at one side of the clearing at the moment Brave got to the other. He squeezed the trigger just as the lion sprang. It was a miss. But the cat turned toward the blast in midair, and Brave was able to duck into the brush.

Before Matthes could shoot again, Brave attacked from behind. The lion whirled, the rest of the pack boiled in, and there was no chance to shoot without hitting a dog. The cat came down on Red with both front feet, and bit him through the shoulder. Brave flew in and grabbed the lion by the back of its neck.

The cat reached back, sank the four-inch-long claws of one paw into Brave's head and jerked him loose.

Matthes, now in the middle of the fracas, shoved the rifle barrel into the giant's mouth and fired. The cat fell. Brave was free, but it looked as if half of his head was gone.

In a wink, the lion was on its feet, only wounded in the lower jaw. Its blazing green eyes locked with Matthes'. Trying to shoot again, Matthes was knocked off of his feet by a dog. He threw himself backward as he fell, did a somersault and stopped with his back against a bush 10 feet downhill from the lion. The rifle lay between them. Paralyzed by fear, Matthes watched the cat stumble toward him, dragging dogs as it came.

At that moment the wounded Brave charged the giant head-on. They went down with jaws locked, and Matthes knew that his dog was being killed. Personal fear vanished. He jumped to his feet, grabbed the gun, and slammed the barrel across the lion's head. The cat didn't seem to notice, much less let go. Only a brain shot would end this struggle before Brave died, but a bullet could deflect into the dog. There was no choice. Matthes held the muzzle to the cat's head and pulled the trigger.

The lion dropped on top of Brave. Neither moved. Matthes grabbed one of the huge forelegs and rolled the cat off of his dog. Brave staggered to his feet, still clinging to the huge animal's lower jaw. The courageous hound slowly released his hold and stood proudly defiant beside the lion. But Brave's life's blood was streaming from his terribly torn head, and Matthes was helpless to hold it back.

Brave was the dog who had traded his life for his master's. ❖

JANUARY 1993

"A GRIZZLY GOT ME"

by Terry Everard, as told to Jim Zumbo

I COULDN'T BELIEVE MY LUCK when I opened the mail that spring day in 1992. Not only had I received a Wyoming sheep tag, but the area I would be hunting was in the Absaroka mountain range, northwest of Cody.

I live across the state in Sundance, Wyoming, but grew up in Cody. In 1978, a few years after leaving Cody, I began working for the Soil Conservation Service. During my time with the SCS I had heard stories of the Sunlight Basin in the Shoshone National Forest, which is the unit my permit entitled me to hunt. It is rich in big game—elk, deer and sheep—and has earned a reputation that has drawn thousands of out-of-state hunters over the years.

I also knew from my time in Cody that this can be a dangerous region, with steep backcountry mountains exceeding 10,000 feet and few trails should you run into trouble. The area is also prime bear country … and I had heard that it also was a spot where wildlife officers dumped "problem" grizzlies from nearby Yellowstone National Park.

But what consumed my thoughts in the following weeks was that I had finally been lucky enough to draw a tag that would allow me to conduct my first-ever sheep hunt in this game-rich area about halfway between Cody and Yellowstone Lake. And as if in confirmation that I was on a roll, the mailman also had delivered me a bonus in the form of a moose tag.

I would be hunting with two longtime friends, Don Viktorin from Worland, Wyoming, and Lonnie Schultz, from Laramie. Like me, Schultz is a former resident of Cody, but unlike me, he had been on a number of sheep hunts in the area.

The plan was for Viktorin to arrange for horses to pack us into a main camp about five miles from the trailhead. We would base ourselves here for the nine-day hunt, and if we found distant sheep we'd backpack into the higher elevations and hunt out of spike camps.

The signs that my luck might change began right from the start of our hunt on September 1. At a bad spot in the trail, one of the packhorses slipped off a ledge and injured its hip. We were only halfway to the area we had planned for our base camp and had to quit for the day and set up in this spot.

We decided that the best plan would be for Viktorin to stay in camp with the horses while Schultz and I hiked in deeper and made a small spike camp. That change was a bit disappointing, but I was still plenty excited. Schultz had already spotted a bunch of sheep as we were riding in and that only added to my hopes for success. I had a hard time getting to sleep that night.

As Schultz and I hiked in the next morning, I spotted fresh bear scat and later we found a place where bears had been digging for squirrels. They weren't welcome sights, but Schultz wasn't concerned.

"I wouldn't worry about it," he said. "I've been hunting here for 15 years, and I've never had any trouble with bears."

His words were reassuring, but the stories I had heard about this being an area where problem bears were released kept playing across my mind.

We crawled into our sleeping bags early that night because the next morning was opening day, and we wanted to make the most of our time. I couldn't shake the thought of bears even after I had turned in. We had followed all of the rules and cached our food up high and away from our sleeping area, and this was hardly the first time I had been on a wilderness hunt. Still, the feel of my .270 rifle lying next to me in the small tent was reassuring.

Opening day began so full of promise that I had little time to think any more about bears. Early on, I saw a small ram but decided to pass him up. Later another ram appeared, and this one very definitely caught my interest. It had a very good full curl. Unfortunately, we spooked him out of the drainage he was in. We figured there was a chance to cut him off on a high pass, but he beat us to it and disappeared.

That would be the last legal ram we that would see for the next three days. Three days of hard hunting. Schultz was disappointed and theorized that the Yellowstone fires of 1988 had caused the sheep to change their habits. This was the first time that he had been back in the area since the fires had burned almost half of Yellowstone and tens of thousands of acres of the Shoshone National Forest.

Whether that was why we couldn't find the sheep or not, we decided to pull our spike camp and head back to the base camp. From there maybe we could figure out a successful new strategy.

On the way back down, near the area where I had spotted the bear scat four days earlier, we jumped a black bear across a deep gully. We had not gone but a couple of hundred yards farther down the trail when Schultz tugged at my backpack. I looked up to see a grizzly sow with two cubs only 80 feet away and running parallel to us.

This was no vague apprehension. This was the real thing. Seeing a grizzly up close, especially a sow with cubs, had me spooked.

The grizzly stopped. She stood on her hind legs and stared directly at us. Schultz and I chambered live rounds with as little movement as possible. But then the sow just dropped down and ran into the timber with her cubs trailing.

"That's the closest I ever want to come to a grizzly," I said to Schultz.

In just hours I would come even closer. A lot closer.

When we got into the base camp we learned that Viktorin had experienced bad luck, too. He had suffered a kidney stone attack and had painfully ridden out to our truck and then driven to the hospital in Cody. He had been admitted, but the attack was not a serious one so he was released after an overnight stay. Viktorin was washed out, but he had come back into the base camp, figuring he would have time to rest up before we were scheduled to return.

This was not what any of us had hoped for. Schultz was so disappointed that he decided to go home early. Viktorin and I would stay on for a few days and look for sheep at lower elevations. Then I would help him get his lame horse out.

After dinner, I spotted some sheep in the valley above camp. It was too far to tell if there were any rams with them, but I was excited all over again.

I was out of camp before daybreak the next day, guiding myself in the dark with a small flashlight and lugging a backpack loaded with 20 pounds of gear. Viktorin was asleep when I left, still exhausted from his bout with the kidney stones.

I worked my way uphill for a couple of hours with no sign of sheep. When I dropped off the ridge from where I had been scouting and walked into a finger of pine trees, I noted that the wind was at my back. It would carry my scent in front of me, and I figured I wouldn't see any game close up.

I came to a small clearing and stopped to enjoy the majestic view of Sunlight Basin and take a few pictures. Moving on, I saw a deep ravine that I would have to cross and thought I saw a place to do so about 150 yards below me. To reach it, I would have to go into the timber and work down in a switchback fashion. The ground was damp, making it easy to walk quietly.

Suddenly I saw a movement. A brown-colored bear stood on its hind legs in a patch of downed timber just 40 feet downhill from me. I stood rooted to the spot.

When my eyes locked on the bear's, I knew I was in trouble.

In one terrible moment that I'll never be able to forget the bear charged. It was only then that I realized that I had not chambered a round. I had carried my rifle that way for safety's sake in this rugged country.

The charge was so incredibly fast that I had no time to load my rifle. My brain told me to play dead. Throwing my arms around my head, I dropped to the ground and braced for the worst. As I hit the ground, the bear struck my right side, growling and biting my head. Its weight and strength completely overpowered me. But even though I was helpless, I was keenly aware of my rifle that now lay on the ground next to me. I had to stay within reach of that gun. It was my only hope.

I felt the grizzly's big teeth ripping and grating across my skull as it tried to bite into my head. I struggled desperately to keep my arms clasped around my skull. Blood poured from my scalp and gushed down over my face.

The bear seized my upper right arm and yanked on it. The grizzly was trying to drag me off. I fought to stay close to the gun. A couple of times I even dropped my right hand for an instant to feel for the rifle. It was still there.

But each time I dropped my hand, the movement seemed to provoke the bear and it increased the ferocity of its attack.

The grizzly bit my right hand hard, then suddenly jumped over me, biting into my left shoulder. The strength in its jaws convinced me that it would rip my arms off. Numbness overcame me. I knew I was going to die. I said a quick prayer.

Suddenly something inside me snapped. No longer was I willing to be torn apart like a rag doll. "If I'm going to die, you're dying too," I thought. Or maybe I shouted it aloud. I can't be sure.

Was it Providence? New resolve? My shout? Whatever it was, it made a difference. The grizzly stopped tearing at me.

I grabbed the rifle with both hands, worked the bolt to chamber a cartridge and lifted the gun. The grizzly reacted to this movement by tearing into my left shoulder again. But now I was determined to fight.

I managed to fire the rifle. The frenzied grizzly reacted immediately. It instantly stopped the attack and loped away. I couldn't tell if it was hit. Nor did I much care. All I knew was that I was free of the animal.

The bear ran only about 25 feet when it stopped to look back at me. Again we locked eyes. Despite the horrible pain and fear, I was alert enough to see that the bear's fur was splattered with blood and a dark streak ran down its left side.

I chambered a new shell. "Come on, bear, this time I'm ready." Adrenaline had taken hold. Paralyzed fear had been overwhelmed by the will to live.

The grizzly leaped over a downfall and vanished into the forest.

It was over.

I would not die. At least not yet. I could feel my skull—the bear had nearly scalped me. Blood ran down my face and neck, soaking my down jacket. I tried to stop the bleeding by applying pressure, but the head wounds were too extensive for me to do much.

If I didn't get help soon, I'd bleed to death. A new panic started.

Camp was a little more than a mile away, all downhill. I dropped the backpack and started running. My headlong rush off the mountain might not have been the wisest thing to do because I'd lose blood even faster, but I didn't care. I knew the grizzly could still be around, stalking me in the timber. My only thoughts were to get out of the area, and forever away from that bear.

About a third of the way to camp I stopped in a clearing and fired three quick shots. Viktorin heard them and started hiking in my direction.

I had only one shell left. I resumed hiking toward camp, stumbling as I went. The bleeding seemed to be slowing down, and for the first time since the attack I thought that I might survive. I fired my last shot about a quarter-mile from camp and heard Viktorin's wonderful voice not too far off.

"Terry, are you all right?" he shouted.

"A grizzly got me," I hollered back.

When Viktorin reached me, he tried to get me to lay down, but I would have none of it. I just wanted to get to camp. The realization of what had happened was starting to sink in. And with that recollection had come excruciating pain.

Viktorin carried my rifle and helped me back to camp. As I hobbled along, we counted our options. Should he leave me at camp and go for help? Should we ride out together? I chose to ride out.

Viktorin quickly saddled up Rusty and Sugar, the two fastest horses. He pushed me up onto one of them and I held on as best I could.

It took a little more than an hour for us to reach the trailhead, where Viktorin helped me get into the back of my pickup truck. Fifteen minutes later we were at the Sunlight Basin Ranger Station, where a call was put in for an ambulance. Viktorin kept driving me on toward Cody so that we could meet the ambulance en route. I arrived at the emergency room at 1:30 p.m. It had been nearly four hours since the attack.

West Park County Hospital in Cody is where many victims of bear attacks and buffalo gorings from Yellowstone are admitted. During three hours of surgery, it took Dr. Jeffrey Balison more than 250 stitches and staples to repair nearly three feet of lacerations and close several puncture wounds, the majority of them to my head. I'd lost four units of blood. But there were no broken bones and I would have no facial disfigurement.

Viktorin returned to camp the following day with Wyoming Game and Fish Department and U.S. Forest Service personnel. They found grizzly tracks in the snow and confirmed that they had come from a sow with two cubs. They also concluded that the sow had not been hit with my bullet. Somewhere, she was still feeding in the area. The blood that I'd seen on the bear was mine.

I was dismissed from the hospital after 48 hours. Two weeks later I returned to the attack site and retrieved my backpack, which was 150 feet downhill from the spot I'd dropped it. I figured that the bear had returned and rolled it down the hill in its fury. Amazingly, the pack was virtually undamaged, with only a bent frame. I credit it for saving my life by protecting my neck during the attack.

It was not even a month later when I took a moose with a respectable 37-inch-wide rack. Then, with just four days remaining in the season, I killed my first sheep, a nice three-quarters-curl ram. The area I hunted had only a 33 percent success rate that season.

I remembered how lucky I felt the day that my sheep tag arrived. Even after what happened, I still consider myself lucky. Very lucky indeed. ❖

JULY 1994

I SURVIVED
a Fatal Arctic Hunt

by Tony Sulak

THE LATE-MARCH MORNING was clear and cold. Far below us, the vast ice fields and jagged snow peaks of Alaska's Brooks Range stretched away, east and west, as far as we could see.

Beyond the mountains the flat arctic tundra ran to the horizon. From our Wien airliner, winging north from Fairbanks to Point Barrow, the whole world seemed frozen and empty, dazzling white, but lifeless as the moon.

No, not quite lifeless. Far ahead a cluster of black dots appeared on the snow-covered barrens and grew swiftly into a herd of caribou, thousands of them feeding slowly across the flat and lonely land. They didn't even break ranks as our giant bird droned high above them. Such herds are a major spectacle of the far north.

I had never enjoyed a plane ride more, and never looked forward to a hunt as much as I was looking forward to this one. It's a good thing we can't see ahead to what's in store for us.

This trip had been years in the dreaming stage for my hunting partner, Bill Niemi, and me. I was 56 at the time and had operated a tool-and-die plant in Seattle, Washington, more than 25 years. I'm also fond of flying, and have a Beechcraft plane dealership at Boeing Field. Bill is from Seattle, too, and is a partner with Eddie Bauer in the manufacture of down clothing and sleeping bags.

I've hunted as far back as I can remember, and so has Bill; we've had some fine trips together. Our trophies include moose, elk, goat, black bear, and grizzly. Now we were off on what we both regarded as the adventure of our lives—a hunt by plane for polar bear on the arctic ice pack off Point Barrow, Alaska.

In my opinion, and in Bill's, the white bear is the most majestic trophy a hunter can collect anywhere in North America. He may well be the biggest bear on earth, outranking even the Alaska brown. He has beauty unmatched by any other game animal I know of. Hung on any wall, his lustrous white pelt is a breath-stopper. And he roams a remote and forbidding world where man is an unwelcome intruder. You hunt him at your own risk, in the face of bone-chilling cold, treacherous sea ice, terrible winds, and gale-driven snow that turns the air to milk. If you take him, you earn him. Make the smallest error, and the odds are good you'll pay with your life.

Bill and I had debated a hunt for big browns that spring, weighing it against this arctic trip, but had finally voted to go after polar-bear rugs while we had the chance. The brownies could wait.

We left Seattle on Monday morning, March 24, 1958, riding an airliner to Fairbanks by way of Juneau and Whitehorse. We stayed overnight at Fairbanks, and took off the next morning for the three-hour flight to Barrow in a plane loaded mostly with Eskimos. Our big adventure lay just ahead, and we were as excited as kids.

Our departure from Seattle had been on a warm, spring morning, with early flowers blooming in the yards. We touched down at Point Barrow in a white, bleak world where snow covered everything. Arctic ice lay piled along the beach, the thermometer stood at 18 below, and a bitter 12-mile wind was blowing out of the northeast.

There was no hint that spring would ever come here. Bill and I had flown north in light clothing and were close to freezing before we could change into more suitable outfits. But we didn't feel like complaining. This cold, desolate land of flat shore and empty sea ice was the only place where we could hope to find what we'd come for.

Months ago we'd mapped our plans and made the necessary arrangements with Frank Gregory, Point Barrow pilot and guide, who'd had plenty of experience in handling polar-bear hunts. He met us at the airport with a second pilot, Jack Hovland, and two planes—a pair of two-place Aeronca Champions—from which we'd scout the arctic pack for bears. They flew us three miles to Browerville, half a mile from the Point Barrow settlement, landing on a frozen lagoon there. We lugged our gear into a cozy frame building known as the Lodge, where we'd put up for the duration of our hunt.

When we rolled out the next morning, the temperature had dropped to 26 below, and a terribly cold wind was still whipping in from the ice fields. One of the Eskimos told us that here at the farthest-north tip of Alaska the wind blows one way for six months without let-up, then turns around and blows the other way for six months. I suspect he came close to the truth.

In such weather, men and planes require special equipment and care. Warming up the Aeroncas for take off that morning was a two-hour job. The oil had been drained the night before and left on top of a stove. Meanwhile, the engines were protected by canvas covers. The first step in the morning was to light gasoline burners—always carried in each plane—and put one under each cover. When the engine was warm, the heated oil was poured in and we were ready to go.

As for Bill and me, we'd brought outfits that we thought would equip us for anything. We were wearing down-filled nylon underwear, heavy wool outer clothing, three pairs of woolen socks, factory-made mukluks with rubber soles and wolfskin tops, and down-filled parkas with wolverine fur around the face. That's one fur that won't ice up from a man's breath.

Only one item proved unsatisfactory: the rubber-soled mukluks weren't up to the weather. We came in from our first flight with our feet close to freezing, and promptly switched to Eskimo mukluks.

We realized all along that there would be some danger on a hunt of this kind. From Barrow to the North Pole there's nothing but ice—a vast, desolate, drifting field of it—swept by polar winds, seamed with pressure ridges and leads of open water, a broken white plain that stretches north, east, and west for about 1,000 miles without a dot of land. Somewhere in that unpeopled and hostile world we hoped to collect our bearskin rugs. If necessary, we'd fly 400 miles out over the frozen sea to do it.

We had prepared for emergencies as best we could, and Gregory and Hovland made it plain that they intended to take no chances. The greatest danger would be unsafe ice, but Gregory explained that the color of sea ice is a fairly reliable guide to its thickness. If it's white, it's normally safe; if dark or grayish, it's likely to be thin.

Of course, there was always the risk that good ice might have a crack or crevice hidden under snow, big enough to catch and snap a ski. And since we'd be far offshore, a disabled plane could mean tragedy unless help was at hand. So we'd fly always as a team, the two Aeroncas together, in constant touch by radio. When we were ready to land, one would go down while the other circled overhead. Under no circumstances would the second plane touch its skis to the ice until the first was definitely safe. And our stops on the ice would be short, for if we allowed an engine to cool we might not get it started again.

With all these precautions, the chance of mishap seemed slight. Pressed as we were, we could survive for a reasonable time on the ice, and we knew search planes would be up promptly in the event of trouble.

There was, however, one kind of disaster that we gave little thought to. That was the possibility that we might be dunked into the icy sea. There wasn't much use thinking about that. We were told frankly that a man plunged into frigid sea water at that time of year couldn't expect to live more than three to eight minutes. Men had been pulled from the water dead, even when rescued almost at once. The cold was just too much for the human body to endure. Well, if that happened, at least it would be over quickly.

But, as we made final plans, we didn't think there was a chance it would happen.

Jack Hovland had spent some time around Boeing Field at Seattle, and I'd met him there, so it was arranged that I'd fly with him. Bill would fly with Gregory.

We took off in midmorning on Wednesday, March 26, and headed northeast over the pack. We'd been flying an hour when Jack banked the plane and pointed down. There on the ice along an open lead was the first polar bear I'd ever seen outside a zoo.

I can't remember anything that's ever happened on a hunting trip that gave me a bigger thrill. The bear looked yellowish, and loomed up plainly on the ice. To me, he seemed as big as a short-legged horse. When Jack announced that he wasn't more than seven feet long and definitely not in the trophy class, I found it hard to believe. But he was at least big enough for pictures, so we dropped down and followed him until he ducked behind a pressure ridge and found a hiding place among the tumbled, upended blocks of ice. We found another bear of about the same size a little later, but didn't bother him.

Shortly after noon we landed, one plane at a time, and refueled with extra gas that we always carried. We were in the air again by 2 o'clock, and within an hour Frank Gregory and Bill located a good-size bear and went after it. Gregory thought it would go at least 8½ feet, and that's big enough. They followed it across thin ice, where the bear lay flat on its belly and crawled along with a swimming motion to keep from breaking through, but finally lost it in an area of ice too rough and broken for a dog sled, let alone a plane.

We were back at Barrow in time for supper that first day, and despite cold feet that we blamed on our factory-made mukluks, Bill and I were about as enthused a pair of hunters as Alaska will ever see. In a single day of flying we'd spotted three bears, one a good trophy. This hunt was in the bag, we told each other.

Our luck the next day wasn't quite so good. We headed northwest over the ice, and saw more watery leads, but we were 80 miles offshore before we spotted our first bear. By that time I'd had enough experience to size it up as a six-footer.

Shortly after that, we found a fresh track that looked promising, and kept it in sight for 50 miles until it ended in an open lead. We could not pick it up again. Jack explained that it's not unusual for a polar bear, hunting for food, to travel that far without a halt.

We flew back to the Lodge for lunch, and went out again in midafternoon. We were two hours finding a bear, and it was another six-footer. We agreed at supper that it hadn't been a productive day, but Bill and I weren't discouraged. Bears were scattered all over the ice, and it was just a question of time before we'd find two good ones in areas where we could land and stalk them on foot.

On Friday morning the temperature was 18 below, and the wind blew as hard as ever. We headed north and west, the two planes flying within sight of each other as always. We were 135 miles out when we spotted our first bear. He was around eight feet long, hardly what we were willing to settle for at this stage of the game, but good for pictures. The planes spooked him, and he lit out at a steady run. We followed, circling overhead. The chase ended when he splashed into a big lead a quarter of a mile across and stayed there, swimming around as if he thought nothing could get at him in the water.

It was now about 11 o'clock. Gregory called Hovland on the radio, suggesting that we go down, stretch our legs, refuel, and have a try at this bear with the cameras from the ice. Hovland agreed.

Gregory went first, putting his green Aeronca down on old ice three or four feet thick. He coasted to a stop, made a sharp U-turn to the left, and taxied back near the place where he'd landed. When he stopped and we were sure everything was all right, Jack Hovland nosed our plane down.

We made contact with the ice and then—to my surprise—we started a slow, 90° turn to the right, away from the other plane and toward the open lead.

Riding in back, I couldn't see what was going on in the cockpit, and no one will ever know just what happened. But we hit bumpy ice, and it's my opinion that Jack decided to make a go-around, gun the plane back into the air, and come in for a fresh landing.

If that was his intention, he didn't make it. We coasted across the rough ice, closer and closer to open water. Then there was a sudden, splintering crash, almost like an explosion. We'd smashed through!

Skis have no buoyancy. The cabin of the Aeronca seemed to go down like a stone until the wings came to rest on the ice and stopped our plunge. Gray-green water swirled in around my feet, my knees, then up to my belt. It must have been terribly cold, but I didn't feel it. Things were happening too fast and I was too busy to feel anything.

"Kick the door out before the ice jams it," Jack yelled.

"The door, hell!" I barked back. "I'll kick out the whole side of the plane."

I reached for a down-filled sleeping bag that lay rolled behind my seat and handed it to him. "Use this for a life preserver," I urged. I figured my down clothing and parka would serve me in that capacity, at least for a few minutes.

The cabin was chest-deep in water now. I kicked savagely at the door, it gave way, and more water poured in. It came up to our necks, but I still didn't notice the cold. Jack went through the door first. He'd told me he was a good swimmer, and two or three strokes took him to an aileron. He grabbed it and hung on. By that time I was out of the drowned cabin and in the water behind him. I'm a strong swimmer too, and at the moment I didn't feel any fear. I swam past Jack, worked my way around the wing to the engine, and climbed up on it. Next I walked out on the wing, got a grip on Jack's hands, and helped him up beside me.

We were out of the water and safe—for the time being. But it would not be for long. The ice around us kept cracking, and gurgling noises came from the cabin as the plane settled slowly into the sea.

Numb from our icy dunking, we both realized our chances were slim. Close to 250 feet of unsafe ice lay between us and the solid white of the old pack. Our companions couldn't get across it to rescue us. The temperature of the salt water under that new ice wasn't more than 28°, probably less. Air temperature was still 18 below, and a 10-mile wind was scouring the ice. We knew how long a man could expect to survive in the water under those conditions—not long enough for us to smash our way to solid footing. And I wasn't sure we could do that anyway. The ice around the plane was too thin to support us, but maybe too thick for a swimming man to break.

Nevertheless we'd have to try, unless we wanted to stay huddled on the wing and drown right there when the plane sank. Neither of us said much, but I kept thinking, "This can't be happening to me. It's a nightmare. I'll wake up."

Deep down, though, I knew it was no dream and I wasn't going to wake up. Live or die, this was stark reality.

"Shall we take off our boots?" Jack asked after a minute.

I shook my head, and he slowly nodded agreement. We both knew better.

Over by the other plane we could see Frank Gregory and Bill Niemi working frantically, breaking out gear that might help them in attempting a rescue, shouting encouragement to us as they worked.

But there didn't seem much they'd be able to do. Our emergency equipment had been planned for rescue from the ice, not from the water. We watched Bill and Frank empty gas cans but I knew that wouldn't do us any good. Next they unrolled the motor cover that was always carried in the plane, a rectangle of canvas about 15 x 4 feet. At the time, I didn't think it would be of use either.

I figured Jack's chances were better than my own. The son of Mr. and Mrs. Gilman Hovland of Fargo, North Dakota (the Hovlands were planning to visit their son three months hence and tour Alaska), Jack was only 27, almost 30 years younger than I was, and in top condition. Unmarried, he had been flying six years in Alaska, two in the U. S. Air Force, the rest of the time for airlines or the territorial government, or as a bush pilot on errands such as this hunt. He was resourceful and physically tough, and although I'm no pantywaist myself, the odds seemed in his favor.

Jack was dressed in sheepskin parka and pants, boots, and heavy gloves. I was wearing a down parka and wool pants over down underwear, but I'd made one mistake. Because the wool pants were old and soiled, I had run them through the washer and dryer the night before I left Seattle. That had robbed them of their ability to repel water, and they'd soaked through instantly. But I still wasn't in too bad shape, thanks to the down-filled nylon underneath.

The plane kept settling lower and lower, and water was up almost to the cabin roof. We couldn't wait much longer. Our guns, cameras, and the rest of our outfit were already beyond hope of salvage.

Jack and I tightened our belts, boots, and collars to keep the water out, and emptied our pockets to rid ourselves of every ounce of surplus weight. Men have queer reactions at such a time, and the next thing we did made no sense: we set our knives, ammunition and the other small odds and ends in a neat row along the edge of the wing as if we expected to come back and claim them.

The last thing I did was strip off my parka and roll it tight. It would be helpful as a life preserver, and I'd learned in my short swim around the plane that I could make no headway with it on. Jack still had the rolled sleeping bag to help him.

It was time to go.

"I'll try it," I told him. "If I can get through the ice, follow me."

I eased off the wing, hoping the ice might hold me. It was too thin. I broke through into the freezing water and struck out for the solid ice where Bill and Frank were watching, about 250 feet away.

The ice in front of me was only about half an inch thick. I started breaking it with my hands, but quickly found I couldn't do that effectively with gloves on, so I stripped them off and tossed them aside. Then I went on with my bare hands, breaking the ice, shoving it aside, throwing chunks back over my shoulders, kicking myself forward, getting a fresh hold, breaking more ice. I was smashing a path through, an inch, a foot at a time, and leaving a plain trail of blood where the sharp edges gashed my hands. But I felt neither the pain of the cuts nor the sting of the salt water in them.

I was maybe five yards from the plane when I looked back the first time. There wasn't much of the little red Aeronca showing now, but the slight figure of the pilot was still erect on the wing.

"Come on, Jack," I called. "We can make it."

I didn't look back again. I concentrated every ounce of strength and determination I had on beating my way ahead, breaking ice, throwing it out of my way, kicking forward, over and over again in a steady rhythm. I didn't know when Jack slipped into the water behind me, or when the plane dropped quietly out of sight a minute later.

Bill and Frank were working cautiously out toward us now, probing the ice with their hunting knives to make sure they didn't break through and doom us all to certain death. They crept on until the knives were punching through, and the ice was swaying up and down. That was as far as they dared come. The rest was up to Jack and me.

I heard them yelling encouragement. They told me later that Jack shouted back he didn't think he could make it, but I didn't hear that. It was many hours before I learned what happened. My pilot swam slowly about 25 feet from the plane, and went down. One second he was dog-paddling through the broken ice; the next the rolled sleeping bag was floating by itself.

All the tortured weeks I lay in the hospital afterward, I kept asking myself whether I could have done anything to help him. Common sense supplied the answer. There was nothing anyone could have done except what I did—try to break a path to solid ice for the two of us, sure we'd both get out or both die. All the same, you don't lose a partner under those circumstances without doing some sober thinking later on.

As I fought that ice, I lost all sense of time. They told me afterward it took me 20 minutes to hammer my way to Gregory and Niemi. When I was close enough, they tossed me an empty five-gallon gas can, thinking it might help me keep afloat. It came within reach, but I didn't touch it. I was afraid my wet hands might freeze to the metal and leave me helpless.

I was getting very tired now. I tried breaking ice and swimming more slowly to conserve what strength I had left. But slow swimming wouldn't keep me afloat, so I went back at it hammer and tongs. The ice was so thick toward the end that I had to break it with my fists and push it aside with my arms. I tried to climb up on it, but that was too much for me.

Then at last I was close enough for Frank and Bill to help. They flipped the canvas motor cover across the ice, within my reach. I tried to grab it and learned for the first time that my hands had turned into frozen white clubs, devoid of all feeling, with hard ice between the fingers.

I lunged ahead, got my arms on the canvas and pulled it to me, and caught it between my teeth. Bill and Frank tugged me two or three feet closer, relaxed their pull, and I got a better hold with teeth and numbed arms. Then, God knows how, they pulled me up on the ice and dragged me to them. I felt them grab me by the wrists; then I passed out cold. The rest I learned hours and days later.

While they'd waited for me to struggle to them, Gregory had run back, started the motor, and taxied the plane as near the scene of the accident as he dared. There he broke out an extra sleeping bag, socks, and boots. Now they skidded me to safer ice and cut my wet clothes off. My pants and underwear froze stiff in the bitter wind, even as they were slashed away. Frank and Bill worked desperately, knowing that an extra minute or two of exposure might mean the difference between my living or dying.

They pulled Frank's overpants and Bill's parka onto me, and got me into dry socks and mukluks. I half regained consciousness once or twice, enough to mumble at them but not to be of any help. Then they started to drag and carry me 300 feet to the plane. Halfway there they had to lift me over a rough shelf of ice a couple of feet high. As they did that they saw that the pants had slipped down and I was being dragged on my bare bottom. It was frozen white and slashed bone-deep by the sharp ice.

They worked the pants back into place, and went on. I weigh over

200 pounds, and when they got to the plane they tried to revive me enough to get me on my feet. They told me I stood erect for a second or two, then folded like a wet dishrag. None of us can say to this day how they got me up through the door and into the two-place Aeronca, but somehow they managed it. They buckled me into the rear seat, and Bill Niemi crawled in over me and inched himself feet first back into the luggage compartment. Frank Gregory managed without help the job of lifting the tail and turning the plane around into the wind, despite its full load of two men. Then he climbed in, gave the motor the briefest warmup he dared, and gunned us off the ice. Two thousand feet up, he radioed Point Barrow, reported what had happened, and asked for help when we came in. Almost before we coasted to a stop on the frozen lagoon, Wien pilots and a visiting hunter were hauling me out.

I was dimly aware of hands tugging at me. Then there was a warm room, a doctor, nurses, running footsteps, blankets, hotwater bottles, and strong black tea—all recorded through a fog, as if I were half asleep. I gagged on the tea, but someone said, "Drink it if you want to live." I tried again and got some down. Next came violent nausea, and I got rid of the sea water I'd swallowed. I started to shake as if I'd never stop, and a nurse jabbed a needle into me.

Then somebody asked where all the blood was coming from. The doctor ordered me rolled over, and saw my lacerated bottom. "Good Lord," he blurted, "that's hamburger!"

Bill and Frank spent the rest of the afternoon at the hospital, but I wasn't aware they were around. They came back at 9 o'clock that night and broke the news about Jack Hovland.

The Point Barrow hospital, operated for the benefit of the natives, was staffed with a doctor, a dentist, and five nurses. I'll never be able to repay the debt of gratitude I owe Dr. Clyde Farson and those nurses. I was in the hospital eight days, and couldn't have had better care.

The day after the accident, Frank Gregory and Joel Thibedeau, a Wien pilot, flew back to the scene with two territorial police officers to make the necessary investigation. They learned nothing that helped explain the tragedy, but they did find tracks where a polar bear had dragged something off across the ice. They got their rifles and followed, thinking they might come on Hovland's body, but found only the underwear that Frank and Bill had cut off me.

The rest of the story is the usual one of a man who has been through an ordeal of that kind and had a very close call. My frozen hands swelled to double their normal size, turned black, and were covered with huge blisters. They stayed that way for weeks, but in the end suffered no permanent damage. I lost all 10 nails, but they regrew. The medics told me it was fortunate my hands had bled so profusely while I was in the water. They believed that had helped to prevent frozen blood vessels.

When I was ready to leave for Seattle, the airline sent over big fur gloves to cover my bandages. The nurses put pain pills in one pocket and sleeping pills in another. The airliner was waiting with engines running when a jeep delivered Bill (he had one hand bandaged as a result of frostbite, too) and me to the field. The flight back to Fairbanks, and from there home, wasn't as bad as we expected. There was quite a contrast, however, between our takeoff from Seattle on March 24 and our homecoming on Easter morning, 13 days later.

I spent the next five weeks in a Seattle hospital undergoing skin grafts and operations. Recovering from frostbite is far more painful than suffering it, and my bottom gave me worse trouble than my hands. Every day was an agony, and there were times when I think I even envied poor Jack Hovland his quick and merciful end. But by early May I was back home, not quite as good as new, but in better shape than I had any right to expect.

Why did I survive in the face of almost impossible odds? How did it happen that I was spared while Jack died? What were the factors that tipped the scales in my favor?

I think I owe my rescue to the bravery of Bill Niemi and Frank Gregory, to the buoyancy of my down underwear, to a tremendous will to live, and to great physical endurance that backed it up.

Men who know the arctic have advanced another theory, too. They say my weight may have played a part.

Seals and walrus live in those northern seas, naked of fur, because a layer of fat under the skin insulates them. Might not the same thing be true of a man? Isn't it possible that I was better protected from the killing cold of the icy sea than Jack Hovland, who was thin and spare? I don't know, of course, but it seems logical.

Finally and above all, I realize I can thank Someone who has greater authority in such matters than any human. ◈

SEPTEMBER 1959

That Lonesome Pine

by John Caldwell

❖

*T*HE SILENCE WAS SHATTERING. All you could hear was the dull crunch of hoofs on the crusted snow and the scurrying of our dogs as they labored up Horse Draw's harsh ascent. No sign of life flickered in the vast, craggy wilderness, yet the three of us, Dad, Marvin Dilly, and I, felt sure that somewhere we'd come onto the tracks of the mountain lion we'd been trailing since yesterday.

I pulled out my cigarettes, and my ungloved hands stiffened. It was forty below, cold even for the arid Colorado Rockies.

Dad reined up abruptly, squinted ahead, and put a hand to his forehead to protect his eyes from the glare of the morning sun.

"Here we go again," he announced.

Almost sixty yards beyond, I could see tiny depressions in the snow which to Dad's trained eyes spelled CAT.

Dad swiftly interpreted the tracks. "Big male. Maybe 150 pounds. Passed by sometime during the night. Same one we trailed yesterday."

A slow grin spread over his leathery face. "No smokes this time, boys," he said. "We'll take this one alive."

We're not exactly boys. We've both voted once. But both Marve and I knew that was Dad's way of kidding us about the female cat we roped last year. We hog-tied her hind feet and, figuring she was fast, stopped for a cigarette. But the lion suddenly revived and took a swipe at me with a free forepaw. As I jumped back Marve grabbed the hemp. In the ensuing scramble the cat tumbled over a cliff and hung herself.

Our determination to take a mountain lion alive was provoked two years ago when the town of Rangely built a million-dollar high school after its oil boom. One night at a school gathering a rancher recalled that Dad had once figured out a way to catch lions alive. Somebody suggested a live one would make a fine mascot for the Rangely High Panthers. In that isolated community, practically snow-bound four months a year, the result was inevitable. Ever since then hunters have been vying for the honor of supplying the school with a mascot.

The pressure was on us because we had some advantages. Everyone agrees that Dad, who's been hunting lions all his life, probably knows more about them than anyone in our area. And our dogs are tops. Toughie, the Airedale, is phenomenal, while

Buster and Lead were bred to Dad's specifications. They're a cross between bloodhound, for size and speed, and fox hound, for just plain cussedness. In a dozen battles, no lion has ever stayed with them.

Now, as anyone who's tried it knows, capturing 150 pounds of screaming, clawing mountain kitty ain't easy. It's one of the most dangerous sports in North America. Normally a lion will stay clear of humans, but when he's cornered he'll take on anything and anybody. A more worthy or more destructive opponent would be hard to find.

Ranchers and government trappers have driven them from many ranges, but they still flourish in the wild, rocky heights of northwestern Colorado, and the state still pays a $50 bounty for each one killed. It's strictly a winter sport since in summer the lion has no rival to dispute his reign over the hard timberline ledges which hold no spoor for dogs to follow.

We'd been in the high country three days when we picked up the cat's trail a second time. We'd wasted a whole Saturday working back and forth on the mountain with Doc Monahan and Hank Storey. Then, after a night's rest, we'd switched horses and started out again. We ran onto tracks in midafternoon. But after cold-trailing the big cat for three hours, Hank and Doc said they had to get back to work. So we returned to the jeep and took them buckety-buckety down the long wagon trail to town.

"Listen you bandy-legged, weasened-up little varmint," Hank said to Dad when we dropped him off in front of his house, "just leave that old tomcat be. We'll get him next week."

"Git the bur out from under your saddle," Dad replied. "Why if we git the chance you had. . . ."

We all laughed, remembering the "expedition" Hank led the year Dad was in the hospital. The dogs chased a big kitty up a large ponderosa pine. Hank grabbed a stick, gulped, and climbed after him.

The trick in getting a lion like this is to keep him bluffed with the stick the way a wild-animal trainer fools the big cats with a chair. You let him bat at the stick like a kitten does a broomstraw. Then you lure him back from the limb, where he usually retreats, until he's close enough for you to flip a lariat over his head. After he's fast, the ground crew hauls him off his perch, using a crotch in the tree as a fulcrum. He's lowered slowly, and as he comes within reach his hind legs are roped and tied.

The only trouble with Hank's lion was that it didn't retreat. Hank was pretty well up in the pine when the lion started down. They passed on opposite sides of the trunk—Hank climbing, the cat descending—and then the lion crawled out on a lower limb and left Hank treed. A volley of carefully placed shots ended the trouble.

Dad fumed about that and vowed that when he came out of the hospital he'd show us how it was done. And that was the very thing he was doing right now.

A glow of excitement lighted Dad's keen eyes when we struck the trail again. As for me, my stomach was as calm as a bucketful of rattlers. And the next hour of hard, silent riding didn't help it any. That spoor was plenty fresh.

Finally Dad pulled up for a breather.

"Notice how there's no break in the tracks?" he asked. "That cat has not stopped once. He's heading directly for the deer herd around Douglas Pass. He's hungry and likely mean."

He gigged Baldy forward. Soon the tracks veered upward onto a ledge. We strung out Indian fashion, dodged around jagged rocks, and held a parallel course while the dogs scampered along the thin shelf. Toughie set a steady, jogging pace.

We covered six miles in the first two hours, a lot of it over boulder-infested, sharp-angle grades which forced the horses to mince slowly. For 100 yards we traipsed along a ledge in the rimrock that had a sheer drop of 200 feet to the jagged stones below.

"Anybody ever fall off this?" Marve yelled with false bravado.

"Nobody ever claimed to have done it," Dad shouted back.

Toughie became impatient, as he always does when the scent gets warm. Suddenly he let out a yelp and took off like a big-tailed bird with Buster and Lead right behind him.

"We'll see kitty soon," Marve cried, grabbing his saddle horn as his horse swerved around a bold upthrust of rock.

Sure enough, we caught a quick look at him a minute later. He was about a quarter of a mile ahead, a beautiful, tawny brute running belly low to the snow. He bounded over some shale and streaked around a ridge out of sight.

The chase really got going then. The horses lathered and the dogs yelped as we dashed around piñons and stony outcroppings and galloped through interlocking washes. Occasionally we got glimpses of the cat as he leaped over rocks and tore over wind-swept ledges, in attempts to confuse the pack. Rounding a sharp turn, my horse skidded and fell kicking to the ground. I lit free. Seconds later we were going again.

We covered three miles this way, miles of treacherous, tortuous running. Once the lion paused dramatically on the edge of a shelf, silhouetted against the drab sky, to survey the enemy below. Then he disappeared.

Moments later the dogs boiled over the same spot, but the footing was too tough for the horses. We circled the blunt face of Patch Mesa and picked our way up a centuries-old landslide at the side. The yapping of the hounds sounded farther and farther away.

I was the first to make the mesa, and by then the yammer of the dogs had a new shrillness. The noise seemed to hover in one place.

"He's treed," Dad yelled, spurring Baldy. Speed became more essential. Often when a cat gets his second wind he'll shove off again with a flying leap which sometimes leaves a dead hound in his wake.

We found our dogs leaping around the base of a fifty-foot ponderosa. Dad shot off his horse with his carbine in his hand. At first the dogs seemed to be jumping at nothing. Then I saw the cat. He was stretched along a limb twenty feet above, half hidden by the gray needles.

"Want to try him, son?"

Did I want to try him! I nodded.

"Keep your stick pointed."

Still facing the lion, Dad backed over to where Marve was tying the horses and extracted a yard-long piñon whip from his scabbard.

I'd done it once before and Dad's done it a dozen times, but I'd be lying if I said I wasn't scared when I started up that pine. The cat crouched as though about to spring. His murderous yellow eyes kept staring at me. But I knew Dad had his carbine ready. I kept the stick pointed and climbed slowly, paying out rope with my left hand and staring as steadily at kitty as kitty stared at me.

It may be true that a mountain lion won't attack a human unless he's provoked. But, durn it, I was provoking him. He was eight feet long but looked eighty. At 160 pounds I had about a ten-pound edge on weight. For what was seconds, but seemed like hours, he crouched there while I inched toward him. Then, with a low growl, he gave way and retreated a couple of steps along the limb.

I felt young again.

Working to a crotch just above him, I poked at the lion with the whip. He swiped it like a monstrous kitten. Since his head was obstructed by little twigs I didn't have any play for the rope. I rapped the limb in front of him. He slithered out to grab the stick. I tried to coax him nearer to the base of the tree where the limb was bare. But he hunched back and looked around nervously.

"Steady, son," Dad yelled above the dogs' yelping.

I poked at the cat again. A second later he quit the tree with a power-ful leap which carried him over a boulder. He lit running. Toughie went berserk with rage at the cat's surprise move and went squirting after him while Dad and Marve ran for the horses.

The second race stopped short when the lion ran out on a long, rock ledge which simply stopped in mid-air. When he tried to double back the dogs cut him off, so he leaped into another pine.

Dad had run ahead on foot while Marve tended the horses, and when I reached the scene the cat was pacing the limb in plain sight. An easy shot.

"This will be tough," Dad counseled. "He's trapped good, but in a spot like this a cat don't always behave like he ought to. Don't press him too fast."

Fast? I started up that tree so slowly Toughie practically boosted me with his frenzied leaps. And I kept that whip pointed—my puny bluff against the lion's steel-muscled might.

In an eternity of seconds I got close to him. He hissed and spat like a tomcat, batting the stick with blows that would have stunned a horse. The rod burned my hand, but I hung on and kept jabbing it in his face.

"Don't crowd him," Dad coached.

I teased that cat for five tedious minutes. Twice I had my hand raised ready to flip the loop of rope over his head. But he finally decided to make another run for it. He made a wild leap. The cat-crazy dogs practically met him in the air, but he dodged like an All-American halfback and darted under a ledge.

Toughie followed and got a raking wound on the head. All three dogs made suicide charges at the lion's narrow cell. The cat clamped down on Lead. Toughie grabbed the cat's jaw and was maneuvering for his throat. But the quarters were too cramped, so he just hung on to the jaw and ripped the skin. Lead finally broke free. Almost instantly all three dogs had grips on the cat and they dragged him out on his back.

They'd have killed him, but Dad rushed up, roped the cat's hind feet and tried to jerk him out from under the dogs. I looped his front feet and we stretched him tight, bracing ourselves against his wild thrashing. Marve dashed in to beat off the dogs. I kept wondering what would happen if the ropes slipped, but Marve stood almost within range of the cat's glistening teeth. Once he was raked on the hand. Toughie finally retreated, curled back his lips, and looked as disgusted as an Airedale can look.

Holding the lasso tightly with his left, Dad did an expert one-handed job of hog-tying the cat's hind feet.

"Rope his head," he ordered.

Marve complied and held those wicked jaws out of the way while I moved in to bind the forepaws. Dad and Marve kept the lion taut between them while I looked for a stick.

His fur was silky to my touch, and I felt his chest straining against my legs as, working from behind, I jammed a thick stick into his mouth. He struggled violently even though every movement he made almost choked him. After a while I got a half hitch around his jaws so he couldn't spit out the stick. As soon as I completed the knot Marve dropped the rope and clamped a hammer lock on the kitty's neck. Dad sat on him while I bound the makeshift bit over his head.

"You and Marve make darn sure those front feet are tied securely," he warned, busying himself with the rear ones. We used enough rope and knots to bind eighty bales of cotton. That turned out to be fortunate.

We stepped back to look at him, an eight-foot, 150-pound beauty built like a greyhound. His ribs heaved like his lungs were about to burst, and a crimson smear spread in the snow under his lacerated jaw.

I think the letdown hit us simultaneously. Suddenly I was so tired my knees almost gave in. Marve reached for the smokes.

"Not yet," Dad directed. "That cat's just calm because he's winded. He's still got plenty of fight left. We'll get him on a horse before he fires up again."

He strode over to Baldy. The old mare walked stiff-kneed against coming close to the lion, but Dad talked her into it.

Marve took the hind legs and I grabbed the front ones and we swung the lion over the saddle. He twisted in mid-air and gave Baldy's flank a sharp scratch. The mare shot from under him like a greased pig. Then the lion put on a real show of strength.

Even though his feet were bound together he had enough balance to gallop down a little grade. Marve and I dashed after him while Dad headed off the dogs.

We caught him after about fifty steps. Marve bowled him over with a kick and held him down while I checked over the ropes. Dad led the very skittish mare up again. This time we hung the lion over the saddle and tied his feet together underneath.

Dad overruled our protests and took the first turn walking as we started the five-mile trek back to camp.

The sun was sinking behind Texas Mountain and the raw cold bit us as we transferred the lion to the jeep and roped him down. In the distance, a coyote yowled mournfully. The gagged cat growled a disdainful answer. Dad made a fire while Marve and I unsaddled the horses. We warmed up over steaming cups of coffee before starting the jolting forty-mile trip to Rangely.

Marve was so tired he sagged against the lean-to while Dad slapped some iodine on his scratched hand.

"Do we try for another one tomorrow?" Dad asked.

Marve grunted. "They only got one high school, ain't they?" ❖

MARCH 1952

SECURELY TRUSSED, the eight-foot, 150-pound cat poses with the author.

I Had to Have
MOOSE

by *Olive A. Fredrickson*

*T*HE CANOE WAS A 30-FOOT
dugout that the Indians had "given"
me. They'd be along in the fall to
claim payment in potatoes.

It had been hollowed out from a big cottonwood with a hand ax, but the tree wasn't straight to begin with, and the canoe had inherited the character of its parent. Otherwise the Indians would not have parted with it. As a result it was not only heavy and unwieldy but also so cranky you hardly dared to look over the side unless your hair was parted in the middle.

I was in the stern, paddling. My six-year-old daughter Olive was wedged firmly in the bow. Between us were Vala, five, and the baby, Louis, two. We were going moose hunting, and since there was no one to leave the children with, we'd have to go as a family.

We weren't hunting for fun. It was early summer, and the crop of vegetables I had planted in our garden was growing, but there was nothing ready for use yet, and we were out of food.

The moose season wouldn't open until fall, but at that time British Columbia game regulations allowed a prospector to get a permit and kill a moose any time he needed one for food. I was not a prospector and, anyway, I had no way to go into town for the permit unless I walked 27 miles each way. But my babies and I were as hungry as any prospector would ever be, and we had to have something to eat. I was sure the good Lord would forgive me, and I hoped the game warden would too, if he found out about it.

So one hot, windless July day—shortly before my twenty-eighth birthday—when fly season was getting real bad, I called the young-sters together.

"We've got to go try to kill a moose," I said. I knew the moose would be coming down to the river on that kind of day to rid themselves of flies and mosquitoes.

I had never shot a moose, but necessity is the mother of a lot of new experiences, and I decided I could do it all right if I got the chance. I got Olive and Louis and Vala ready, loaded them into the big clumsy canoe, and poked four shells into my old .30/30 Winchester Model 94. I jacked one into the chamber, put the hammer on half cock, and started upstream against the quiet current of the Stuart River.

It was a little more than a year after the June day in 1928 when a neighbor, Jack Hamilton, had come to our lonely homestead 40 miles down the Stuart from Fort St. James, in the mountain country of central British Columbia. He had a telegram for me from the Royal Canadian Mounted Police at Edmonton, and had to break the news that my husband, Walter Reamer, a trapper, had drowned in Leland Lake on the Alberta-Northwest Territories border. Walter's canoe had tipped over in a heavy windstorm.

That was almost 40 years ago, but I still remember raising my hand to my eyes to wipe away the fog that suddenly clouded them and Hamilton leading me to a chair by the kitchen table.

"You'd better sit down, Mrs. Reamer," he said.

I looked around at my three children. Olive, then only five years old, stood wide-eyed, not quite taking it all in. Vala was playing with her little white kitten, and Louis lay on his back, reaching for his toes. What was to become of them and me?

Olive leaned her head against my skirt and began to cry softly for her daddy, and I felt a lump in my chest that made it hard to breathe. But that was not the time for tears. If I cried, I'd do it out of the children's sight.

"Will you be all right?" Jack Hamilton asked before he left.

"I'll be all right," I told him firmly.

All right? I wondered. I was 26 and a homesteader-trapper's widow with three little children, 160 acres of brush-grown land, almost none of it cleared, a small log house—and precious little else.

That was just before the start of the great depression, the period that Canadians of my generation still call the dirty thirties. There was no allowance for dependent children then. I knew I could get a small sum of relief money each month, maybe about $12 for the four of us, but I did not dare to ask for it.

Olive and Louis had been born in Canada, but Vala had been born in the United States, as had I. I was afraid that if I appealed for help, Vala or I or both of us might be sent back to that country. In the very first hours of my grief and loneliness, I vowed I'd never let that happen, no matter what. It was the four of us alone now, to fight the world of privation and hunger, but at least we'd stay together.

My father had been a trapper, and my mother had died when I was eight. We had been a happy family, but always poor folk with no money to speak of. And after I married Walter, his trapline didn't bring in much. I had never known anything but a hard life, but now I was thankful for it. I knew I was more up to the hardships that lay ahead than most women would be.

I don't think I looked the part. Please don't get the idea that I was a backwoods frump, untidy and slovenly. I was small, five feet two, and weighed 112, all good solid muscle. And if I do say it, when I had the proper clothes on and was out dancing, I could compete with the best of them in looks.

There were a lot of moose around our homestead, some deer, black bears, wolves, rabbits, grouse, fox, mink, and muskrat. I decided I'd become a hunter and trapper on my own.

We had a little money on hand to buy food with. We had no horses, but I dug potatoes, raked hay—did whatever I could for our few neighbors to pay for the use of a team. By the next spring, I had managed to clear the brush and trees from a few acres of good land.

Olive was housekeeper, cook, and baby-sitter while I worked outside. I planted a vegetable garden and started a hay meadow. I hunted grouse and rabbits, and neighbors helped out the first winter by giving us moose meat. We managed to eke out a living. It was all hard work, day in and day out, dragging myself off to bed when dark came and crawling out at daylight to begin another day. But at least my babies and I had something to eat.

Then, in July of 1929, our food gave out. I couldn't bring myself to go deeper in debt to my neighbors, and in desperation I decided on the out-of-season moose hunt. With the few odds and ends we had left, we could make out on moose meat until the garden stuff started to ripen.

We hadn't gone far up the Stuart in the cranky dugout before I began to see moose tracks along shore and worn moose paths leading down to the river. Then we rounded a bend, and a big cow moose was standing out on a grassy point, dunking her ungainly head and coming up with mouthfuls of weeds.

I didn't want to kill a cow and maybe leave a calf to starve, but I don't think I was ever more tempted in my life than I was right then. That big animal meant meat enough to last us the rest of the summer, and by canning it I could keep every pound from spoiling. I paddled quietly ahead, whispering warnings to the kids to sit still and keep quiet. The closer I got, the more I wanted that moose. She finally saw us and looked our way while I wrestled with my conscience.

I'll never know what the outcome would have been, for about the time I was getting near enough to shoot, Olive let out a squeal of pure delight, and I saw a little red-brown calf raise up out of the tall grass. That settled it.

The children all talked at once, and the cow grunted to her youngster and waded out, ready to swim the river. We were only 200 feet away at that point, and all of a sudden she decided she didn't like us there. Her ears went back, the hair on her shoulders stood up, and her grunts took on a very unfriendly tone. I stuck my paddle into the mud and waited, wondering just what I'd do if she came for us.

There was no chance I could maneuver that cumbersome dugout out of her way. But I quieted the youngsters with a sharp warning, and after a minute the cow led her calf into deep water and they struck out for the opposite side of the river. I sighed with relief when they waded ashore and walked up a moose trail out of sight.

A half mile farther up the river we landed. I took Louis piggyback and carried my gun, and the four of us walked very quietly over a grassy point where I thought moose might be feeding. We didn't see any, and now the kids began to complain that they were getting awful hungry. I was hungry, too. We sat down on the bank to rest, and I saw a good rainbow trout swimming in shallow water.

I always carried a few flies and fishhooks in my hatband, and I tied a fly to a length of string and threw it out, using the string as a hand-line. The trout took the fly on about the fifth toss, and I hauled it in. I fished a little longer and caught two squawfish, and we hit back to the canoe.

I built a fire and broiled the rainbow and one of the squawfish on sticks. The kids divided the trout, and I ate the squawfish. As a rule squawfish have a muddy flavor, and I had really caught those two for dog food. But that one tasted all right to me.

A little farther up the Stuart, we came on two yearling mule deer with stubby spikes of antlers in the velvet. They watched us from a cut bank but spooked and disappeared into the brush soon after I saw them. A little later the same thing happened with two bull moose. They saw us and ran into the willows while I was reaching for my gun. I was so disappointed and discouraged I wanted to bawl.

That made four moose we had seen, counting the calf, without getting a shot, and I decided that killing one was going to be a lot harder than I had thought. And my arms were so tired from paddling the heavy dugout that they felt ready to drop out of the sockets.

I had brought a .22 along, as well as the .30/30, and a little while after that I used it to shoot a grouse that was watching us from the bank.

I had about given up all hope of getting a moose and was ready to turn back for the long paddle home when I saw what looked like the back of one, standing almost submerged in the shade of some cotton-woods up ahead. I shushed the kids and eased the canoe on for a better look, and sure enough, I was looking at a young bull, probably a yearling. Just a dandy size for what I wanted.

He was feeding, pulling up weeds from the bottom and putting his head completely under each time he went down for a mouthful. I paddled as close as I dared, and warned Olive and Vala to put their hands over their ears and keep down as low as they could, for I had to shoot over their heads.

I put the front bead of the Winchester just behind his shoulder, at the top of the water, and when he raised his head I let him have it. He went down with a great splash, and I told the kids they could raise up and look.

Luckily for us, the young bull did not die right away there in deep, muddy water. I don't know how I'd ever have gotten him ashore for dressing. When I got close with the dugout he was trying to drag himself out on the bank. My shot had broken his back. I crowded him with the canoe, feeling sorry for him all the while, and as soon as I had him all the way on dry land I finished him with a head shot.

I had always hated to kill anything, and by that time I was close to tears. Then I saw Olive leaning against a tree, crying her heart out, and Vala and Louis with their faces all screwed up in tears, and I felt worse than ever. But I reminded myself that it had to be done to feed the children, and I wiped my eyes and explained to them as best I could. About that time a porcupine came waddling along, and that took their minds off the moose.

Dressing a moose, even a yearling bull, is no fun. I went at it now, and it was about as hard a job as I had ever tackled. The kids tried to help but only succeeded in getting in the way. And while I worked, I couldn't help worrying about my out-of-season kill. What would happen if I were found out? Would the game warden be as understanding as I hoped?

When the job was done, I built a small fire to boil the partridge I'd shot and a few pieces of moose meat for our supper, giving Louis the broth in his bottle, I felt better after I ate, and I loaded the meat into the dugout and started home. But it was full dark now, and I was so tired that I soon decided not to go on.

We went ashore, spread out a piece of canvas, part under and part over us, and tried to sleep. The mosquitoes wouldn't let us, and I finally gave up. I sat over the children the rest of the night, switching mosquitoes off with a willow branch. Daylight came about 4 o'clock, and we got on the way.

I'll never forget that early-morning trip back to our place. My hands were black with mosquitoes the whole way, and the torment was almost too much. Joel Hammond, a neighbor, had given me some flour he'd made by grinding his own wheat in a hand mill, and the first thing I did was build a fire and make a batch of hot cakes. The flour was coarse and sort of dusty, but with moose steak and greens fried in moose fat, those cakes made a real good meal. Then I went to work canning meat.

That was the only moose I ever killed out of season. When hunting season rolled around that fall I got a homesteader's free permit and went after our winter's supply of meat. It came even harder that time.

The first one I tried for I wounded with a shot that must have cut through the tip of his lungs. He got away in thick brush, and I took our dog Chum and followed him. Chum drove him back into the river, and he swam across and stood wheezing and coughing on the opposite side, too far off for me to use my only remaining shell on him. Chum swam the river in pursuit, and started to fight him in shallow water.

Another neighbor, Ross Finley, who lived on the quarter section next to ours, heard me shoot and came up to lend a hand. He loaded Olive and me into our dugout, and we paddled across to where the dog was badgering the moose. When we got close, Finley used my last shell but missed.

The bull, fighting mad by now, came for the canoe, throwing his head this way and that. I was scared stiff, for I couldn't swim a stroke and neither could Olive. I knew that one blow from the moose's antlers would roll the dugout over like a pulpwood bolt.

I had the bow paddle, and I moved pretty fast, but at that the moose didn't miss us by a foot as I swung the canoe away from him. He was in deep water now, and Chum was riding on his shoulders and biting at the back of his neck. The dog took the bull's attention for a second or two, and I reached down and grabbed Finley's .22, which was lying in the bottom of the dugout.

I shot the moose right at the butt of the ear, with the gun almost touching him. He sank quietly out of sight, leaving Chum floating in the water. The dog was so worn out from the ruckus that we had to help him ashore.

We tried hard to locate the dead moose. But the current had carried it downriver, and it was days before we found it. The carcass was lying in shallow water at the mouth of a creek, the meat spoiled.

There were plenty more around, however. We could hear them fighting at night, grunting and snorting, and sometimes their horns would clash with a noise as loud as an ax hitting a hollow log. In the early mornings I saw as many as five at one time along the weedy river shore. I waited and picked the one I wanted, and that time I killed him with no trouble.

The Stuart was full of ducks and geese that fall, and there were grouse everywhere I went in the woods. I had plenty of ammunition for the .22 and always a few .30/30 shells around. I canned everything I killed and no longer worried about a meat shortage. Life was beginning to sort itself out.

A few unmarried men came around and tried to shine up to me, but I wasn't interested. All I wanted was to get more land cleared and buy a cow or two and a team of horses of my own. The young homestead widow was proving to herself that she could take care of her family and make the grade.

But before the winter was over I had another crisis. By February most of our food was gone, except for the canned meat and a few cans of vegetables. We had used the last of the hand-ground flour that Joel Hammond had given me and were desperately in need of groceries. I had no money, but I decided to walk the 27 miles to Vanderhoof, on the Prince George-Prince Rupert railroad, and try to get the supplies we needed on credit. I knew I could pay for them with potatoes the next fall, for by that time I had enough land cleared to grow a bigger potato crop than we needed for ourselves.

I left the three children with the George Vinsons, neighbors a mile and a half downriver, and started out on a cold, wintry morning. I had a road to follow, but only a few teams and sleighs had traveled it, and the walking was hard, in deep snow. Two miles out of Vanderhoof I finally hitched a ride.

I didn't have any luck getting credit against my potato crop. Those were hard times, and I guess the merchants couldn't afford much generosity. I tried first to buy rubbers for myself and the kids. We needed them very badly and they were the cheapest footgear available. But the store turned me down.

A kindly woman who ran a restaurant did well by me, however. She gave me a good dinner, and when I put her down for 50 pounds of potatoes she just smiled and shoved a chocolate bar into my pocket. I saw to it that she got the potatoes when the time came, anyway.

Another storekeeper told me that he couldn't let me have things on credit, but be gave me $2 in cash and told me to do the best I could with it. I knew where part of it was going—for the oatmeal and sugar I had promised Louis and Vala and Olive when I got home. But I couldn't see any way to pay for another meal for myself or a room for the night, and I walked around Vanderhoof thinking of how wet and cold our feet would be in the slush of the spring thaw.

I was about as heartbroken as I've ever been in my life.

Finally I decided to make another attempt. Some of my neighbors on the Stuart River traded at a store at Finmoore, 19 miles east of Vanderhoof. I also had a friend there, Mrs. John Holter. I'd walk the railroad track to Finmoore and try my luck there. At the time I didn't know how far it was and I expected a hike of only 10 miles or so.

It was about dark when I started. The railroad ties were crusted with ice, and the walking was very bad. My clothes were hardly enough for the cold night, either: denim overalls, men's work socks, Indian moccasins, and an old wool sweater with the elbows out, worn under a denim jacket.

I had never been brave in the dark, any time or any place, and I can't tell you what an ordeal that walk was. All I could think of were the hobos I had heard stories about, the railroad bums, and I was afraid of every shadow.

I got to the lonely little station at Hulatt, 15 miles from Vanderhoof, at midnight and asked the stationmaster if I could rest until daylight. I lay down on the floor by the big potbellied stove. It was warm and cozy, and I was worn out. I started to drift off to sleep but then I began to worry about the children and the likelihood that if I was later in getting home than I had promised, they might come back to the house and get into trouble starting a fire. Things were hard enough without having the place burned down. I got up and trudged away along the track once more.

It was 2 o'clock in the morning when I reached the Holter place. Mrs. Holter fixed me a sandwich and a cup of hot milk, and I fell into bed. She shook me awake at 9 o'clock, as I had told her to. Those scant seven hours were all the sleep I had in more than 36.

Mrs. Holter loaned me another $2, and I went to the general store and struck it rich. The proprietor, Percy Moore, stared at me in disbelief when I poured out my hard-luck story.

"You've walked from the Stuart River since yesterday morning?" he asked in amazement. "That's forty-six miles!"

"No, forty-four," I corrected him. "I got a ride the last two miles into Vanderhoof." Then I added, "I've got fourteen more to walk home before dark tonight, too."

The first thing he let me have, on credit, was the three pairs of rubbers we needed so desperately. Then he took care of my grocery list. Eight pounds of oatmeal, three of rice, five of beans, five of sugar and—for a bonus—a three-pound pail of strawberry jam.

I plodded away from Finmoore at 10 o'clock that morning with almost 30 pounds in a packsack on my back.

Three inches of wet snow had fallen that morning, and the 14-mile walk seemed endless, each mile longer than the one before. My pack got heavier and heavier, and sometime in the afternoon I began to stumble and fall. I was so tired by that time, and my back ached so cruelly from the weight of the pack, that I wanted to lie there in the snow and go to sleep.

But I knew better. After each fall, I'd drive myself back to my feet and stagger on.

To this day I do not know when it was that I reached our place, but it was long after dark. Chum met me in the yard, and no human being was ever more glad to fumble at the latch of his own door.

I slid out of the pack, pulled off my wet moccasins and socks, and rolled into bed with my clothes on. The last thing I remember was calling the dog up to lie at my feet for warmth. The children awakened me at noon the next day, fed me breakfast, and rubbed some of the soreness out of my swollen legs and feet.

Next fall, when I harvested my potato crop, I paid off my debt to Percy Moore in full, except for one item. There was no way to pay him, ever, for his kindness to me when I was broke and had three hungry children at home.

I was to make many more trips to Finmoore in the years before I left the Stuart, for I did most of my trading at his store. And when times got better, he and his wife and daughter Ruth often came out and bought vegetables and eggs from me. I remember walking back to his place the next year, carrying six dressed chickens, selling them for 50¢ apiece, spending the money for food and packing it home. Three dollars bought quite a heavy load in those days. ❖

MAY 1967

50

KING of the SWAMP

by Homer Croy

❖

OLD BULL, THE ALLIGATOR, LAY motionless in the water, with only his eyes and nostrils out, looking and listening. But he was always doing that—always on guard, every minute of the day and night. Even when he was asleep the slightest sound aroused him. He had to do this; if he didn't, he died. That was what it cost to live in the quiet, peaceful swamp.

He was the king of the swamp, the enemy of almost every living creature he knew, and almost every living creature that knew him was his enemy. But no swamp creature was so ferocious, so ruthless, so sinister. And he was the strongest. Nothing could stand before him. He lived and hunted both on the land and in the water, as fierce as a lion, as strong as a shark. He was fifteen feet long, fifteen feet of muscle, and cruelty, and cunning.

In comparison, the crocodile was a gentle maid out for a stroll. He was larger, his snout was shorter and broader, and his teeth were arranged differently. And he was far more cruel.

His enemy was coming. Hunters. Men in boats with high-powered rifles. But he was not afraid. In fact, he was afraid of nothing—one of his scant virtues. He did not court danger, but when the show-down came he gave all he had, which was plenty. It was startling to think that one so slimy, so scaly, so grotesque in appearance should have so much intelligence tucked away in that nauseating body. But he was what he was.

He was not afraid, for the hunters had come many times before and he had always got away. As he had always escaped from all his enemies.

All sorts of creatures had hunted him when he was an egg. The minute he was born new troubles beset him, muskrats, for one. Another was his own cannibal father, who considered him a most pleasing delicacy and would have gobbled him down, if his mother hadn't spirited him out of sight.

And so, like a monstrous hen with her brood, the mother waddled off to the brackish water with his brothers and sisters around her. Once he got to the water, things were not so bad, because, for some strange reason, the father seemed to look on him in a different way. His son could swim, he might amount to something some day.

The boat with the hunters came closer, but the alligator just waited. That was what he did best. He would wait motionless for hours for a toothsome dog to come sniffing along the edge of the water. He liked dog best of all. Second best, he liked the razorback hogs which ran wild in the lonely parts of the swamp. Men feared them, for they were fleet and strong, and as merciless as himself. He had, however, to keep his wits about him, for a drove needed watching. But, if he could entice them into the water, then he was master, no matter how many there were, nor how savage.

The sound of the hunters' boat grew stronger. The younger alligators, who were not so cunning, began to notice it. That was another strange thing about this ancient alligator. As he grew older, his hearing became more acute, his eyesight improved, and his cunning grew greater, and his temper worse. He fought the other alligators in the swamps and marshes more than he did the young alligators. He was seventy years old. He had not become full grown till he was twenty-five, and he would live to be a hundred, if nothing happened. Even when he died he would not rise to the top, as fishes do, but would sink to the bottom and be eaten by others of his kind.

The hunters' boat came closer. The men were watching, their guns were ready. The alligator's teeth, when put in the ground and rotted from the jaw bone, would sell at fancy prices for ivory; his skin would make a lovely suitcase. But some hunters did not want him for these purposes; they wanted to pin his hide on the wall to show how well they could shoot with their big guns.

It was almost a game with the king, a game far too hazardous for the alligators to play. The point was to see how near he could let the boat come before he slid out of sight. Closer and closer it came, making an incalculable amount of noise, although the hunters thought themselves craftily silent. Then, at the last possible moment, the king slid into the water and made no ripple all. What other animal could do that? And that was not the only astounding thing the killer could do. He could fight fiercely on both land and sea. But he was better—far better—in the water. His toy legs were his great trouble on land. They were far too uncertain, and carried him along at a miserable rate. They were puny and tiny for one of his tremendous strength, but they got him from one bayou to another. No fish could do that.

Old Bull and his kind were clever and crafty beyond believing in many things, but in others they were just plain dumb. One was the staked-dog trick. They could never learn it. The hunters would stake a dog out on the bank, then get behind a blind. But Old Bull learned it. Sometimes the temptation was almost beyond his powers of resistance, but he did resist. Foolish young alligators waddled toward the dog. That was the end of the foolish young alligators.

The hunters' boat went by, and Old Bull came to the top again, without a ripple, and those two eyes, which looked so much like knots on a log, again surveyed his enemy. Suddenly one of the men leaned forward. Bang! Instantly there was a tremendous threshing in the water. A young alligator had been shot. The boat came joyously back, and in a short time the young alligator was on the bank, its mouth spread with a stick. It made the king mad. If they hadn't pulled the young alligator out, Old Bull could have had food for several days.

"There's a lot more 'gators here," said one of the hunters. "We could come back at night and jack 'em."

"Let's do that," said another. "That's the best way to get them. They can't stand up against a light."

There wasn't any sense in staying, after the hunters had frightened everything away, the old king decided. He swam slowly off, looking for something to eat. He was always either eating, or resting after a full meal. That was the biggest want in his life. Food. Always food. And lots of it. Those mighty muscles had to have it.

Old Bull had other wants, too. One was to impress the dainty female alligators, full three feet shorter than himself, with his mighty prowess. He had his own way of doing that. It was by the simple process of bellowing—a terrible, earth-shaking, primeval sound. When that mood came over him he filled up with air, opened his mouth, braced his legs and violently expelled his breath. To one who heard it from nearby, it was almost deafening, the most lonesome, awe-inspiring sound of the swamp.

But the king was not to have the female for the asking. There were other bull alligators around, and, when he went toward her, one of them challenged his way. The two drew up and looked at each other, nose to nose, silently, making no motion at all except, now and then, the slightest fleck of the tail. Suddenly all was changed; the two bulls were at each other. The water heaved, it churned, red streaked it. The bulls did not stop. At last Old Bull triumphed, swam bloodily off. But Old Bull knew it would end that way; it always had been; it always would be. King of the swamp.

He had to rest a while before he could go to the female. Two days he idled and sunned himself while his cuts grew better. Later, the female would lay eggs; the process of life would go on. This urge, however, seldom came over him. But the food urge was always there.

A week later he went back to the river where the hunters had been. Everything was quiet and peaceful, except for one hunter's boat. A shot from one hunter's rifle nipped him, but he had sweet revenge.

One flip of his mighty tail and the boat was in the water. And he got one of the Negroes. There was a terrible fuss about that. More hunters came and probed the water. That made him mad. Anything, or any act, that took food from him made him furious.

His appetite was ferocious, and the way he hung onto life was astonishing. He could be proud of himself, in that respect. He was a true survivor of the age of monsters. Most creatures had succumbed, but Old Bull and his kind hadn't.

He swam silently under water up to the edge of the land, and lifted his eyes and nostrils, and became silent. Snakes slid by, birds screamed. A young alligator came nosing around, and Old Bull flashed over to call on him. The foolish young alligator went off to look for other pastures and Old Bull came back and again took up his patient vigil.

He was rewarded at last, for a drove of wild hogs began to drift down to the water's edge. Must be careful. They were ferocious creatures themselves. A diamond-back rattlesnake was a titbit to one of them. They had long, cruel tusks which could tear any living creature to shreds, and razor hoofs to stamp him. But Old Bull wasn't afraid. He had dined off many a razorback, the finest dish in all the world, except dog. But dogs were much harder to get. Fewer of them, for one thing. Didn't come in droves. But, on the other hand, the wild hogs had an ancient feud with alligators, which did not enter into the make-up of a dog. In the first place, a dog couldn't fight back. No tusks. The process was simple. His powerful tail tapped the dog into the water, his mighty jaws opened, they snapped shut, and he swam away with the dog under water.

Patiently he waited. The high-backed, thin-flanked, steel-muscled, mighty-tusked creatures came toward him making to his sensitive ears enough noise for an army. They had been eating nuts; they were thirsty. They came closer, the leader a little ahead and proceeding cautiously—for them. Closer.

Old Bull shot forward with incredible speed and switched his tail. The lead hog was hurled into the air and fell neatly into the water. Another dart forward, the great jaws opened, and he swam away with the wild hog as easily as a cat trotting away with a mouse. Instantly there was a mighty squealing among the wild hogs, but they retreated, as they always did, for he was in the water, which was his home. Nothing in that country could stand against him.

He did not devour the wild hog immediately, for his gullet was very small. Jaws big. Throat tiny. But there were other ways of taking care of that. He carried the hog along to where the river branched off and grew narrower, and then, nosing out a hole in the bank, he packed it in, and nosed back the dirt again as neatly as a mason smoothes mortar. A few days later, when he came back, the razorback was so decayed that he could easily pull it to pieces and get it down his strangely inadequate throat. And he kept it there, in his private cupboard, nibbling from time to time at his dainty.

That monstrous appetite must be appeased. The swamp where he was accustomed to rule had too many alligators in it. He would change his feeding grounds. At last, he started for another arm of the bayou 200 yards away. Sometimes the ground was flooded. At such times he could manage handsomely. But now it was dry, and the path he set for himself led through the pine forest, a beautiful, peaceful glade.

He left a broad, flat trail behind him, with little footmarks along it like prints on a pound of butter. He moved slowly, due to his immense weight and to his bent, awkward, ill-adjusted legs. Frequently he paused, lifted himself up, and looked sharply around. No time to be caught by illwishers. Then his ears picked up a faint but ominous sound. He began to hurry, his toy legs beat faster, but that was hard work, and he paused. There it was again, and it was coming closer. Again he started.

The drove of razorbacks feeding in the pines came closer. Their sharp noses caught the odor. They stopped, their ears went up, and fear laid hold of them. Their ancient enemy. But this was different. No water here...

As they moved toward him, Old Bull struggled harder than ever, but this only took him deeper into the peaceful pines. The hogs came closer and ringed around him. No contented grunting now, but the shrill cries of attack. They came at him, drawing their lips back from their savage tusks, the hair on their backs lifted. They began to run past him, along his side, craftily out of reach of the slashings of his tail, slitting him a little each time. They came at him from both sides, trying to get under his throat and at his eyes.

He began to roar, but it was not the monstrous lyric call he had sent up when he courted in the lagoon, but a terrible shriek, growing high and somehow, pitiful. He tried to run, as they tore at him, but, after a

THEY CAME AT HIM from both sides, drawing back their lips from their savage tusks.

few feet, he had to sink down. Then they were at him again. One of them took an eye; the throat cuts went deeper, blood ran among the pine needles. The shrill, exultant cries of victory rose from the lashing, blood-drenched pack.

A few days later a plantation Negro got a surprise as he came into the pine-covered dell. Both the king's eyes were gone, his throat was open, his legs chewed. The ground was cut by a myriad sharp hooves, but under them all the broad, flat, death trail still showed. Old Bull had died, but not until he had fought to the bitter finish. With tail and teeth, he had made his death a costly victory.

The Negro hurried away. This was a mighty fine specimen.

With shiny, new, glass eyes, Old Bull now glares down at curious passers-by from a pedestal in a great museum. Half fearfully, half admiringly the visitors study his mighty body. Some intrepid hunter, they assume, dared the killing power of those tremendous jaws to bag this monarch of the swamp. Far from their minds is any thought of razorback hogs and their slashing tusks. ◆

MARCH 1936

The HAMMERHEAD

by Hank Bruns

❖

SOMETHING HAD TO GIVE. My fly rod had that deadly arc indicative of ultimate stress. The bend was severe just above the grip, and the rest of the rod lay out almost parallel with the water. But I just didn't have enough strength left in my wrist to raise the thing.

I glanced at the anchor rope, and then I reached for it. My little watch fob of an anchor came easily out of the coral, and somehow I managed to get it into the kayak. The boat began to move toward Hawk Channel, which meant the Atlantic.

Getting that anchor aboard gave me a mild sense of triumph. As I say, something had to give, and it wasn't going to be me. I was determined to land this big shark, but I should have known that my stubbornness was ridiculous and foolhardy.

Key West, Fla., is a long way from New Jersey, which is where I was living then. Some 1,200 miles, I guess. The kayak I'd put together in the garage back home was a boat, and because I knew that I'd be going fishing in Key West and would need a boat I took the kayak with me. It had two pontoons attached to it. They were like miniature kayaks, made of canvas stretched over light wooden frames, and were mounted on a crossbar which placed them about three feet out on each side of the kayak amidships.

The kayak worked fine in New Jersey, especially on lakes like Budd, Swartswood, and Hopatcong. It even carried me on one mildly perilous trip down the Musconetcong River. It was a good fishing boat. Good, that is, for bass and trout.

In Key West it created a small sensation. People turned to stare at it, and sometimes they smiled or laughed. They often looked twice. Small boys followed my car, chattered in Spanish, and pointed in wonder at the thing perched on top. It made me kind of proud. We usually are when we can be safely different.

I was a little nervous when I first put the kayak in the water off the Boca Chica Fishing Camp. Boca Chica was a quiet tropical isle before the Navy took over. I paddled out into the turquoise channel that separates Boca Chica from the island south of it. The long wooden bridge was some distance away, and here and there were flats where the water slowed and spread itself thinly. To my right were tiny dotted mangrove keys that shouldered the water into sectional flows.

The wide, immensely high skies were bigger than anything; the white clouds piled up for miles. I knew that the black, wide-winged bird soaring over my head was a frigate bird. I don't know how I knew. I just did. Terns with cocked, inquisitive heads flew so close that I could see their orange legs plainly. A pelican collapsed into the water with a great splash, then sat and rearranged the fish in his bill. A horde of small silver fish came out of the blue water in one leaping lift. Then they all went down, only to come up again three feet beyond. They were being chased by a swarm of striking jacks. The water boiled, and as it did so the terns left me to join the party. I was bewitched.

At that moment the kayak bumped hard and tipped as far as the pontoons would permit. I came back to my senses and pushed my light craft away from the bridge piling against which it had bumped. I began to paddle back up the channel. Outside that wooden bridge was the Atlantic, and I wasn't ready for it.

I went to work with my casting rod and plugs. It was difficult to keep the kayak from rushing away with the tide. I'd cast once and then have to paddle for three or four minutes. I didn't like it, so I quit fishing.

Then I went exploring, west against the current, toward the backwaters near the little keys. Four tarpon came rolling up out of a deep hole, and my heart leaped. They weren't silver, as I'd read; they were pinkish and yellow. At least their backs were, and that's all I could see.

I approached a tiny key. It wasn't more than fifty feet long, but it had a white sandy beach. As I got closer to it a three-foot barracuda slid out of his hiding place and went past me. When he saw the kayak he kicked his tail, and was gone. I slid the kayak up on the beach and stepped ashore. Instantly I was covered with small black mosquitoes. I got out of there fast, wiping layers of mosquitoes off my arms and face. There was a lot of blood.

I went back to Key West, and that's when I bought the little anchor. It weighed only five pounds. Charlie Thompson sold it to me, and he knew the waters around there. He laughed at the anchor, and called it a watch fob because it was so little. But it was O.K. for my kayak. Charlie suggested that I fish off Rest Beach.

"Lots of coral out there about half a mile," he said. "Take a water glass. Look down into the holes in the coral. Pick the fish you want to catch." He laughed. I bought a bucket with a glass bottom in it. Charlie told me to hold the bottom of the bucket against the surface of the water and to look down. "You can see a fish sigh with that thing," he said.

Next morning I went out off Rest Beach. I carried the anchor, two sandwiches, and a crawfish tail for bait. I had about 150 yards of silk casting line on my fly reel. I didn't take fly line because I didn't expect to cast. I had some drinking water, my big sheath knife, some brass leader wire, and some hooks.

The water off the beach was so shallow I could have waded out in it for a couple of city blocks. I kept looking into the water glass. Charlie was right, I could see everything—even grains of sand which sometimes moved because they weren't grains of sand at all but small mollusks. I saw three big crawfish hiding in crevices. Their long feelers waved fast when the kayak went over.

Then I came to the coral. It was just like in the books. There was a great city of it going out for a long way. There were fish in the dark holes of the coral, small yellowtails, muttonfish, porkfish, angelfish, and grunts. There were sargeantfish, tiny damselfish, and slippery dicks, too. I looked down into the bucket so long I began to get seasick. I didn't know whether it was from my looking down or from the chop. The chop is always bad over shallow water, even on nice days. This was a very nice day.

I dropped the watch fob overboard and paid out line until the kayak was right at the edge of a big hole. Then I cut the crawfish tail into fine baits, tied a wire leader to the end of my line, and fastened a hook to it. A segment of the crawfish tail slipped on the hook nicely. I dropped the line into the water, and placed the rod over the gunwales of the kayak. The boat gave the bait plenty of motion.

The dip and rise of the craft occupied my attention for a time; I felt green. But quickly the tip of the fly rod moved. The kayak went up, but the rod tip stayed down. I picked up the butt and set the hook. The fish fought hard. It bore down, then went round and round like a big bluegill. It put up a good fight, and when I brought it in it turned out to be a black angelfish. When I grasped it, the sharp scalpel-like bone projection on its gills cut my thumb badly. I still have the scar. I put the angelfish in a sack, baited my hook again, and tossed it into the water.

The air smelled like warm seaweed. The clouds were high, white, and round. The terns came to visit me, and I tossed them the shell of the crawfish tail. On the beach I could see the cabanas and little people. They seemed very far away.

My rod tip went down sharply, making an audible swish. Drops of seawater struck my sunglasses. I grabbed the butt quickly and raised it until I felt the fish move. It felt terribly strong. I set the hook. Nothing happened. It was as though the fish hadn't noticed the sting of the steel. Its calm indifference annoyed me, so I struck hard, again and again.

When I was a small boy I once tried to bring a bucket of water up out of a well. I got it half way and then had to let go. Its weight was too much for me. The awful weight of that bucket came as a shock to me, and I never forgot it.

Something like that happened now. The fish I'd hooked shook and then, like that bucket of water, pulled from my grasp and shot away. There was nothing I could do to stop it. I held the rod high, and the reel spun. Since the water wasn't deep, the line tangent was long. It cut the water with an ominous hiss. A wave of fear swept over me momentarily.

Maybe it was fortunate that I couldn't thumb the reel. With no drag beyond the slight one of the line, the fish ran only 200 or perhaps 300 feet. Then it turned. A gull came down the line, but when it approached the fish's end it veered up wildly.

I compressed my lips and pulled the rod tip high. I began turning the red handle. The fish moved off into the direction of the sun. The swing gave me some slack, and I reeled as fast as could.

A second later the fish turned again and came toward me. Realizing that would be impossible to reel line fast enough, I began to strip it in. It fell in coils on my feet. The fish slowed down about thirty feet away. I took in more slack. Then the fish surfaced. I gasped when I saw it. It was a hammerhead shark, and was nearly as long as my kayak.

When I'd got in almost all the loose line the shark submerged and made another run. This time the run was strong and full of panic. The line whipped up and flipped over a button on my shirt. There was a twang, and the button was gone. The shark headed out to sea.

I leaned back on the rod and gave the shark full butt. The effort had no effect on the fish. The line tore out, the reel hummed, and the rod assumed a terrible arc. So I lifted the anchor.

I put my left hand under the butt section of the fly rod, hoping to relieve the near paralysis in my arms. The line dwindled fast, but the fish was slowing. I held hard, desperately.

Suddenly the kayak began to move, but I found that with just the right amount of strain on the line I could save what I had reeled in. After a while I even began to take in more line. But the big fish moved on out.

My right arm began to ache. At first it was just a small ache, like the beginning of a toothache; it spread fiercely and suddenly to my shoulder. I gathered the entire rod into my arms, and pressed the butt into my stomach. This gave me some relief.

At times the fish appeared to rest. When it did I pumped in line until the kayak was almost over the monster. I looked around at the beach, and was frightened when I couldn't see much of the cabanas. I put more pressure on the shark.

It happened while I was attempting to gain a little more line. The shark seemed to be resting, and I was pumping away at the reel handle. The line was straight down. Suddenly the pressure on it lightened. I reeled desperately, hoping that the fish was about to give up. In seconds the hammerhead appeared under the left pontoon.

The shark was long, and utterly horrible. Its eyes stuck out on the extremities of the crossbar that is part of its head. It looked at me, and I at it. Then it turned on its side and moved to the pontoon. It opened its jaws and bit the fragile thing clean through. The kayak immediately listed sharply to the left. Desperately I threw my weight to the right, at the same time letting go of the line.

I no longer felt secure. With only one pontoon for balance, it became imperative for me to keep my weight on the right of the kayak all the time. I'd arrived at the point when the only sensible thing to do was cut the line and paddle home. But I didn't.

I don't know why I didn't. Perhaps I was trying unconsciously to be a hero. Real fear flooded over me, but instead of provoking me to be sensible it only increased my foolish determination to hang on.

My slacking off of line relieved the tension of the moment; the shark turned, went down, and swam leisurely away. I gave line grudgingly. The kayak again began to follow the fish, but this time it acted like a crippled seagull.

I leaned hard to the right. It hurt my side, but I tried not to think of that. A squall came up, and the rain pelted hard. Seconds became minutes, minutes hours. We headed farther out into the Atlantic. I managed to eat a sandwich and drink some water. Nausea gagged me, but I hoped the food would calm the trouble inside me. It didn't.

A black tramp steamer went south far on the fuzzy horizon. I watched it with longing. A great flock of terns followed me for a while. The big blue balloons of Portuguese men-of-war drifted past, and once a stray flying fish lifted from the water.

The water was turning from green to deep blue, and I knew we couldn't be far from the Gulf Stream. My arms hurt terribly. I began to talk to myself, telling myself how stupid I was for not cutting the line. Why don't you cut the line, you fool? But I didn't cut it.

I looked at my watch. It was now five hours since I'd hooked the shark. I couldn't see Key West; it had dropped below the horizon. I began to doze, but suddenly I felt that I was tipping. I came awake with a frightened start and leaned heavily to the right. I was tired, seasick, and hurt, but eventually I fell asleep.

A sudden bump shook me, and I awoke with a shout. Next to me, on the water, was a small platform that reached almost to the kayak. I looked up and saw a small Bahama sloop. It was the dirtiest, most ramshackle boat I've ever seen, but to me it looked beautiful. There were four or five men aboard. One leaned over the gunwale. "Hey mon," he shouted, "you in trouble?"

I shook my head. Then I knew I was being silly, and I think I blushed.

"My outrigger," I answered. "I lost it. Shark bit it off."

I was close to the boat's platform now, and I managed to uncramp one arm from around my rod and grasp it. The pain was awful. The man who had shouted came down the ladder.

"Here mon, why it 'appen you don't let go that pole?" he asked, reaching out for me.

"Hooked big shark," I gasped. "Don't want to lose him."

"Don't want to lose 'im? Why not, mon?"

I was on the platform now, and the man was tying the kayak to the ladder.

"I don't know," I said. I staggered and almost fell, but the man grasped my arm.

"It ain't nothing to eat, mon. Break your line," he urged.

I shook my head. I had my left arm around the rod, and leaned back against it. I reeled. I felt dead, except for the pain. The man scratched his head.

"E won't let 'im go, and it ain't a eatin' fish. God! Where you from?" he asked.

"Key West," I gasped, "Rest Beach."

"In that thing?" He looked at the kayak.

I nodded, working at the reel. The shark was a dead weight, but it moved slowly toward me.

"Get a gaff," I begged.

The man turned to one of the crew. He got a gaff, a great hook on a ten-foot pole, and turned to the water. The hammerhead was close now. I gave the rod all it would take.

"Hough," the man grunted, and struck the gaff into the fish. The water exploded, the pressure on the rod suddenly disappeared, and I fell into the water.

I saw one of the men on the deck grab the gaff, and felt him haul me aboard. That was all. After that all the lights went out.

I awoke just before the boat pulled into the dock at Key West.

"Thanks," I said to the man. He laughed.

"What a sport," he said. "Know how much that 'ammerhead weighed? It weighed one hundred an' twenty-seven pounds."

My good wife took care of me when I got home. She said a great many things, and asked a lot of questions. She kept asking one question I couldn't answer. "What were you trying to prove?"

I still don't know, not well enough to put it into words. But I think other fishermen will understand. ❖

JANUARY 1953

SPEARED BY A SAILFISH

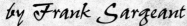

by Frank Sargeant

RON ABBOTT was crouched in the bow of his 23-foot cuddy fisherman, the corner of a cast net clenched firmly in his teeth. The boat floated on the shallow grass flats of Florida's Indian River as dawn began to turn the sky pink.

He waited for the school of silver mullet to draw within range, and then whirled the shining web of monofilament over them. Half a dozen fish were caught inside the net as he quickly drew the lead line to trap them. They fluttered madly on the deck as he shook them free.

Six mullet would be enough because Abbott, as usual, was fishing alone. He flipped the big mullet into his live-well, started the outboard, and pointed the bow out Sebastian Inlet toward the Atlantic. It was an almost mirror-calm day, rare off this part of the Florida peninsula, and the rising sun burned a golden track for Abbott's boat as he raced offshore. The 200-horse outboard motor sent him greyhounding over the low swells.

Abbott, a muscular and athletic 43-year-old, is a saltwater fishing addict. His established business as a mobile home dealer in nearby Melbourne gave him plenty of time to pursue his passion. His boat, the "Miss Carolyn," was an almost new Pro-Line rigged with every fishing option available for offshore trolling.

He followed a 120° course, running for about 45 minutes until his depth recorder marked 240 feet. This put him more than 20 miles off the inlet, near the edge of the continental shelf where the northward flowing Gulf Stream begins to make itself felt. The water was deep indigo, and had long trails of golden-orange sargasso weed where the varying currents met. The fishing should be good, Abbott surmised while he eyed the weedlines.

Always hoping for a trophy fish, a blue marlin or maybe a big shark, Abbott rigged a two-pound mullet on a heavy wire leader and hooked it lightly on a file-sharpened, live-bait hook so that it could swim freely. He dropped the bait back on a 6/0 trolling rig, then set out four lighter rods with rigged balao, the hooks buried in their bellies. He trolled slowly south along the weedlines. Though the water looked alive, with plenty of small baitfish fluttering at the surface, no fish struck Abbott's baits for the first hour of fishing.

At 8 a.m. the big outboard sputtered, then went dead. Abbott, used to taking care of minor problems, quickly checked the fuel lines, the battery hookups, and ignition cables. He found nothing unusual. He reported his position to the Coast Guard, but wasn't worried. After spending years as a Coast Guardsman all over the eastern Atlantic, he had little fear of the ocean. He believed he could get the motor started, or at least get a tow from other boats in the area before long.

As he was working on the motor, his baits drifted listlessly behind the boat. Suddenly he saw the big mullet come to the surface about 50 feet behind the boat, flipping desperately. Seconds later, a club-like bill rose above the baitfish, and then disappeared in a massive boil. Abbott grabbed the rod and fed line to the fish. Then he jammed the reel into gear and slammed the hook home. About 100 yards out a blue marlin weighing at least 400 pounds came raging across the surface, shaking its mighty head. The mullet sailed off the hook, but the barb was solidly fixed in the jaw of the billfish.

The fish went down and began a sizzling run. Without the motor to help him follow the marlin, Abbott knew he had no chance. He swore as line melted from the reel. Soon the metal spool showed through, and seconds later the 80-pound-test monofilament drew taut, hummed, and snapped as the great fish gave a final good-bye leap. The line had broken at the spool.

Abbott had little time to regret the loss. The boat had drifted into a heavy weedline, and there were fish all around him. Two of the smaller reels began to howl at once; fish had struck the balao baits dead in the water and had hooked themselves.

Both fish proved to be leapers. A sizable bull dolphin cavorted in yellow and green flashes at the end of one line. And on the other, a big Atlantic sailfish leaped toward the sky, thrashing to throw the hook.

Unable to handle both rods at once, Abbott had to decide which fish to fight. If he left one rod in the holder to fight the other, chances are the lines would become tangled and he'd lose both fish. Since he already had a good stock of dolphin fillets at home in the freezer, he clipped the line of the dolphin rod and set the fish free. Then he turned his attention to the sailfish.

The fish leaped mightily, its sides and sail glowing an iridescent purple. It was a good sail, close to eight feet long, and it was only 30 feet from the boat. It dashed around the bow, and Abbott moved the rod around his outriggers and aerials, above the cuddy cabin and back into the cockpit. The fish then went straight under the stern, ripping line off the reel.

Then the line went slack, and 40 feet off the transom the water burst open. The sail was tailwalking wildly, and it was headed right at the boat.

Abbott was more intent on catching fish than on the possible danger. Only at the last instant did he realize that the sail was not going to stop.

"My God," he thought, "he's coming straight at me!"

Abbott watched in amazement as the fish came close, it's bill flailing the air wildly. It rose in a last frantic jump just five feet behind the outboard, and then came over the transom in a graceful, arching leap.

Abbott danced on one foot, attempting to pirouette out of the way of the fish. As he did, the sail's sharp bill came down and plunged into his upraised left foot like a dagger. He roared in pain and surprise.

The weight of the fish slammed him to the deck, knocking the rod from his hand. He landed on his back with the fish lying across his chest.

"I grabbed the fish in a bear hug and tried to pull the spear out of my foot," he said. "It wouldn't budge, but I could feel the roughness of that bill ripping into my heel like a buzz saw. Blood began to pour from my foot.

"About that time, the fish started raising all kinds of hell."

The force of the sailfish's twists raised Abbott completely off the deck as he clung frantically to the fish's tail. Abbott ricocheted off the fighting chair and slammed against the gunwales. One violent slash of the tail struck him on the mouth, and he could feel his front teeth give way from the blow. Rods snapped and tackle flew out of the boat. The deck turned crimson with blood from the gills of the hooked fish and Abbott's heel.

"I was bouncing around, as if the deck was a trampoline," Abbott recalls. "He ping-ponged me off just about everything hard that he could find, and almost threw me out of the boat. He had me three or four feet off the floor sometimes. One thing was sure. Wherever he went I went, because that spear was stuck in my foot like it had been welded there. I knew if we went over the side, that would be it, so I made darn sure that didn't happen. But there wasn't much else I could do. The power in his body was unbelievable. "

For what seemed like hours but was certainly not more than minutes, the fish battered Abbott, slamming his leg to the deck with each convulsion.

Finally the mad flailing ceased as the fish began to tire. Moving carefully so as not to arouse a final effort from the sail, Abbott again grasped its body near the tail and attempted to pull the bill from his agonizing wound. The coarse texture of the spear gripped his flesh, tearing at it like sandpaper.

"I have never felt pain like that. I heard myself screaming, and felt tears pouring from my eyes, and then everything went black," he recalled.

He came to slowly. The powerful smell of the big sail washed over him, mingled with the iron-tinged scent of his own blood. Midmorning sun poured into the cockpit, turning it bake-oven hot in the calm ocean.

Abbott opened his eyes, but his vision was blurred by a mixture of blood and fish slime. Wiping at his eyes, he finally saw the fish lying next to him, the large, round eye slowly glazing in death. The tip of its spear was broken off.

Abbott looked at his injured foot and saw several inches of the thumb-thick stump protruding from his tennis shoe. The rest was inside his heel, and bright red blood was shooting from the wound with every beat of his heart, gushing around the spear and out the top of the shoe.

"Blood was everywhere," Abbott recalled. "It looked like somebody had taken a five-gallon bucket of red paint and spattered it all over the cockpit." Broken tackle littered the floor, and the line from the hook in the fish's throat trailed over the gunwale. It had knocked the rod out of the boat.

But Abbott had a lot more to worry about than broken gear. "I felt myself growing weak," he said. "The sun seemed to be burning me up, but my skin was white and clammy." He fought down a rising sense of panic when he realized that he was going into shock. He had spent years as a Coast Guard corpsman, and he recognized the symptoms. If he did not do something quickly he was likely to die from shock and loss of blood before help could find him. He wiped at the film in his eyes, and crawled to the big ice chest near the console. He opened the lid, thrust his bleeding foot in the ice cubes, and hoped that the cold would stanch the flow.

In a few minutes the chill of the ice took away some of the blinding pain from his foot, but he noticed from the pink water flowing out the drain hole of the chest that the foot had not stopped bleeding.

He slid his way around the ice chest to where he could reach his radio transmitter. Fighting back the urge to pass out, he flipped the dial to channel 16 and spoke into the microphone.

"Mayday, Mayday, Mayday, this is the "Miss Carolyn" calling the Coast Guard. Mayday! "

He slumped in the cockpit, waiting a long minute until the receiver crackled into life and he heard a response.

" 'Miss Carolyn,' this is the Coast Guard. State the nature of your distress and your location."

"I've been speared by a sailfish," Abbott whispered.

"Say again?" the Coast Guard operator replied in disbelief.

"A sailfish, right through my foot. I'm bleeding, and I'm getting shocky. My motor won't start. I need help quick. "

"What is your location?"

"I'm not sure. I've been adrift for almost two hours. But my recorder reads 300 feet, and I was about 20 miles off Vero Beach last time I checked."

"Keep talking. We'll get a radio fix on your position."

Abbott talked. He mumbled the happenings that had led to his predicament; the breakdown of the motor, the escaped marlin, the dual hookup with the dolphin and the sail, and then the accident. In a few minutes the Fort Pierce Coast Guard had a line of position, and by getting a second line from another station farther down the coast, they established the location of the "Miss Carolyn" some 27 miles offshore.

The Coast Guard personnel could not respond, however. Its offshore rescue boat was trying to save a sinking yacht at Sebastian's Inlet, and all of the helicopters normally based within range of the wounded angler had been transferred to Miami to cover the Cuban freedom flotilla. If Abbott was to be saved it would have to be a fellow fisherman who was a Good Samaritan. The Coast Guard sent out an appeal to all boats within miles of Abbott's position to render assistance.

By rising to a sitting position, Abbott could see boats far away across the indigo water, their outriggers bobbing as they trolled rigged baits, but none drew any closer. Abbott sank into a daze as he waited, first 10 minutes, then 20.

All the while, the pink flow from the cooler continued, though it appeared at last to be thinning out a bit. Perhaps the bleeding was slowing down. The blood ran through the overboard drain, and Abbott could hear small fish splashing next to the boat as they came to the chum made up of his own blood. He wondered idly if the blood would eventually bring sharks, and whether it would matter to him by that time.

Eventually the ice began to make his foot ache, and he carefully withdrew it.

To his relief he saw that most of the bleeding had finally stopped. He propped his foot on the cooler so it would be higher than his heart and the flow wouldn't start again. His vision had cleared, and the fear he had felt earlier had subsided. Abbott now felt certain that he would survive, provided help came soon.

But he was to have a long wait. Though there were a number of boats trolling close to the "Miss Carolyn," no angler had their radios turned on. Abbott lay in pain for an hour and a half, talking with the Coast Guard station and making futile calls to other fishermen. He watched in frustration while his depthfinder registered ever-increasing depths as the boat drifted farther and farther offshore.

Denny Sada had been fishing for five- to six-pound school dolphin when he heard the Coast Guard call after turning his radio on during a lull in the fishing. When he checked the location of his 25-footer he realized that he should be somewhere near Ron Abbott.

Sada took in his lines and began to search for the "Miss Carolyn. " Abbott was not far off and a short run put him in view. Sada was prepared to give any aid he could, but he was not prepared for the sight that met his eyes.

The boat seemed to be covered with blood from bow to stern. Smashed tackle was everywhere, and in its midst lay Ron Abbott smeared with blood from head to foot. For a moment, Sada thought the wounded man was finished. But then Abbott sat up, wiped at his crimsoned face, and managed a grim smile.

"I'm sure sorry to spoil your fishing trip," he said.

Abbott was lifted aboard Sada's boat for the long run back to land. Another boat, arriving shortly after Sada's, towed in the "Miss Carolyn." As they started to pull away Abbott shouted: "Take care of my fish. This one's going on the wall!"

The emergency room doctor at the Indian River Medical Center in Sebastian worked for more than an hour trying to remove the embedded bill from Abbott's foot, but with no success. The four-inch segment had penetrated almost completely through the foot; its tip was visible under the skin on the outside of his heel. The thousands of tiny spines on the bill made it impossible to withdraw it. A surgeon was called in, and after making several deep incisions, he was able to remove the spear. Abbott was on the operating table more than 3½ hours.

He went home the next day, and the first thing he did was call the local taxidermist to make sure his sailfish had been picked up for mounting. It had.

Abbott spent a few more days on crutches, but otherwise recovered without complications.

Though veteran charterboat skippers and mates believe that on rare occasions sails and other billfish will attempt to slash or spear anglers in their boatside battles to escape, Ron Abbott is convinced his ordeal was caused by nothing more than bad luck.

"That sailfish meant no harm; he was only trying to get away," he said. "You could fish out there a hundred years and never have anything like that happen again. "

Probably so, but several lessons are clear from his experience. First is that any big-game fish is capable of inflicting serious injury, even on experienced anglers. Second is that fishing far offshore alone subjects an angler to some unusual risks—boat breakdowns and medical problems or accidents are far worse when there is no one to help. And third, though a radio transmitter is a great safety asset, it's no guarantee of a quick rescue when trouble strikes.

But Ron Abbott's love of saltwater fishing is irrepressible. Within two weeks of the accident, he was looking for more blue water adventure. And, once again, he was fishing alone. ❖

JUNE 1981

Tragedy of
TOP SLIP

by Cyril E. Holland

*I*N THE COIMBATORE DISTRICT of South India, the Anaimalai Hills rise to an elevation of 7,000 feet. From 50 miles away, they are a smoky blue mass forming a sawtooth skyline; from five miles away, trees take shape on the slopes, and the feathery bamboo shows as a lighter shade woven into the dark green forest.

Two roads wind up the hills from near the small town of Pollachi at their foot. One road climbs up to serve the many tea estates on the plateau; the other goes to Top Slip, an elephant camp maintained by the government. Wild elephants are plentiful on these hills, and the camp workers trap them in pits.

Normally the work of training elephants and the care of government teak plantations goes on peacefully from sunup to sundown at Top Slip; but when something unusual happens here, tragedy is generally involved. A rogue elephant was the cause of it this time. He started by killing a forest guard, a man of the Malayalam sect from the West Coast. Most forest guards are from that community. For about $1 a week they look after the trees, the game, the grazing rights, and see to forest fires. They walk miles in the course of their duty and, being denied the use of firearms, risk their lives a dozen times a year.

Unni Nair, the forest guard, was returning at dusk from the teak nurseries down near the river. His uniform—khaki shirt, shorts, and green turban—was inconspicuous enough, but the crunching of his army-pattern hobnail boots advertised his presence for 100 yards in all directions. Yet as he came clodding up the path, he must have had no reason to think that in a few seconds he'd die.

As he entered a clump of giant bamboos an elephant stepped out. In his sudden panic, the guard took a few paces backward—and found his retreat cut off by an impassable wall of bamboo stems.

The rogue swept him into the air, where his turban and part of his hair caught in the thorns, then dashed him to the ground, placed one massive foot on his body, and tore him limb from limb.

Next morning two men from the elephant camp went to look for the guard. From the hair in the tree to the heel marks against the bamboo, the story was only too clear. They left the remains where they lay and hurried to report to the head of the Top Slip forest camp. This gentleman with very commendable courage returned unarmed to the spot. With two or three helpers, he gathered what was left of the body in a blanket, and brought it to the camp. For all the men knew, the elephant was still in the vicinity.

Now, a few years before this incident took place a boyhood friend of mine, Terence O'Neil, had gone up as an assistant engineer to a group of estates on the far side of the Anaimalais from Top Slip. He and I had started our shooting careers together. Many a time, while still in our teens, we heard a bamboo creak while we were hunting. We'd whisper "elephant" and be off as fast as our legs would carry us. Some of that fear of elephants persists in us both to this day.

One day, shortly after the forest guard had been killed, O'Neil crossed from his neck of the wood, where the tea estates were situated, to Top Slip, where the guard had lost his life. He was spending a day deerstalking with his ancient .405, and had come across a small herd of axis deer grazing at the edge of a swamp below him.

O'Neil was waiting, hoping a stag would show, when he whispered something to his tracker, who should have been standing behind him. Getting no response from the tracker, he repeated the question and then turned his head. Where the tracker's face should have been was the red, open mouth of an elephant.

O'Neil hadn't heard the faintest sound from either the departing tracker or the approaching elephant. It had actually lifted its trunk to grab him before he turned.

Terence sprang over the bushes in front and straight down the hillside, with the elephant after him. Fortunately, it was so steep the elephant was somewhat wary on the descent. O'Neil beat the beast to his motorcycle and got away.

His letter telling me all this went on to say that the forest department had asked the collector—the administrative head of the district—to proscribe (condemn) the elephant. The collector, a man I'd dealt with in undertaking to kill other rogue animals, had suggested that I come up and try for this elephant, O'Neil added. And he concluded his letter by saying he couldn't join me in this venture.

I immediately contacted the forest official concerned and he informed me that the tuskèr had now been officially proscribed and hoped I'd come up and shoot it. I applied to him at once for a general forest license and got his help in booking the forest bungalow and obtaining a tracker. Then I wrote to some friends in the district capital of Coimbatore requesting them to buy me a very cheap but serviceable car. In a few days I left my home in Madras and took the train for Coimbatore, where I was to pick up the car and proceed about 50 miles to the Anaimalais.

While I was on my way the rogue struck again. The local tribe on Anaimalais are the Kadirs; a wooly headed, dark-complexioned, happy-go-lucky lot. One morning a roving Kadir took a fancy to a particularly straight bamboo pole, which he started to cut down. He didn't hear the elephant coming up behind him as he worked, but a black trunk suddenly appeared in front of his chest. The next minute he was up in the air. The rogue carried him to a big mango a few yards away and beat his body to pulp.

Terror now set in around the locality, and where you and I were discussing the impending Munich meeting between Chamberlain and Hitler, the people of Top Slip could talk of nothing but the rogue. It was at this stage that I arrived at Mount Stuart bungalow, a short distance from the Top Slip elephant camp.

The bungalow was a comfortable one, except that I first had to dispossess a family of bears that had taken over the place in the years since a human had occupied it. The two trackers assigned me were Kadirs, but I knew nothing of their capabilities.

I'd arrived at Mount Stuart shortly after lunch, and in the early evening I went to the elephant camp at Top Slip to get the latest news of the rogue. I was told he was now near Tekkadi, another forest establishment back down the road I'd driven to Mount Stuart.

So the next morning I drove in the old car to Tekkadi, and there I saw an astonishing sight. The forester was sitting on the roof of the bungalow, refusing all entreaties to come down. The forester was a young man just out of college. He'd hardly been in the jungle a week, and when two elephants started to fight near the bungalow just before I arrived, he'd taken refuge on the roof.

After a little gentle talking, I got him down from his perch. He thought—as did the local Kadirs—that one of the fighting elephants was the rogue. I asked about the fight, and he said that after 20 minutes or so one elephant had run away.

All this had happened a couple of hours previously, so my trackers and I got onto the spoor at once.

But the tracks we followed, those of the elephant that had run away, finally led into a herd of a dozen elephants. It was unlikely that the rogue had joined a herd; a rogue is usually ousted by the herd leader. Anyhow, we decided to watch the herd awhile.

There's no more pleasant or exciting study in the jungle. Contrary to popular belief, the herd is not led by an old bull, but invariably by a cow. The tuskers follow after the herd in a leisurely manner, and if the herd takes fright these bulls get away fast, leaving the mothers with calves to bring up the rear. There's a reason for this female leadership—the herd mustn't move too fast for the calves to feed.

Elephants communicate with one another and express feelings by uttering a great variety of sounds with the trunk or throat. An angry elephant will trumpet shrilly. One brooding over his wounds will grumble constantly. And sometimes—through fear or impatience—elephants produce a roar that can be heard for miles. They also make a peculiar warning sound, as when a tiger is near, by tapping the end of the trunk on the ground and at the same time blowing little gusts of air through it. This sound has a hollow and strangely metallic quality.

Right now I was watching a little calf nursing when his mother suddenly sensed danger. She had carried this little fellow for about 22 months and was not going to let harm come to him now. Knowing that there's no more dangerous or persistent beast than a cow elephant with a calf, the Kadirs and I beat a quiet but hasty retreat.

We returned to Tekkadi and investigated the other set of tracks. As they seemed to follow the road, I decided to take the car, piling the two Kadirs and another local man in the back.

We tracked the elephant down the road for three or four miles, to where the construction of this new road ended. Here we faced the car about and walked on into the forest. But all we saw were some bison and sambar deer, and as dusk closed in we turned back to regain the car.

We'd stayed a bit too late, but I'd had the forethought to bring an electric torch, and I was just getting ready to use it as we approached the car. Just then we heard a most unusual sound. I switched on the flashlight and there, 40 or 50 yards away, was an elephant at the car. He had his trunk under the running board and was lifting and dropping the vehicle, at the same time uttering little squeaks. The sound we'd heard was the thump as the car fell back onto its tires.

My first thought was not of danger with the rogue, but of the car turning turtle so that I'd have to walk miles to find some other transportation. I grabbed the 12 gauge shotgun—loaded with slugs—from one of the Kadirs and fired into the road near the elephant's feet. He backed away from the car and shook his head. Before he had time to think, I fired the second barrel. The beast turned and ran down the road for 100 yards.

I rushed to the car and switched on the lights. There he was standing on the road, trying to make up his mind. If I'd been sure at that moment that he was the rogue, I think I could have shot him that night, for my heavy .404 Mauser rifle has a light-reflecting platinum sight, and I might have got up close enough to put a 400-grain bullet between his eyes.

But I wasn't positive he was the rogue. As he stood there I started the engine, blew the horn, and drove straight at him. He stuck it out until I was perhaps 30 yards away and thinking of stamping on the brakes to leap out of the car. Then he stepped into the heavy forest— and my trackers and I got out of there and drove back to Mount Stuart.

I was now convinced that this elephant was the rogue, so next morning I returned to Tekkadi. We picked up the tracks and I measured a clear print with my pocket tape. The diameter was 17 inches, so this made the elephant eight feet 11 inches at the shoulder—twice the circumference of an elephant's forefoot is its height at the shoulder. We followed the tracks for a few miles and then lost them on hard ground. Finally, just before noon, we gave up and turned back for Mount Stuart.

Before having lunch and a lie-down that afternoon I went into the jungle near the bungalow to see the grave of a fine and popular forest officer, Hugo Wood, who had recently died and had expressed a wish to be buried in his beloved jungle. It was a touching sight to see this lonely new tombstone in the deep peace of the forest he had tended so carefully.

Later—I don't know just when—I was standing in an aisle of bamboos, and the rogue elephant, with a puckish smile on his face, was nodding at me. I was trying to put two cartridges into the breech of my double-barreled 12 gauge, but each time I did they slipped right through and fell out the other side. Next the rogue smiled again and said, "Come closer, I don't want to catch you." When I refused to believe him he put out his trunk and caught me round the leg with a jerk. I believe I screamed; I know I spluttered and choked. Then I opened my eyes.

I'd fallen asleep and one of the Kadir trackers was shaking my leg. He was greatly agitated and told me to come quickly.

Outside stood a little knot of people who'd come to tell me that the rogue had just made a triple killing. A few hours earlier, and just after I'd driven up the road from Tekkadi, an old Kadir man, his young daughter, and her child had been coming along the road from one of their hamlets toward Top Slip. As is common in India, the man was walking 20 yards ahead of the girl, who was carrying her year-old child. As the man came around a blind corner the elephant stepped out, caught the old man, and dashed him to pieces on the road. The girl, still carrying her child, turned and fled.

The elephant worked 10 minutes on the man, but he hadn't forgotten the mother and child, and he went down the road after them. In less than a mile he caught them. To think of the horror that girl must have gone through is in itself a horror.

That evening, with one tracker (the other had refused to come), I scouted the hillside and the valley below the road where the three had been killed. We tracked until dark—and then we got lost.

Eventually we found ourselves in a swamp in pitch dark. Every step took us down almost to the waist, and I had to hang onto the tracker to tell where he was. Mosquitoes swarmed over us. We were looking for a patch of dry ground on which to spend the night when, faintly in the distance, we heard the river and got our bearings. We were out of the swamp and headed for the river when we heard the tonk, tonk of a tame elephant's bell. I felt relieved but soon discovered my guide wasn't; he explained that these tame elephants were let out to feed at night and were—during the hours of darkness—as dangerous as the wild ones. We skirted the tame elephant and finally hit the road that led us back to the car. I flopped into the driver's seat while the tracker got in the back.

I was just reaching for a flask of tea when there was a scream and an elephant rushed down the road from behind us. There was no sound of a bell this time. I flipped the switch, jabbed the starter, and we shot forward just ahead of the elephant. It was a terrifying ending to a harrowing day, and I slept badly that night.

Next morning we returned to the spot where I'd left the car the night before. From the sign, it became apparent the elephant had located the car and waited in ambush. He'd evidently come to associate the vehicle with human beings. That gave me an idea. It was a slim chance, but the more I thought about it the better it seemed.

Around 5 o'clock that afternoon I came back to the spot with the Kadir tracker. We turned the car where I'd turned it the evening before, and I raced the engine and blew the horn. Somewhere down in the valley near the river was the elephant, and he could hear such sounds three miles away.

We left the car and climbed the bank beside the road. Behind us the hill rose steeply, too steep even for an elephant. We were perhaps 20 yards from the car and above it. Here I decided to sit until late dusk.

I didn't have to wait that long. Within 20 minutes I saw a huge shadow come around the corner—followed by the elephant.

It has always amazed me how silently an elephant can tread when he doesn't want to be heard. This rogue had come pussyfooting up through dense bamboo and undergrowth like a ghost, and I had no idea he was in the vicinity until I saw his shadow.

I slowly raised my .404, which I'd loaded with five 400-grain solids. He was bobbing his head and I couldn't get a bead on a vital spot. Upon reaching the car he ran his trunk along the edge of the folded-back canvas top. Then he put his trunk inside the car for a few seconds and felt around. Finally he walked to the other side. I saw his ear and fired.

The rogue let out a scream and went back along the road. I jumped down the bank and cautiously peered around the corner, to see him pivoting around like a top. Then he went down the bank with blood running down the side of his head and staining his tusks and his great trunk.

He slipped and slid unsteadily for 40 or 50 yards while I tried to get in another shot, then he swung around and faced me. I was above him, so I fired high between his eyes. For a moment he swayed, and then with a shudder his back legs gave way and he toppled over.

I went in close and fired another round into his brain near the temple, but it wasn't necessary.

I jumped on top of the carcass, which was five feet high as he lay on his side, and from there I could see the head and shoulders of the Kadir, who had so bravely followed me unarmed all through the hunt. He came running down to greet me and was beaming with delight.

I examined the elephant, trying to discover what had turned him rogue.

His tusks—of medium size—seemed in order. The left one was broken off at the tip, but not so short as to have caused him any pain. He had no visible wounds. But I could perceive an oily secretion exuding from a tiny hole on the side of his head, and I concluded he was going into must—a periodic condition probably associated with the rut, when this secretion is noticeable. Possibly he'd become quarrelsome, two or three bulls had driven him from the herd, and he'd gone off to sulk. Then killing the unfortunate forest guard had whetted his appetite, and he'd gone around hunting for trouble and not stopping until he found it.

He was old, as I could see from his loose skin, bony head, and torn and folded-over ears—probably 50 years old when the first World War broke out; twice as old even then as I was the day I ended his reign of terror. ❖

MARCH 1956

KIDNAPPED!

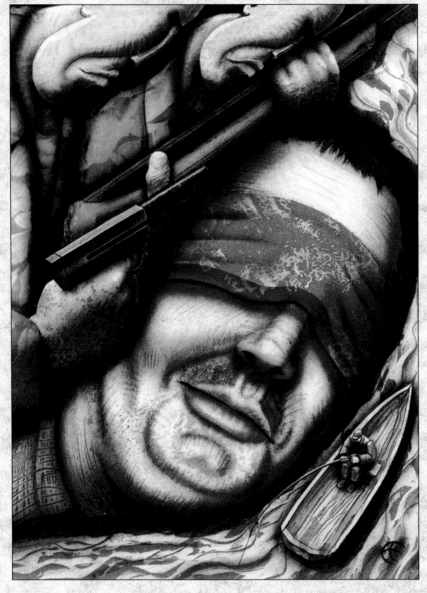

by Jerry Gibbs

*T*HE NEW CAMP IS A 300-MILE rifle shot from the Orinoco River border between Colombia and Venezuela. Figure 700 miles by road. It is where Kjell (pronounced "Shell") Erland von Sneidern started again, fishing for *pavon*, the peacock bass.

This camp is on the Paragua River in Venezuela, near the gold and diamond mining village of Paragua. High up near the Uraima rapids there is an untapped mother lode of magnificent, record-breaking fanged payara, the fish with fangs so large it has holes in its head to store them. For von Sneidern there is something else very important about this location: It is far away from the nightmare that began on November 15, 1992.

On that day, driving in Puerto Carreno, Colombia, near the Orinoco River, von Sneidern was blocked by recently-felled trees. He and his passenger—an Italian interested in starting a fishing camp—were forced from their vehicle and taken hostage. For 72 days they suffered unremitting psychological terror and physical deprivation. To understand how it is to live in such close company of the angel of death for so long and, two breaths later, to go back to business as usual running a fishing lodge, is to know something of von Sneidern.

Initially the high-register, Spanish-inflected English speech comes as a surprise from the big, broad-shouldered, blue-eyed man you see before you. But then you remember that Erland von Sneidern grew up in Colombia. His father, also named Kjell, was an internationally recognized ornithologist who immigrated there from Germany in the 1920s, when he entered the coffee trade ... and as a sideline opened a fishing camp. A fishing houseboat on the Orinoco soon followed, as did a billfishing operation at Solono Bay, then world-class dove shooting out of Cali. All the operations were successful and formed the backdrop against which young Erland became impassioned with the life—and the business—of the outdoors. But it was the camp in the northeastern border country that intrigued him the most, with its potential and its outstanding peacock bass fishing. And, eventually, it was this camp that nearly claimed him.

"My dream was to develop sportfishing there, to give the poor families jobs guiding and working in my camps," von Sneidern says. "The government was never interested. Now they say 'why don't you come back and reopen the camps; we'll help.' Maybe in another lifetime. They left me alone, and because of that, what happened, happened."

Trouble started even before von Sneidern was kidnapped. The Orinoco Arc, his popular houseboat base for peacock fishing, mysteriously sank—or was sunk. He ordered an elaborate new custom houseboat before realizing the dynamics of change that were subtly at work all around him. "Local Indians were pressed by guerrillas to grow cocoa for cocaine," he says. "[The guerrillas] didn't want fishermen in the area.

"But I had this new boat and had to pay for it. We leased it, and I discovered the renters turned it into a bordello. It was the hottest thing in town for a while. You never saw any drunks on the boat because the customers knew they'd throw you overboard if you created trouble. But then one evening a dissatisfied customer set the boat on fire and that was the end of the houseboat."

Von Sneidern's answer was to start the El Morichal peacock bass lodge, unfortunately still within the trouble spot. He hired his cousin Erik Bennettsen, a wry, chain-smoking, philosophical type, to help run the operation. Bennettsen grew up in the former Tanganyika of British East Africa and left during the independence turmoil. Like von Sneidern, he had no idea what was coming, but, again like von Sneidern, his background would help resolve an unthinkable situation.

When he wrenched his vehicle to a stop in front of the roadblock that mid-November day, von Sneidern and his passenger were immediately surrounded by a group of well-armed men. He saw they were mostly young—16 to 19 years old. There were three young women with them, armed as well. "There were 17 of them all together. They took us and my car, and when we went into the bush they abandoned the vehicle, which I never saw again," von Sneidern remembers. "I know it was disassembled quickly and sold for parts. You have to understand about these people. In this remote area, a young woman has eight or nine children by different fathers. They have little to eat. At 4 or 5 years old, a boy has to help mamma find food. There is no school, no church, no sense of value, nothing. They are like animals. The people who took us didn't know the days of the week, but they could handle an AK-47 very well, and they knew the country."

The impoverished illiterate of the area are pawns for more organized guerrillas who train them in weapons' handling. But lacking the purpose and iron-handed control of the famed drug cartels, guerrillas often lose their pawns to splinter factions. Such was the case here. Rather than leverage for some ideological cause or drug deal, the kidnappers wanted only money. They pegged the ransom for von Sneidern at $500,000.

Immediately, von Sneidern's sister Margit Ridgeway flew from the United States to Colombia. There, along with von Sneidern's wife, Lilliana, and his father, a rescue plan began to be hammered out.

The border country of the Orinoco is flat, semi-arid savanna. It is enriched wherever there are springs and small rivers by stretches of open, low-treed jungle called morichales. These jungle strips are as narrow as 200 yards on either side of the watercourse but may run for miles. In them the ground is always wet, like soaked carpet. This was the country that would hide the kidnappers and their hostages for more than two harrowing months.

From the start, von Sneidern and the Italian sportsman were bullied and barraged with threats. One of the gang took pleasure in displaying a human skull punctured by a bullet hole for emphasis. Dry leaves and twigs were scattered beneath the hammocks in which the hostages slept to alert guards should either of the two men move. They slept by day and traveled only at night, walking in water when possible to avoid leaving tracks. When stringing the hammocks was impossible, they lay on the wet jungle floor or leaned against trees attempting to sleep. Though mosquitoes were a problem, only once were they bothered by predatory wildlife.

"One of the jungle strips had a beautiful spring where we bathed," says von Sneidem. "It was deep and usually crystal clear. But sometimes we saw the pool would be muddy. We found out why. We heard screams from the guerrilla girls who were bathing there. They came running. The spring was the home of an anaconda, and it went for them. The men hunted the snake and killed it. It was 5½ meters long [23 feet].

"But other than that, we really became *part* of the wildlife. There were deer, tapir and jaguar. The bird life was fantastic." Von Sneidern chuckles as he says this. "It's a pity I had to enjoy nature in those circumstances."

The retrospective humor with which he can relate the tale is in stark contrast to the realities of the experience. Back then, von Sneidern focused exclusively on staying alive. As food became an ever more crucial factor, he worried about water, too. "I had no purification tablets but found a big bottle of Bayer aspirin in my bag. I dissolved two tablets in each bottle of water I drank with my fellow hostage. We never had dysentery, but once I ate a piece of rotten fish and twisted over from the pain. I had terrible cramps for 11 hours.

"Then the food became even more scarce. When the men were guarding the food I could sometimes get a piece of meat or something. But with the women guarding ... you couldn't kid them, they were mean and would be happy to shoot you. They were bad, bad, bad."

Back in Cali, while Lilliana von Sneidern attempted to raise ransom money, Erland's frustrated father called cousin Erik Bennettsen and Erland's brother, also named Erik. Officials had yet to begin rescue operations, and the elder von Sneidern told the two men, "You've got to do something."

Experienced outdoorsmen, the two men understood rough savannas and jungle country, but guerrilla tactics were not in their repertoire. They located eight "professionals," as Bennettsen calls them, and with Erland's sister Margit organizing supplies, broke into two groups and attempted to locate the kidnappers.

"We were better equipped," says Bennettsen. "They had some automatic weapons; we had plenty—AK-47s, Colt AR-15s and grenades."

Realizing they were being tracked, the gang moved continually, restocking from local farmers through threat or theft. "Sometimes they would steal a cow and kill it, or find a deer or tapir in the jungle. Then we would eat like crazy for two or three days. Then came days without anything," von Sneidern says. He estimates covering more than 600 miles on foot before the ordeal ended. "I had a pair of Sperry Topsiders that unbelievably lasted the entire time.

"But the fungus! Not only on your feet, it was all over us. Crazy. Crazy. Some of those guys had it bad. It was eating them away so you could see their bones in places. I tried to dry my feet any time we could sleep in those hammocks.

"Once you were in a hammock, you didn't want to take the trouble to get out. One time, for some reason, they had given me some rum they'd taken with supplies. This real bastard was on guard. He knew I had rum and came over for it. I had finished it; in fact I had used the bottle to relieve myself. I gave the bottle to him. He had no experience with alcohol. He drank and didn't like it, but knew he was supposed to. He was trying to take it like a man. It was a small victory, but the knowledge of it helped."

Von Sneidern's will to survive was paramount. He was confident he could mentally outlast his younger captors. Above all, he had not succumbed to panic. His positive mind-set insulated him from the Stockholm Syndrome, which results in the captive gradually identifying with the captor. In fact, von Sneidern worked the reverse. "I gave one guy my comb. It was the biggest present he'd ever had," von Sneidern says. "He agreed to help me but ended up running away himself. One of the women guerrillas knew he was going to run but didn't know why. When he did, the others suspected she knew or had helped him, so they shot her and threw her into a lagoon. One of them, one of these kids, said 'the piranha will take care of her.' It was terrible. When I was finally free I heard the guy who escaped was in jail."

With their physical condition deteriorating and no response to their demand for money, the kidnappers became increasingly anxious. They were able to get word to the von Sneidern family that the ransom was halved. But Lilliana had conferred with an expert on kidnapping in South America who warned her that a payoff would not necessarily buy von Sneidern's freedom. Standard operating procedure among abductors was to eliminate any chance for identification—ie. kill the victim no matter what.

By now the rescue group with Bennettsen and Erik von Sneidern had closed in. "There was a fire fight," says Bennettsen. "We took, well, prisoners of war. We cut off all their potential for supplies on the Colombian side. The next day we came to an abandoned house where they had held Erland and the Italian fellow the day before. They had abandoned everything and run. I stayed at the house with the prisoners because I could no longer walk from foot fungus. The others went on."

The kidnappers, still holding von Sneidern, commandeered a boat, intending to flee across the Orinoco to Venezuela. The outboard failed in midstream, stranding the group for three hours in the night. Finally the current brought them across to shore, but the gang was disoriented. Von Sneidern had been working on another of the abductors, who agreed to help the hostages escape should an opportune moment occur. It would come soon. The group was in total disarray—a condition escalated even further when a limb slammed the Italian sportsman in the eye, nearly blinding him.

"They wanted to leave him," von Sneidern says. "I told them I began this episode with him and would end it with him. So I made them wait and help him. In a way it was me running with them now. I could almost command them—except when it came to my liberty."

From the Venezuelan side a wave of troops from the National Guard moved in on the gang. The kidnappers reversed course and headed back for the Orinoco where Bennettsen's group and the Colombian Army were blocking off escape from that side.

And then the shooting began.

In a maelstrom of crossfire von Sneidern, the Italian, and a male and female kidnapper broke for the jungle and kept going.

"Suddenly these military helicopters were overhead," von Sneidern says. It was like a James Bond movie. In one minute I went from the worst position you can be in to flying on top of all these guys who held me—like in Goldfinger being rescued in the middle of the ocean. The only thing missing were the beautiful women. They did not come with the helicopter." In the months that followed, rumors had it that members of the group of kidnappers who had escaped being imprisoned or killed began casting blame on one another for the failed ransom attempt. One splinter group that wanted to assassinate von Sneidern began retribution. It is not precisely known who or how many may be left, though the gang leader and one of the women kidnappers are thought to be among them.

With his two other successful Colombian sporting operations going well, how would a man fresh from an ordeal like von Sneidern's find the energy and courage to launch a new fishing camp in Latin America interior, albeit it far from the troubled border area? Erik Bennettsen calls it the von Sneidern family disease—The Passion.

"It's the adventure. The fishing that's in my blood and the idea of developing something," says von Sneidern. "I could not just sit around dreaming about it, so I went and did it."

Von Sneidern offers several trip packages to sample a variety of waters and species from the main Paragua lodge and outpost camps. A one-day air charter to Angel Falls, the world's highest waterfall, is available. The best season for both peacock and payara seems to be from November to May, though exploration continues. ◈

DECEMBER 1995

This Happened TO US!

by Jim Carmichel, Todd Smith, Bob Brown, Jerry Gibbs, Pat McManus, Larry Mueller, Vin T. Sparano, and Jim Zumbo

❖

SCARIEST THING THAT'S happened to me? Not much I can think of except the odd times I've almost gone over cliffs, been caught in avalanches, nearly frozen on mountaintops, gotten lost in dark caves, been chased by moose, bears, elephants, buffalo, lions and revolutionaries, had deadly snakes, spiders and scorpions visit me in my tents, huts and sleeping bags, or watched a boat sink under me in crocodile-infested water.

Not to mention the charming fevers, skin eruptions and bowel corruptions I've collected, like trophies, in faraway rivers and jungles and deserts. Or the time insane tribesmen in northern Iran took me ibex poaching on a Soviet artillery range. And the bush plane crashes and near crashes too numerous to remember.

Point-Blank Lion

One incident that sticks in my memory, however, happened on a cool morning in Central Africa a few years back. We were hunting giant eland and picked up the tracks of a couple of lions. The prints were fresh and promising so we followed for a mile or so and spotted two big males across an opening in the scrubby forest. They spotted us at the same time and, for some reason, it was murderous hatred at first sight. The bigger of the two lions didn't hesitate, he simply set his sights and came at me like a rocket. My professional hunter got off one wild shot and the front sight flew off his ancient .375, rendering him hors de combat and leaving me to fend for myself. (Our trackers were already enjoying the view from the tops of local trees.)

About then a pint or two of adrenaline hit my veins and everything switched to slow motion. The lion seemed to be swimming in molasses and I had hours to shoot. My first bullet went into his chest but the lion didn't notice. He didn't seem to mind the second bullet, either, and was getting close when I closed the bolt on my last round and put the crosshairs on his nose. Then, suddenly, his fight was gone and he stopped, a gun-barrel length away. We searched deep in each other's eyes for a moment, trying to understand what had happened, and in another moment he was dead on his feet.

"There's another lion," I suddenly remembered, and swung to meet his charge. He was crouching, head and tail low, eyes aimed at my guts. He was coming too and there was only one cartridge in my rifle...

But that's another story...

JIM CARMICHEL

Snakes in the Bathroom

"I hate snakes!"

Indiana Jones's fateful words whirled through my head as I started back to my hut. My Zambian safari had gone great—great that is until one of the camp staff beat the stuffing out of a five-foot mamba that had taken a shine to hanging out around the propane freezer where we kept the cocktail ice.

Our skinner brought the still-wriggling body to us over lunch. The snake was as gray as the dirt floor of the dining hut and my first thought was, "My God, you'd never see one of the buggers until it was too late." You see, the black mamba has a rather impressive batting average. Only a handful of people have ever survived a mamba bite, owing to the snake's frighteningly powerful venom, which sends bitees into a convulsive, frothing death the likes of which I had no mind to see (or experience) firsthand.

"Probably another one lurking about," my professional said casually, his voice sounding more British than South African as he calmly examined the coffin-shaped head of the deceased. "Not uncommon for them to travel in pairs. Best take a bright torch when you head off to bed tonight."

"A bright torch?" I thought. "How about aircraft landing lights?"

"And mind that you give your duffel a good bash before you go rummaging around inside it. They do love dark places."

"Wonderful," I thought, as I headed for my cot and a noontime siesta, picking up a four-foot branch along the way.

The Zambian locals do fabulous things with thatch. My hut was more like a house, with a bedroom in front and a shower and latrine area built off the back. You had to step through the shower area to get to the latrine, which I had just finished doing when something came flying out of the shower outlet. The something moved liked lightning, was pencil-thin and as gray as the charcoal ground, but oh that coffin-shaped head.

"Mamba!" I thought, and I felt my body go stiff as stone. The snake whipped around like a snapped cable and rose up on its tail, its eyes locked on the bare legs below my bush shorts, only three feet away from it.

"Don't move or you're dead," I told myself, eyeing the useless stick that lay propped against the wall just out of reach.

Time stopped. The trilling noise of the crickets outside ceased. And in the nanosecond that followed I could hear the blood hiss through my veins. The snake moved first: In between heartbeats, he swapped ends and flew back out the drain hole like he owned the place.

My shouts brought the entire camp staff running. I blurted out my story, and our trackers started beating the grass behind my hut with long sticks. Sure enough, my old friend surfaced and was quickly thrashed into pulp. (We later discovered that he'd been living in the filled-in remains of a latrine that had been built off the back of a hut that had stood where mine was a few years before.)

"Probably came in to feed on the field mice nesting in the thatch," my professional said. My stomach did a back flip.

"What's the matter with you, man? Looks like you've seen a ghost."

"I have," I gasped.

Back in the dining hut, over four fingers of Dewars, I related how I had been awakened the night before by the sound of a mouse screeching from one end of my hut to the other and then back again.

"I've never heard a mouse scream before," I said.

"And you probably never will again," my professional answered. "Odds are that bloody snake was in there chasing him around."

I took a deep gulp of air and drained my glass, feeling the whiskey burn all the way down.

TODD SMITH

Trapped on the Nissequogue

Had I read the tide tables I would have known how much time I had left to live.

More to the point, had I read the tide tables I wouldn't be in this fix.

The fix being up to my crotch in sucking, viscous muck. Stuck firm. Each move of my legs to free myself causing me to sink an inch or more into the water.

The rising water. As the tide had turned and the current was now rushing into the Nissequogue River, an estuary into Long Island Sound.

De dum, de dum...de dum, de dum. The theme from The Twilight Zone began to play ominously in my head as the incoming tide recalled the one about the wayward husband being playfully buried up to his neck in sand and left there by his knowing wife as the tide rolls in. I had always considered it one of Rod Serling's most terrifying episodes.

And for me, the cause of death would be a fishing spoon. It had gotten hung up on a submerged branch to which I had been casting, thinking it would be a good lie for sea-run brown trout. This was new water to me, running through a mile-wide marsh. It was late fall and the eight-foot high flagellum that surrounded the meander where I fished had already turned to a wall of thatch.

When I waded deeper, hoping to retrieve the ultralight spoon given to me by a Welsh coworker a few years earlier, the sandy bottom abruptly ended and my left leg plunged into bottomless muck. Quicksand.

I lurched, pile-driving my leg deep into the mud and, worse, reflexively causing myself to step forward with my right leg to keep balance—ramming it even deeper into the quicksand than my left leg.

Now, entombed up to my hips as the tide rose on my torso, I fought with panic, the only possible witnesses to my predicament the snapping turtles whose nests pockmarked the riverbank. Any effort to free myself simply drove me deeper into the muck. I could safely move only my hands and arms.

I could still see the spoon fluttering from the snag about 20 feet downstream. S-l-o-w-l-y, I started to reel in line. I had no idea how big the entire branch might be, but if I could work it toward me, I might be able to brace it on the bottom and push myself out of this mess before the now fast-rising tide was over my head.

I felt the branch begin to lift, and I could see that it was crowned by a tangle of branches that would offer the widebased support that might allow me to pry myself loose. But it was all attached to a substantial branch, one that probably weighed 30 pounds. Inch by agonizing inch, line came back on the reel and the branch rose farther off the muck bottom.

The speed with which it wrenched free and then was caught by the current took me by surprise. Desperately I lunged as the branch drifted by. My legs drove deeper with the violence of the effort.

I had the branch. Cautiously, trying not to put too much downward force into my legs, I wrestled the branch into position, even as the current tried to rip this only hope from my hands. But I had to work quickly, too, as the water was now trickling over the top of my waders. In ultra-slow motion it all came together. I strained—evenly, methodically—as I used just my arms to lever loose my legs. Finally my front foot gained a slight hold on a stone or branch (I'll never know which) buried deep in the muck that held me. From this small and unexpected platform, I could carefully rock forward and back, working my lower body upward against the cloying quicksand.

Unlike the branch, I did not pop free. Anything but. It was a slow-motion race with the incoming tide. Finally, sweat-drenched and shaking, I was able to reach to the side and grab a heavy root exposed in the undercut riverbank. I could pull myself free.

Exhausted, with black mud coating me to my armpits, I looked at my watch. It had taken more than 35 minutes to work myself free. When I looked in the newspaper that evening, I saw that the tide would have continued rising for another 50 minutes. It would have risen another foot and a half in that time. De dum, de dum...de dum, de dum.

BOB BROWN

Bad News Bear

It was a bad time to be on the Brooks. The old alpha bear called Scar had lost his first battle and was in a vile mood. Across his forelegs, gashes from the fight gaped like slashes in whale blubber. He had killed a cub that had wandered into his fishing territory, and for a time the mother sow raged down the riverbanks. The bear of my trouble, however, was a teenager pumping more testosterone than was good for himself or anyone around him. His shtick was false-charging anglers. So far, the charges had been bluffs.

It was sockeye time on the little river in Alaska's Katmai National Park. The great bears were fishing, tolerating (under stress) the near-ness to one another as well as to humans. When a bear came down the bank you moved from the river to the opposite shore. Fixed on the fish, they usually ignored you—except for the teenage male coming toward us now. My guide, Ron, was into a fish.

Seeing a good photo opportunity, I dropped my rod on a midstream bar and grabbed my camera. "Go right," I said, directing. Suddenly both Ron and the bear were sharp as tacks in the viewfinder. "Right, hell," he sputtered, breaking off the fish. I looked up. The bear was too close and still coming. It had not committed to one bank, and was quartering like a hunting dog across the river, his head swinging.

Ron gambled on the left bank. I stayed in the water, grabbing my rod as I passed the bar. I was last in line now, the straggler in the school—the appetizer. Then Ron slid fast off the bank into the river, heading right, and over my shoulder I saw that the bear had changed course. Farther upstream, anglers were swinging in a bizarre conga line as the bear switched banks. My wife, Judy, was in that line, and I thought this might be ugly for her. I glanced over my shoulder and knew I would not turn again.

The water had gone from calf deep to crotch deep. Wading fast against it reminded me of the slow-motion flight from faceless horror in a childhood nightmare. I thought I ought to talk, yell at this bear, tell it something. In those slow-mo nightmares you always wake up just as the thing catches you, or just before, and you're okay even if you do have the sweats. But this wasn't dreamtime.

"Left," Ron screamed. "Go left!"

I did, panting hard, and saw the bear an awfully easy cast away as it ghosted by in the water. It looked at me, eyes devoid of expression, then cut to the far bank, moving on.

We clustered with the others then, everyone talking in the nervous relief that comes after a close one. "I really thought you might be eaten," my wife told me seriously. "What could I have told the boys?"

"That the insurance is paid up," I said, "and that the rubber waders probably gave the bear worse heartburn than your spareribs could." She hit me with something, but I couldn't feel it.

JERRY GIBBS

Grazed by a Gator

September 1983. Mac Beatty and I are fishing the Cuiabá River deep in the interior of Brazil. Our boat resembles a very long and skinny canoe, except it is powered and steered by what looks like a Chevy engine on a stick. The craft gives the sense of being highly unstable, as does the guide.

His attention occupied by a search for signs of baitfish, the guide suddenly swerves the boat straight toward a high bank. Sunning itself atop this bank and directly ahead of us is the largest alligator I've ever seen. Mac, sitting with his back to the bow, is totally unaware of what only the alligator and I know is about to occur. Then the boat hits the bank. The situation couldn't be worse—unless, of course, I was the one sitting in the bow.

The alligator launches itself right over the top of Mac, missing him by a good two or three inches. I judged from Mac's reaction that he'd never before had an alligator leap over the top of him. Odd. Shucks, that sort of thing happens to me all the time.

PAT McMANUS

Surfing the Levee

For several years, until the flooded brush died and rotted away, our mostly shallow Brush Lake was a dog man's duck-hunting paradise. An L-shaped levee impounded 40 acres of overgrown, frequently flooded Silver Creek bottoms. One spring, however, an especially high flood threatened to destroy our paradise. It crested over a low spot in the levee, and the spillway couldn't handle the volume, so the water cut another exit.

My brother, Willie, and I inspected the levee cut and concluded it wasn't terribly deep and could be sandbagged. I presented a carefully engineered plan. We would use the small johnboat with the little motor that could be turned around to face backwards. A sandbag would be placed on the bow seat, Willie would sit in the center and I would idle the motor, letting the current carry us to the cut. Then I would rev up the engine to hold us in place while Willie deposited the sandbag.

We did a careful test run—in and back out—to get a feel for motor speeds. I instructed my crew to stand by for the first drop as we eased back to the cut. I could see Dad watching from the spillway. I smiled with satisfaction. You know fathers, forever expecting sons to unconsciously neglect important details. But this was working.

Willie moved forward. Suddenly the bow dipped to the gunwale under his extra weight, the stern rose, and the motor's prop was spinning in thin air. In a blink, the current shot us through the cut on a gush of water that drenched us, filled the boat and carried us out into the unknown depths of the flooded timber. The bow slammed into a tree. We could feel the flooded boat sinking. Could we swim in this current? The boat hit bottom.

"Hey! The water's only a couple of feet deep," I said. "We can walk out of here." I could see Dad coming across the narrow plank that spanned the spillway. His hipboots were flapping, the plank was bouncing under him like a diving board and his lately acquired bay-window belly was flopping in alternating rhythm with the plank. I almost wished we had to be rescued. You know fathers. After finding us safe, he'd be mad as hell.

LARRY MUELLER

May Day

My most terrifying day came about a decade ago when my son Matt and I were fishing in a tournament from my 24-foot boat. We left Little Egg Inlet in New Jersey at daybreak and headed southeast in search of fish. At about 1 p.m. and more than 20 miles offshore, we heard a loud boom and my single 175-horsepower engine quit. We made all the obvious engine checks, but it was a major lower-unit breakdown. We were dead in the water.

There were no other boats in sight and it would be dark in about four hours. Worse yet, the previously calm sea was now becoming a mass of whitecaps with the winds building. To my horror, I discovered that the fuse connector on the VHF radio was corroded. I could only contact the Coast Guard sporadically, if I squeezed the connector tightly in my fist. Water was coming over the transom, the fish boxes on deck were now full of water and the bilge pump was running continuously, draining the battery and our only source of power for the VHF radio.

The Coast Guard asked for my position. I said southeast of the inlet when, in fact, we had drifted northeast of the inlet. I had a new Loran unit but it had yet to be programmed and the manual was back at the car, so we couldn't give them a Loran position.

The Coast Guard began using triangulation to pick up our position and I was instructed to shoot flares when they thought they were close enough for visual contact. I had only two flares left.

Matt and I were now in life jackets, the wind was still increasing and it was getting dark. How much power was left in the battery? What if we lost contact with the Coast Guard? It was too deep to anchor and we were being blown out to sea. How long would we last in the cold fall water?

Just when I thought that prayer was our only salvation, the Coast Guard asked me to fire one of my two remaining flares. Within seconds, a voice came over the radio: "We have you in sight." As darkness approached, a Coast Guard cutter arrived and towed us back home. Winds reached gale force that night and a Northeaster blew for three days.

I sometimes joke about that day at sea, but it's always a very shallow cover-up for a truly terrifying experience.

VIN T. SPARANO

Flameout

"Doug, your truck is on fire!" I shouted.

That statement galvanized my pal and me into action, and together we raced wildly for the pickup. Black smoke was rising from underneath it, and flames licked along the driveshaft and around the oil pan. The gas tank was inches away.

Desperately we scooped up handfuls of sand and tossed them at the fire, but the flames grew larger. We worked like madmen for a few seconds, and then prudently decided to get the hell out of there.

Backing off 20 yards, we assessed the predicament. A whole lot of things go through your mind when your truck is on fire, you're in a desert wilderness, the temperature is 110 degrees, camp is 23 miles away and your only water is in the burning vehicle.

My rifle was in the truck, too—my beloved .30/06 that I had hunted with for 20 years. Doug and I knew that we had to get the water out, so we dashed to the vehicle and grabbed canteens, coolers, gear and everything of value, including my rifle. The flames grew stronger, and we quickly placed the recovered equipment as far from the truck as possible. I expected it to blow at any second.

Suddenly Doug raced back to the truck, yelling something about a handgun his grandfather had given him that was still in the glove compartment. The heat was too intense and he turned away. The flames were now 30 feet high and the truck was engulfed in a furious fire.

My Utah desert sheep hunt was over. Facing us was a long hike to camp, and then a horrible drive down a rockstrewn hillside in my vehicle to collect our gear. We were whipped when we got the job done, but there was even worse news to come.

Another hunter camped near us had killed a ram, and a companion ram had been laid down close by. A member of the party drove hurriedly to fetch me, but Doug and I had already left, headed home in defeat. Only two of 17 hunters took rams in that unit. I wasn't one of them. ❖

JIM ZUMBO

JUNE/JULY 1997

Classic Adventures

THE GIANT
of the South Seas

by Zane Grey

*T*IME IS PROBABLY MORE generous and healing to an angler than to any other individual. The wind, the sun, the open, the colors and smells, the loneliness of the sea or the solitude of the stream work some kind of magic. In a few days my disappointment at losing a wonderful fish was only a memory, another incident of angling history.

On the 15th of last May, which was the seventh day of clear, hot, sunny weather, I stayed in my camp near Tahiti, in the South Seas, to do some neglected writing, and let Cappy run out alone off the east end, where we had not scouted for several weeks. He returned to report a rather choppy sea, but he had raised two marlin, one of which was a good-sized fish that came for his bait three times, to refuse it, no doubt because it was stale. Tuna, a small species, were numerous, and there were some bonito showing.

"Same old story," averred the Captain. "If I'd had a fresh bait I'd have hooked that bird. A lunker, too. All of 500 pounds."

Just what had transpired in my mind I was not conscious of then. It all came to me afterward, and it was that this game was long, and some day one of us might capture a giant Tahitian marlin. We would go on trying.

That night the dry spell broke. The rain roared on the pandanus roof, most welcome and dreamy of sounds. Morning disclosed dark, massed, broken clouds, red-edged and purple-centered, with curtains of rain falling over the mountains. This weather was something like March come back again for a day! Wondrous South Seas!

I took down a couple of new feather gigs—silver-headed with blue eyes—just for good luck. They worked. We caught five fine bonito in the lagoon, right off the point where my cottage stands. Jimmy, one of my natives, held up five fingers: "Five bonito. Good!" he ejaculated, which voiced all our sentiments.

Cappy had gone up the lagoon toward the second pass, and we tried to catch him so as to give him a fresh bait. As usual, however, Cappy's natives were running the wheels off his launch, and we could not catch him. The second pass looked sort of white and rough to me. Cappy went out, however, through a smooth channel. Presently we saw a swell gather and rise, to close the channel and mount to a great, curling, white-crested wave which broke all the way across. Charley, who had the wheel, grinned up at me: "No good!" We turned inshore and made for the third pass, some miles on, and got through that wide one without risk. Afterward Cappy told me Areiareia knew exactly when to run through the second pass.

We headed out. A few black noddies skimmed the dark sea, and a few scattered bonito broke the surface. As usual—when we had them—we put out a big bonito on my big tackle and an ordinary one on the other. As my medium tackle holds 1,000 yards of 39-thread Swastika line it will seem interesting to anglers to speak of it as medium. The big outfit held 1,500 yards of line—1,000 of 39-thread and 500 yards of 42 for backing; and this story will prove I needed hardy rod and reel, and the great Swastika line.

Off the east end there was a brightness of white and blue, where the clouds broke, and in the west there were trade wind clouds of gold and pearl, but for the most part a gray canopy overspread mountain and sea. All along the saw-toothed front of this range inshore the peaks were obscured and the canyons filled with down-drooping veils of rain. What a relief from late days of sun and wind and wave! This was the kind of sea I loved to fish. The boat ran easily over a dark, low, lumpy swell. The air was cool, and as I did not have on any shirt the fine mist felt pleasant to my skin. John was at the wheel. Bob sat up on top with Jimmy and Charley, learning to talk Tahitian. The teasers and heavy baits made a splashing, swishy sound that could be heard above the boil and gurgle of water from the propellers. We followed some low-skimming boobies for a while, and then headed for Captain M.'s boat, several miles farther out. A rain squall was obscuring the white, tumbling reef and slowly moving toward us. Peter sat at my right, holding the line which had the larger bonito. He had both feet up on the gunwale. I noticed that the line on this reel was white and dry. I sat in the left chair, precisely as

Peter, except that I had on two pairs of gloves with thumbstalls in them. I have cut, burned, and skinned my hands too often on a hard strike to go without gloves. They are a nuisance to wear all day, when the rest of you, almost, is getting pleasantly caressed by sun and wind, but they are absolutely necessary to an angler who knows what he is doing.

Peter and I were discussing plans for our great round-the-world trip next year, boats, camp equipment, and what not. And, although our gaze seldom strayed from the baits, the idea of raising a fish was the furthest from our minds. We were just fishing, putting in the few remaining hours of this Tahitian trip, and already given over to the hopes and anticipations of the new one. That is the comfortable way to make a trip endurable—to pass from the hard reality of the present to the ideal romance of the future.

Suddenly I heard a sounding, vicious thump of water. Peter's feet went up in the air.

"Ge-suss!" he bawled.

His reel screeched. Quick as thought, I leaned over to press my gloved hand on the whizzing spool of line. Just in time to save the reel from overrunning!

Out where Peter's bait had been showed a whirling, closing hole in the boiling white-green water. I saw a wide purple mass shooting away so close under the surface as to make the water look shallow. Peter fell out of the chair at the same instant I leaped up to straddle his rod. I had the situation in hand. My mind worked swiftly and coolly. It was an incredibly wonderful strike. The other boys piled back to the cockpit to help Peter get my other bait and the teasers in.

Before this was even started the fish ran out 200 yards of line, then, turning to the right, he tore off another hundred. All in a very few seconds! Then a white splash, high as a tree, shot up, out of which leaped the most magnificent of all the leaping fish I ever saw.

"Giant marlin!" screamed Peter. What had happened to me I did not know, but I was cold, keen, hard, tingling, motivated to think and do the right thing. This glorious fish made a leap of 30 feet at least, low and swift, which yet gave me time to gauge his enormous size and species. Here at last on the end of my line was the great Tahitian swordfish! He looked monstrous. He was pale, shiny gray in color, with broad stripes of purple. When he hit the water he sent up a splash like the flying surf on the reef.

By the time he was down I had the drag on and was winding the reel. Out he blazed again, faster, higher, longer, whirling the bonito round his head.

"Hook didn't catch!" yelled Peter, wildly. "It's on this side. He'll throw it."

I had instinctively come up mightily on the rod, winding with all speed, and I had felt the tremendous, solid pull. The big Pflueger hook had caught before that, however, and the bag in the line, coupled with his momentum, had set it.

"No, Peter! He's fast," I replied. Still I kept working like a windmill in a cyclone to get up the slack. The monster had circled in these two leaps. Again he burst out, a plunging leap which took him under a wall of rippling white spray. Next instant such a terrific jerk as I had never sustained nearly unseated me. He was away on his run.

"Take the wheel, Peter," I ordered, and released the drag. "Water! Somebody pour water on this reel! Quick!"

The white line melted, smoked, burned off the reel. I smelled the scorching. It burned through my gloves. John was swift to plunge a bucket overboard and douse reel, rod, and me with water. That, too, saved us.

"After him, Pete!" I called, piercingly. The engines roared, and the launch danced around to leap in the direction of the tight line.

"Full speed!" I added.

"Aye, sir," yelled Peter, who had been a sailor before he became a whaler and a fisherman.

Then we had our race. It was thrilling in the extreme, and, though brief, it was far too long for me. A thousand yards from us—over half a mile—he came up to pound and beat the water into a maelstrom.

"Slow up!" I sang out. We were bagging the line. Then I turned on the wheel drag and began to pump and reel as never before in all my life. How precious that big spool—that big reel handle! They fairly ate up the line. We got back 500 yards of the 1,000 out before he was off again. This time, quick as I was, it took all my strength to release the drag, for when a weight is pulling hard it releases with extreme difficulty. No more risk like that!

He beat us in another race, shorter, at the end of which, when he showed like a plunging elephant, he had out 750 yards of line.

"Too much—Peter!" I panted. "We must—get him closer! Go to it!"

So we ran down upon him. I worked as before, desperately, holding on my nerve, and, when I got 500 yards back again on the reel, I was completely winded, and the hot sweat poured off my naked arms and breast.

"He's sounding! Get my shirt—harness!"

Warily I let go with one hand and then with the other, as John and Jimmy helped me on with my shirt, and then with the leather harness. With that hooked on to my reel and the great strain transferred to my shoulders, I felt that I might not be torn asunder.

"All set. Let's go," I said, grimly. But he had gone down, which gave me a chance to get back my breath. Not long, however, did he remain down. I felt and saw the line rising.

"Keep him on the starboard quarter, Peter. Run up on him now. Bob, your chance for pictures!"

I was quick to grasp that the swordfish kept coming to our left, and repeatedly on that run I had Peter swerve in the same direction, so as to keep the line out on the quarter. Once we were almost in danger. But I saw it. I got back all but 100 yards of line. Close enough. He kept edging in ahead of us, and once we had to turn halfway to keep the stern toward him. But he quickly shot ahead again. He was fast, angry, heavy. How his tail pounded the leader. The short, powerful strokes vibrated all over me.

"Port—port, Peter," I yelled, and even then, so quick was the swordfish, that I missed seeing two leaps directly in front of the boat, as he curved ahead of us. But the uproar from Bob and the others was enough for me.

As the launch sheered around, however, I saw the third of that series of leaps—and if anything could have loosed my chained emotion on the instant, that unbelievably swift and savage plunge would have done so. But I was clamped. No more dreaming! No more bliss! I was there to think and act. And I did not even thrill.

By the same tactics the swordfish sped off a hundred yards of line, and by the same we recovered them and drew close to see him leap again, only 200 feet off our starboard, a little ahead, and of all the magnificent fish I have ever seen he excelled. His power to leap was beyond credence. Captain M.'s big fish, that broke off two years before, did not move like this one. True, he was larger. Nevertheless, this swordfish was so huge that when he came out in dazzling, swift flight, my crew went simply mad. This was the first time my natives had been flabbergasted. They were as excited, as carried away, as Bob and John. Peter, however, stuck at the wheel as if he were after a wounded whale which might any instant turn upon him. I did not need to warn Peter not to let that fish hit us. If he had he would have made splinters out of that launch. Many an anxious glance did I cast toward Cappy's boat, 2 or 3 miles distant. Why did he not come? The peril was too great for us to be alone at the mercy of that beautiful brute, if he charged us either by accident or design. But Captain could not locate us, owing to the misty atmosphere, and missed seeing this grand fish in action.

How sensitive I was to the strain on the line! A slight slackening directed all my faculties to ascertain the cause. The light at the moment was bad, and I had to peer closely to see the line. He had not slowed up, but he was curving back and to the left again—the cunning strategist!

"Port, Peter—port!" I commanded.

We sheered, but not enough. With the wheel hard over, one engine full speed ahead, the other in reverse, we wheeled like a top. But not swift enough for that Tahitian swordfish.

The line went under the bow.

"Reverse!" I called, sharply.

We pounded on the waves, slowly caught hold, slowed, started back. Then I ordered the clutches thrown out. It was a terrible moment, and took all my will not to yield to sudden blank panic.

When my line ceased to pay out, I felt that it had been caught on the keel. And as I was only human, I surrendered for an instant to agony. But no! That line was new, strong. The swordfish was slowing. I could yet avert catastrophe.

"Quick, Pete. Feels as if the line is caught," I cried, unhooking my harness from the reel.

Peter complied with my order. "Yes, by cripes! It's caught. Overboard, Jimmy! Jump in! Loose the line!"

The big Tahitian in a flash was out of his shirt and bending to dive.

"No! Hold on, Jimmy!" I yelled. Only a moment before I had seen sharks milling about. "Grab him, John!"

They held Jimmy back, and a second later I plunged my rod over the side into the water, so suddenly that the weight of it and the reel nearly carried me overboard.

"Hold me—or it's all—day!" I panted, and I thought that if my swordfish had fouled on keel or propellers I did not care if I did fall in.

"Let go my line, Peter," I said, making ready to extend the rod to the limit of my arms.

"I can feel him moving, sir," shouted Peter, excitedly. "By jingo! He's coming! It's free! It wasn't caught!"

That was such intense relief I could not recover my balance. They had to haul me back into the boat. I shook all over as one with the palsy, so violently that Peter had to help me get the rod in the rod socket of the chair. An instant later came the strong, electrifying pull on the line, the scream of the reel. Never such sweet music! He was away from the boat—on a tight line! The revulsion of feeling was so great that it propelled me instantaneously back into my former state of hard, cold, calculating, and critical judgment, and iron determination.

"Close shave, sir," said Peter, cheerily. "It was like when a whale turns on me, after I've struck him. We're all clear, sir, and after him again."

The gray pall of rain bore down on us. I was hot and wet with sweat, and asked for a raincoat to keep me from being chilled. Enveloped in this I went on with my absorbing toil. Blisters began to smart on my hands, especially one on the inside of the third finger of my right hand, certainly a queer place to raise one.

But it bothered me, hampered me. Bob put on his rubber coat and, protecting his camera more than himself, sat out on the bow waiting.

My swordfish, with short, swift runs, took us 5 miles farther out, and then, welcome to see, brought us back, all this while without leaping, though he broke water on the surface a number of times. He never sounded after that first dive. The bane of an angler is a sounding fish, and here in Tahitian waters, where there is no bottom, it spells catastrophe. The marlin slowed up and took to milling, a sure sign of a rattled fish. Then he rose again, and it happened to be when the rain had ceased. He made one high, frantic jump about 200 yards ahead of us, and then threshed on the surface, sending the bloody spray high. All on board were quick to see that sign of weakening, of tragedy—blood.

Peter turned to say, coolly: "He's our meat, sir."

I did not allow any such idea to catch in my consciousness. Peter's words, like those of Bob and John, and the happy jargon of the Tahitians, had no effect upon me whatever.

It rained half an hour longer, during which we repeated several phases of the fight, except slower on the part of the marlin. In all he leaped fifteen times clear of the water. I did not attempt to keep track of his threshings.

After the rain passed I had them remove the rubber coat, which hampered me, and settled to a slower fight. About this time the natives again sighted sharks coming around the boat. I did not like this. Uncanny devils! They were the worst of these marvelous fishing waters. But Peter said: "They don't know what it's all about. They'll go away."

They did go away long enough to relieve me of dread, then they trooped back, lean, yellow-backed, white-finned wolves.

"We ought to have a rifle," I said. "Sharks won't stay to be shot at, whether hit or not."

It developed that my swordfish had leaped too often and run too swiftly to make an extremely long fight. I had expected a perceptible weakening and recognized it. So did Peter, who smiled gladly. Then I taxed myself to the utmost and spared nothing. In another hour, which seemed only a few minutes, I had him whipped and coming. I could lead him. The slow strokes of his tail took no more line. Then he quit wagging.

"Clear for action, Pete. Give John the wheel. I see the end of the double line. There!"

I heaved and wound. With the end of the double line over my reel I screwed the drag up tight. The finish was in sight. Suddenly I felt tugs and jerks at my fish.

"Sharks!" I yelled, hauling away for dear life.

Everybody leaned over the gunwale. I saw a wide, sheery mass, greenish silver, crossed by purple bars. it moved. It weaved. But I could drag it easily.

"Mauu! Mauu!" shrilled the natives.

"Heave!" shouted Peter, as he peered down.

In a few more hauls I brought the swivel of the leader out of the water.

"By God! They're on him!" roared Peter, hauling on the leader. "Get the lance, boat hook, gaffs—anything. Fight them off!"

Suddenly Peter let go the leader and, jerking the big gaff from Jimmy, he lunged out. There was a single enormous roar of water and a sheeted splash. I saw a blue tail so wide I thought I was crazy. It threw a 6-foot yellow shark into the air!

"Rope his tail, Charley," yelled Peter. "Rest of you fight the tigers off."

I unhooked the harness and stood up to lean over the gunwales. A swordfish rolled on the surface, extending from forward of the cockpit to 2 yards or more beyond the end. His barred body was as large as that of an ox. And to it sharks were clinging, tearing, out on the small part near the tail. Charley looped the great tail, and that was a signal for the men to get into action.

One big shark had a hold just below the anal fin. How cruel, brutish, ferocious! Peter made a powerful stab at him. The big lance head went clear through his neck. He gulped and sank. Peter stabbed another underneath, and still another. Jimmy was tearing at sharks with the long-handled gaff, and when he hooked one he was nearly hauled overboard. Charley threshed with his rope; John did valiant work with the boat hook, and Bob frightened me by his daring fury, as he leaned far over to hack with the cleaver.

We keep these huge cleavers on board to use in case we are attacked by an octopus, which is not a far-fetched fear at all. It might happen. Bob is lean and long and powerful. Also he was mad. Whack! He slashed a shark that let go and appeared to slip up into the air.

"On the nose, Bob. Split his nose! That's the weak spot on a shark!" yelled Peter.

Next shot Bob cut deep into the round stub nose of this big, black shark—the only one of that color I saw—and it had the effect of dynamite. More sharks appeared under Bob, and I was scared so stiff I could not move.

"Take that! And that!" sang out Bob, in a kind of fierce ecstasy. "You will try to eat our swordfish—dirty, stinking pups! Aha! On your beak, huh! Zambesi! Wow, Pete, that sure is the place."

"Look out, Bob! For God's sake—look out!" I begged, frantically, after I saw a shark almost reach Bob's arm.

Peter swore at him. But there was no keeping Bob off those cannibals.

Blood and water flew all over us. The smell of sharks in any case was not pleasant, and with them spouting blood, and my giant swordfish rolling in blood, the stench that arose was sickening. They appeared to come from all directions, especially from under the boat. Finally I had to get into the thick of it, armed only with a gaff handle minus the gaff. I did hit one a stunning welt over the nose, making him let go. If we had all had lances like the one Peter was using so effectively, we would have made short work of them. One jab from Peter either killed or disabled a shark. The crippled ones swam about belly up or lopsided, and stuck up their heads as if to get air. Of all the bloody messes I ever saw, that was the worst.

"Makes me remember—the war!" panted Peter, grimly.

And it was Peter who whipped the flock of ravenous sharks off. Chuck! went the heavy lance, and that was the end of another. My heart apparently had ceased to function. To capture that glorious fish, only to see it devoured before my eyes!

"Run ahead, Johnny, out of this bloody slaughter hole, so we can see," called Peter.

John ran forward a few rods into clear water. A few sharks followed, one of which did so to his death. The others grew wary, they swam around.

"We got 'em licked! Say, I had the wind up me," said Peter. "Who ever saw the like of that? The bloody devils!"

Bob took the lance from Peter, and stuck the most venturesome of the remaining sharks. It appeared then that we had the situation in hand again. My swordfish was still with us, his beautiful body bitten here and there, his tail almost severed, but not irreparably lacerated. All around the boat wounded sharks were lolling with fins out, sticking ugly heads up, to gulp and dive.

There came a let-down then, and we exchanged the natural elation we felt. The next thing was to see what was to be done with the monster, now we had him. I vowed we could do nothing but tow him to camp. But Peter made the attempt to lift him on the boat. All six of us, hauling on the ropes, could not get his back half out of the water. So we tied him fast and started campward.

Halfway in we espied Cappy's boat. He headed for us, no doubt attracted by all the flags the boys strung up. There was one, a red and blue flag that I had never flown. Jimmy tied this on his bamboo pole and tied that high on the mast. Cappy bore quickly down on us, and ran alongside, he and all of his crew vastly excited.

"What is it? Lamming big broadbill?" he yelled.

My fish did resemble a broadbill in his long, black beak, his wide-spread flukes, his purple color, shading so dark now that the broad bars showed indistinctly. Besides, he lay belly up.

"No, Cappy. He's a giant Tahitian striped marlin, one of the kind we've tried so hard to catch," I replied, happily.

"By gad! So he is. What a monster! I'm glad, old man. My word, I'm glad! I didn't tell you, but I was discouraged. Now we're sitting on top of the world again."

"Rather," replied Peter, for me. "We've got him, Captain, and he's some fish. But the damn sharks nearly beat us."

"So I see. They are bad. I saw a number. Well, I had a 400-pound swordie throw my hook at me, and I've raised two more, besides a sailfish. Fish out here again. Have you got any fresh bonito?"

We threw our bait into his boat and headed for camp again. Cappy waved, a fine, happy smile on his tanned face, and called: "He's a wolloper, old man. I'm sure glad."

"I owe it to you, Cap," I called after him.

We ran for the nearest pass, necessarily fairly slowly with all that weight on our stern. The boat listed half a foot and tried to run in a circle. It was about 1 o'clock, and the sky began to clear. Bob raved about what pictures he would take.

"Oh, boy, what a fish! If only Romer had been with us! I saw him hit the bait, and I nearly fell off the deck. I couldn't yell. Wasn't it a won-derful fight? Everything just right. I was scared when he tried to go under the boat."

"So was I, Bob," I replied, remembering that crucial moment.

"I wasn't," said Peter. "The other day when we had the boat out at Papeete I shaved all the rough places off her keel. So I felt safe. What puts the wind up me is the way these Tahitian swordfish can jump. Fast? My word! This fellow beat any small marlin I ever saw in my life."

I agreed with Peter and we discussed this startling and amazing power of the giant marlin. I put forward the conviction that the sole reason for their incredible speed and ferocity was that evolution, the struggle to survive, was magnified in these crystal-clear waters around Tahiti. We talked over every phase of the fight, and that which pleased me most was the old whaler's tribute:

"You were there, sir. That cool and quick! On the strike that dry line scared me stiff. But afterward I had no doubt of the result."

THE GIANT had a tail spread of over 5 feet.

We were all wringing wet, and some of us as bloody as wet. I removed my wet clothes and gave myself a brisk rub. I could not stand erect, and my hands hurt—pangs I endured gratefully.

We arrived at the dock about 3 o'clock, to find all our camp folk and a hundred natives assembled to greet us. Up and down had sped the news of the flags waving.

I went ashore and waited impatiently to see the marlin hauled out on the sand. It took a dozen men, all wading, to drag him in. And when they at last got him under the tripod, I approached, knowing I was to have a shock and prepared for it.

But at that he surprised me in several ways. His color had grown darker and the bars showed only palely. Still they were there, and helped to identify him as one of the striped species. He was bigger than I had ever hoped for. And his body was long and round. This roundness appeared to be an extraordinary feature for a marlin spearfish. His bill was 3 feet long, not slender and rapier-like, as in the ordinary marlin, or short and bludgeonlike, as in the black marlin. It was about the same size all the way from tip to where it swelled into his snout, and slightly flattened on top—a superb and remarkable weapon. The fact that the great striped spearfish Captain Mitchell lost in 1928 had a long, curved bill, like a rhinoceros, did not deter me from pronouncing this of the same species. Right there I named this species, "Giant Tahitian Striped Marlin." Singularly, he had a small head, only a foot or more from where his beak broadened to his eye, which, however, was as large as that of a broadbill swordfish. There were two gill openings on each side, a feature I never observed before in any swordfish, the one toward the mouth being considerably smaller than the regular gill opening. From there his head sheered up to his humped back, out of which stood an enormous dorsal fin. He had a straight-under maxillary. The pectoral fins were large, wide, like wings, and dark in color. The fin-like appendages under the back of his lower jaw were only about 6 inches long and quite slender. In other spearfish these are long, and in sailfish sometimes exceed 2 feet and more. His body, for 8 feet, was as symmetrical and round as that of a good, big stallion. According to my deduction, it was a male fish. He carried this roundness back to his anal fin, and there further accuracy was impossible because the sharks had eaten away most of the flesh from these fins to his tail. On one side, too, they had torn out enough meat to fill a bushel basket. His tail was the most splendid of all the fish tails I ever observed. It was a perfect bent bow, slender, curved, dark purple in color, finely ribbed, and expressive of the tremendous speed and strength the fish had exhibited.

This tail had a spread of 5 feet 2 inches. His length was 14 feet 2 inches. His girth was 6 feet 9 inches. And his weight, as he was, 1,040 pounds.

Every drop of blood had been drained from his body, and this with at least 200 pounds of flesh the sharks took would have fetched his true and natural weight to 1,250 pounds. But I thought it best to have the record stand at the actual weight, without allowance for what he had lost. Nevertheless, despite my satisfaction and elation, as I looked up at his appalling shape, I could not help but remember the giant marlin Captain had lost in 1928, which we estimated at 22 or 23 feet, or the 20-foot one I had raised at Tautira, or the 28-foot one the natives had seen repeatedly alongside their canoes. And I thought of the prodigious leaps and astounding fleetness of this one I had caught. "My heaven!" I breathed. "What would a bigger one do?" ❖

NOVEMBER 1930

Arrows Against
WILD BOARS

THE AUTHOR poses with his old tusker, one of the three killed by his party in the hills of Santa Cruz Island.

by Howard Hill

G RACEFULLY SLIPPING HIS plane down through a hole in the fog, Jerry made a beautiful landing in a sheep pasture on the north end of Santa Cruz Island. Three of us crawled out, and, in a muddle of bed rolls, grub, bows, and arrows, waved good-by as the plane taxied down the field and took off, droning out over the Pacific. Our bow-and-arrow hunt for Santa Cruz wild boar had begun.

The wild boars that range over the fifty square miles of this rugged island grow to considerable size, and, since the sixteenth century, when the Spaniards left them there, they have reverted to type, so that they resemble the boar of the Black Forest of Germany. Their tusks often protrude five inches from the lower jaw, and their temper is anything but pleasant. Even when armed with a high-powered rifle, more than one hunter has been on the losing end of an encounter with a Santa Cruz boar. When a man faces one with a bow and arrow, the chances are at least even that the boar will be able to give a very good account of himself.

Although as deadly as a .30/06, an arrow has no shocking power. Our bows would throw a broadhead clear through the largest boar on the island, but, in the few seconds required for the arrow to carry out its deadly effect, the boar would be able to run several yards, and to inflict much damage. However, Walter and Ken Wilhelm had often hunted with me, using the long bow, and the three of us had made up our minds to pit our skill against any boar we chanced to meet, and to go down together or share in the success, as the case might be.

That night we bedded down in a shallow draw, and, by daylight the following morning, we were moving over the low foothills. We hoped to be able to stalk the hogs within shooting range, and to deliver a telling blow before they had time to charge. About a mile from camp, Walter spotted a big, black tusker, moving along a high range that ran along the east side of the island.

The big boars feed mostly at night, and go back into the hills to sleep during the day among the clumps of scrub oak and pear cactus that grow six or eight feet high in the bottom of the mountain draws. We could see by the long, trotting gait of this boar that he was hurrying to his favorite sleeping ground. Through the glasses, we saw him disappear into a narrow draw that ran straight to the base of an abrupt cliff. When, after several minutes, he did not emerge on either side, we started after him.

When we came within a few hundred yards of where we had last seen the beast, we stopped, and planned our stalk. It was decided that Walt should take the left side of the draw, and I the right, and that Ken should drive straight up the center, along the bottom. The draw was narrow, and the walls steep. At the head, just under the lee of the cliff, nestled a large clump of scrub oak, and giant pear cactus. Here, we felt sure, our quarry must be bedded down. We moved in cautiously, with no more than forty or fifty yards separating any two of us.

Walt and I were now abreast of the bush and cactus patch, while Ken waited below in the bottom of the draw. If the boar was here, we had him surrounded on three sides, and the cliff made impossible any escape on the fourth side. Any way he went, one of us would get a close shot. We were peering cautiously through the brush, anxious to see him before he jumped.

Suddenly I heard a stick crack. Thinking I saw something move, I drew and hurriedly loosed an arrow. It struck an oak limb and glanced to the right. Like a tornado, our quarry sprang into action.

Bounding down the steep mountain side in long, deerlike leaps, the black boar ripped through the scrub oaks and pear cactus, knocking leaves and limbs ten feet into the air. He skipped through an open space fairly close to Walter, but running sidewise to him. In that split second, Walt slipped a broadhead through the boar's ham. The tusker was checking out, but now, straight in line with his retreat, crouched Ken, waiting with bow half drawn.

Without trying to change his course, the enraged tusker bore down on Ken with bristles standing straight up.

I tried vainly from where I stood to get a shot as the boar whisked through the brush, but not until he broke cover, thirty feet in front of Ken, could I shoot. I could see both Ken and the boar plainly. I knew that the beast could hardly miss him, but Ken stood his ground until the hog was almost upon him. Like a flash, Ken sprang to one side, and, as the boar swished through the air on the downhill side, he loosed an arrow that caught the porker high up and just in front of the hips.

The old monarch seemed to stiffen in midair. When he struck the ground with his front feet, he turned a somersault, and then another, which brought him to the edge of a small cliff leading to the bottom of the draw. On his third somersault, the boar went over the cliff, skidded, rolled, and finally came to rest out of sight, in a small stream of water thirty yards below.

We rushed down as fast as we could to where the old boar had stopped. There he stood, on his front legs, with green devils jumping out of his eyes.

Ken's arrow had cut the boar's spinal cord just forward of the hips, paralyzing the hind legs, and making it impossible for him to carry home another charge.

However, during the next couple of days, Walter and I each got a boar, and we had three fierce-looking trophies when Jerry again eased his plane down on Santa Cruz Island. Three wild boar, with long, death-dealing tusks, and razor-sharp teeth, and every tusker brought down with a bow and arrow. It's a risky business tackling game as dangerous as the wild boar without firearms, but the thrills of such a jaunt as ours prove there's no hunting quite like it in all the world of sport. And Jerry, who flies a plane, thinks he has fun. ◆

AUGUST 1937

119

White Spearman OF THE JUNGLE

by Tracy Lewis

❖

"TIGER MAN" THE NATIVES OF Brazil call him, for *tigre* is their name for jaguar and Sasha Siemel is the only white man who has ever killed one of these beasts with a spear. In all, Siemel has accounted for 125 jaguars, twenty-seven of these having been slain with primitive weapons. Of these twenty-seven, he has killed eighteen with his spear, two with bow and arrow and seven with combination attack, of rifle bayonet, arrow, and spear.

Few persons have been on such intimate terms with a jaguar. Fewer still realize the great size and ferocity of these spotted animals as they are found in the Xarayes marshes and the Brazilian jungle near the Bolivian border. Our zoo specimens are no criterion, for these, because of the difficulty of transporting them through the jungle, are captured as near as possible to the coast. The coastal jaguar never grows so large as the beasts farther inland. One jaguar that Siemel killed with his spear weighed 350 pounds and was nine feet long—as big as a medium-sized lion or an average Bengal tiger. And Siemel is convinced that his brand of tiger is superior to the Bengal both in courage and strength. So firmly does he believe it that he has offered to match himself and his spear against either a lion or an Indian tiger. He hopes that the spectacle will be staged sometime in 1936 in Mexico.

Unlike the puma—called mountain lion or cougar in North America— the South American jaguar has little fear. The puma, Siemel says, cannot be speared successfully because it will never charge. But the jaguar is every inch a fighter when wounded or cornered. Besides, he has the strength to back up his courage. It is no trick at all for him to drag off a good-sized cow to the jungle for his dinner. One jaguar in the course of a year will take fifty or sixty head of cattle and for his depredations is bitterly hated by the natives. When you add to the other characteristics of a jaguar an amazing agility, it is not difficult to realize what a dangerous opponent he is when met face to face. He can bound up a tree as easily as a house cat and often takes that means of escape when pressed too closely by hounds. But he is just as likely, when cornered, to take refuge in a clump of bushes on the ground. The hunter cannot afford to take too much for granted when trailing a jaguar.

Siemel, who lately came to the United States to tell his harrowing tales of jungle adventure on the lecture platform, does not look the part of a Tarzan. He is a good-looking, regular-featured man with thick dark hair, and black eyes. A heavy, black beard, touched slightly with gray, covers his chin. He is tall without seeming so and is stronger and more sturdily built than a casual glance would indicate. He would probably appear more in character on a yacht than in the jungles of Matto Grosso. He is an expert amateur boxer and wrestler. The muscles are there. They have to be to hold a savage jaguar on the end of a spear.

Siemel was born in Rega, Latvia, on the Baltic Sea, but has lived from 1910 to 1935 in South America, seventeen of these years in the jungle. He has spent much of his time in big cities, and enjoys meeting persons who are interested in his fascinating sport, but he likes the jungle and its excitement better.

Siemel does not think it odd that such a gentle-mannered and well-educated person as he became the foremost—in fact, the only—exponent of a strictly primitive art.

"When I went to South America" he told me, I heard that there were a few natives called *zagayeiros*, or spearmen, who killed tigers with nothing but a spear. To me it seemed incredible but I intended to find out. So I made the acquaintance of Joaquim, a Guato Indian, who lived in a little hut on the Paraguay River. I showed him my rifle and told him that was my weapon for jaguars. Joaquim was too courteous to be contemptuous. He merely smiled and patted his spear. That was his idea of the proper weapon for such work.

"The spear was seven feet long. The shaft was made of unusually strong wood with a steel head. This head was leaf-shaped, being wider towards the shaft than towards the point. This shape permitted it to be pulled out of an animal's body easily. At the junction of the head with the shaft there was a small steel crosspiece to prevent the head from passing clear through the beast. The spear didn't look like much of a weapon but, after years of dependence upon it in emergencies I have decided that I would rather have that spear than a rifle in my hands if a wounded lion or tiger were in the bush.

"When Joaquim first showed it to me I wasn't so enthusiastic but I told him I liked it and he agreed to demonstrate to me the next day how efficient it could be when properly handled."

The next day Siemel and the *zagayeiro* drifted down the Paraguay in a canoe while the hounds ranged the shore in search of the prey. The country combined stretches of prairie, grown with spear grass, small clumps of woods and the "green hell" of the Brazilian jungle itself. In places the jungle was sufficiently open to permit a well-trained horse to pass through, one that had learned enough to avoid the ever-present branches and bushes. Elsewhere wild pineapples, thorn trees, the parasitic "strangler tree" and a thick underbrush made travel hard even on foot.

After an hour or two, the hunters heard the dogs baying. Hurrying ashore, they forced their way through a jungle tangle towards the sound. They found the jaguar treed, calmly surveying the yapping dogs below him. The hounds didn't bother him much. He had recently dined on an alligator and wasn't particularly interested in the dogs. But, when an arrow from Joaquim's bow pierced his side, that was different, much different.

He leaped from the tree with a snarl and Joaquim rushed to meet him. Then, as the tiger charged, Joaquim stood with his spear almost horizontal, and with his knees slightly bent to absorb the shock of the beast's weight. He didn't jab at the tiger with his spear. To do so would have been suicide. One swift slash of the tiger's paw would have knocked the spear aside, but when the weapon was held motionless, the charging tiger would not notice it, any more than he would a branch.

Before that mad rush, Joaquim stood like a statue. The tiger sprang but, instead of descending upon the *zagayeiro,* he landed with his chest on the point of the spear. At the moment of impact, Joaquim lowered the butt of the shaft to the ground to hold the weight. Then with a heave, he turned the animal over on its back, whirling around as he did so to get near its head and so avoid the saberlike claws of the hindpaws which could easily have disemboweled him.

"That was all," said Siemel. "It was over in twenty seconds. The tiger was dead and there wasn't a scratch on Joaquim. I looked at him. I was stronger than he. I was ashamed to admit less courage. If he could do it, so could I, or any other young man with good muscles and an inclination for sports. But it would be necessary to learn slowly—that was the secret—just as Joaquim had learned from his father. Well, I'd do it!

"So the next day we set out again. The dogs brought another tiger to bay in the bushes. With my heart occupying most of my mouth, I advanced, poked aside the leaves with my spear and then sprang back to assume the position shown me by the *zagayeiro*. None too soon. With a snarl that made the leaves shake, the tiger sprang. I waited for him to leap at my head as the other one had at Joaquim's. But, instead, he dived for my feet and caught me entirely unprepared. I aimed the spear for his head but merely grazed the fur. Good old Joaquim saved me by running his spear through the great cat's open mouth. I had missed him and lived! That doesn't happen often in spear hunting. My instructor explained why I had failed, saying that no two tigers charge alike.

"Joaquim continued to give me pointers and the time finally came when I considered myself able to go out and do the job unassisted.

"Word was brought to me of a cattle killer. He would kill a cow in one village and the next day would slaughter another in a village twenty-five or thirty miles away. I was living on my houseboat, the *Adventuress*, with a native named Apparicio. One night I heard the mating call of the jaguar. As a call it was not impressive, but to me it sounded like a challenge.

"'Tomorrow,' I said to myself, 'you'll try it alone. No Joaquim to help you.' But I decided to have the full benefit of daylight for the experiment."

In the early dawn, with the orchestra of the jungle in full tune, Siemel, with none but his dogs for companions, set out into the jungle. Before long the dogs' baying indicated that they had found a trail. Suddenly Siemel's enthusiasm left him. For the first time he realized how very much alone he was. But there was no turning back. His pride would not let him. He could picture the native's smile at his early return. So on he pushed, through brush that strove to hold him back; past trees full of chattering monkeys, through pineapple-thorn bushes that cut him with their points, until at last he came to where the dogs were making their commotion.

"I was afraid, desperately afraid," Siemel admitted. "I knew the tiger was in the bush and there was no one to help me now. Perspiration broke out on me as I stepped towards the bushes whence came the rumbling snarl of the jaguar. I shouted, partly to relieve my feelings and partly to induce a charge from the tiger. Another shout and there was a deep-throated, answering growl.

"I jumped back to a small clearing and stood ready. The bushes were wrenched aside by three hundred pounds of yellow, black-spotted fury. I looked into pale, yellow eyes that gleamed with hatred. From the beast's red, wide-stretched mouth came a guttural growl that vibrated in my very bones. Then the jaguar leaped. As it did, my fear left me; I became too busy to think of fear. I dropped back as I had seen Joaquim do, and rested the butt of the spear on the ground. There was a mighty scream and the spear shook as the tiger's weight fell upon it and drove it six inches into the soft ground. The tiger's chest had been pierced. Blood rushed from the wound and the dying cat coughed warm, red foam into my face. I quickly turned him over on his back, and held him there, kicking and struggling, as I wheeled to avoid his murderous claws. In half a minute I had killed my tiger. I was a *zagayeiro* at last and may be forgiven, I think, if I celebrated vocally just as a native *zagayeiro* would have done."

Part of Siemel's equipment when he goes spearing is a bow and arrow of the native type. He has killed two tigers with this weapon but does not carry it for that purpose. An arrow will kill more certainly, some archers claim, than a bullet. The wider opening it makes, they say, permits air to escape from the lungs and causes them to collapse. But a bullet has more shocking, or stopping, power. There is less danger of a charge by the wounded animal. While a beast hit by the arrow would soon die, it might often finish the archer before it did, unless the archer carried some other means of defense.

Because the guests that Siemel escorts into the jungle aren't anxious as a rule to follow tigers any longer than necessary, he finds a properly placed arrow useful in getting quick action. Needless to say, Siemel won't allow any of the white men in his party to try the spear. He prefers to bring back his tigers dead and his guests alive.

ONE OF SIEMEL'S LARGER PRIZES. Some of the big Brazilian cats weigh 350 pounds.

125

After the members of his party have shot their tiger, Siemel shows them how it is done with a spear. Often the guests prove quite as dangerous as the jaguars themselves. There was, for example, the hair-raising occasion on which he had two students and a college professor out with him. All of them, he assured me, were good sports but had too much courage.

Siemel had just received the charge of a tiger on his spear's point. On trying to turn the animal on its back, his foot slipped and he sank to his knees. Holding the tiger with one hand, he reached for his heavy machetelike knife with the other. He would have had little difficulty had it not been for the boys who rushed to his "rescue" with their revolvers. The bullets plunked about Tiger Man and tiger alike. Siemel's spear could hold the tiger off, but it wasn't much protection against bullets. Siemel lives to tell the tale but he wishes that his college friends had been cowards and, on that occasion, at least, had run away.

One mistake is a spear hunter's full quota, even in the life of such an expert *zagayeiro* as Joaquim whose skill had been passed on to Siemel. A skull and a broken spear, revealed the tragic tale to the Tiger Man.

Word had been brought to Siemel of the depredations of an immense three-toed tiger, the animal about whom he had heard Joaquim speak at their last meeting a long time before. Siemel set out to get "Old Three Toes" on horseback accompanied by his little terrier Tupi and his hounds.

The next day he came across the rusty spear head, lying in the grass. Nearby was a skull, bleached a dull white. He identified the broken spear as Joaquim's. Clearing a small space he buried the skull and set up the spear for a headstone.

When he set out again, the disquieting thought occurred to him that it was perhaps "Old Three Toes," the very jaguar he was hunting, that had killed Joaquim. Several hours later Siemel found the half-consumed body of a tapir. He knew that the tiger was not more than two hours ahead of him for the naked-headed vultures that were flying overhead had not yet stripped the bones of the tapir clean.

Siemel cantered for two hours more, following the dogs through marshes and clearings. Finally the hounds turned into the forest. Even here Siemel stuck to his horse, for his mount was trained to the forest. But, penetrating more deeply, he came to wild-pineapple growth that proved too much even for the horse. So tying his mount, he ran after the dogs on foot. As the tiger they were chasing ran in diagonals and stopped at intervals, he was able to cut down the distance between them even though he was outmatched in speed by the flying jaguar.

By now he had lost the dogs. If he did not find them soon the tiger would make short work of some of them. The hounds, unless the hunter is present to direct them, approach the jaguar too closely and Siemel in this way loses several dogs every year. In this instance he blew his horn and was reassured when he heard the dogs bay in reply.

"I was pretty well out of breath," said Siemel in describing the experience, "when I finally came to the tree into which the dogs had chased the tiger. I stopped to rest a bit. I would need all my strength for that tiger snarling up in the tree was a 350-pounder. I nocked an arrow, let fly and hit him in the flank. He came out of that tree pronto, smashing the skull of one dog that rushed at him and to disembowel another that came too near. Then he rushed for me.

"Four times in quick succession, I let him bound upon my spear, each time wrenching the spear clear and jumping back to receive another charge. The fifth time I caught him squarely under the foreleg, turned him, kicking, snarling, and spouting blood, over on his back. That did the trick. He died at last.

"When quite confident that the tiger breathed no longer, my little dog Tupi came over and mounted his side in triumph. Then I looked at the tiger's paws. One of them had only three toes! The old boy had paid for his sins at last!"

Siemel has no desire to visit Africa and try his spear against the big game there. Tourists have spoiled Africa, he says, and he does not wish to shoot his game from automobiles. Because it has so far escaped exploitation, the "Green Hell" of Brazil and Bolivia is far more interesting and fascinating to the Tiger Man.

And when he leaves this country, he will return once more to the land of pumas, alligators, anacondas, anteaters, armadillos, monkeys—and tigers. And there he expects to be joined by Kermit Roosevelt, one fortunate man who will see the Tiger Man in action. ❖

MAY 1935

Most Dangerous Shooting in the Americas

by Grancel Fitz

❖

*I*N THE JUNGLES OF INDOCHINA, back in 1958, I had my first experience with wild Asiatic water buffaloes. It was nearly three years later, however, that my hunting for this species reached its climax—in Brazil. If that seems an improbable place to find them, it's no stranger than all that happened earlier. Those beasts gave me a whole series of surprises.

The first surprise came in the South Viet Nam city of Saigon. On a torrid afternoon, I sat in a sidewalk cafe, talking with an old-timer from the back country. The issuing of my rifle permits and shooting license would take several days. Communist guerrillas were making things unpleasant in the neighborhood of my companion's rubber plantation, so he had come to the city.

"If you get into the right places," the planter said, "you can find plenty of wild elephants, tigers, leopards, guars, buffaloes, and bantings. There are even a few Malaccan rhinos. On the average, water buffaloes are the most dangerous of the lot. They stay in thick cover where they're hard to stop."

I hadn't thought the buffalo would rate so much respect against such competition. I had seen docile buffaloes working in Cambodian rice paddies, and herded like cattle in India. But I recalled that in World War II survival training, our troops in Asia were warned that to strangers, these "tame" buffaloes could be more dangerous with horns and hoofs than any jungle animal. Like the buffalo of Africa, the much larger Asiatic kind is single-minded and thorough.

A week later, on a day when I was hunting with a couple of Moi trackers, I learned how fast a wild buffalo can be. In the early morning we saw plenty of old gaur and banting spoor. The gigantic gaur—known as sladang in the Malay countries—commonly weigh more than 3,000 pounds. They're the world's tallest wild oxen, sometimes measuring nearly seven feet at the withers. In the next hour, though, we found some differently shaped footprints that made those of the largest gaur look small. Only a water buffalo could make a track like that. A height of six feet is about their limit, but really big buffaloes of this species are probably a bit heavier than gaurs. They also have much larger horns and hoofs.

For nearly three hours the buffalo led us through dense jungle, but it was easy to follow so large an animal.

Toward the end of their trailing, the Moi—armed with crossbows— turned off on a smaller game trail. This soon brought us to a creek, hardly knee-deep where it flowed past us and not more than 20 feet wide. Here the men stopped to look. Then one of them touched my arm and pointed excitedly upstream with his chin.

We could see upcreek for nearly 100 yards, but the jungle on both sides came straight down to it. I tried for a minute to spot a tall, bulky animal. When I suddenly saw it—about 80 yards away—I could hardly believe my eyes. No part of that buffalo was more than a few inches above water. He'd found a hole, and there he was, in profile, with his nostrils only a yard from shore. Nothing else could be seen except the bridge of his nose, his eyes, the flat upper surfaces of his back-sweeping horns, and the tiny island between them that marked the top of his withers.

Now what? I had no ambition to follow a wounded buffalo into that jungle. I'd simply have to wait until I could plant a bullet that would anchor him. Undoubtedly I should have waited until he got up, but that called for more patience than I had.

"If he heard just enough noise to alert him," I reasoned, "he might show me a vital spot."

Raising my rifle, I spoke to him softly. Nothing happened. I tried again, a trifle louder. After an instant of motionless quiet, the buff exploded from the creek. In one great splash he hit the thicket, giving me no chance for a well-aimed shot. I turned to the Moi. They shrugged, smiled, and shook their heads; our hunt was finished. That was the only wild buffalo I saw in Asia.

I thought little more about them until last winter. Then, in a most unexpected way, my interest was revived. A letter arrived from Alberto L. Machado, a prominent Rio de Janeiro sportsman I'd never met. He enclosed pictures of his trophy room; these showed some notable African specimens and an extremely fine collection of practically all the big game of South America. In the place of honor hung the head of a water buffalo. He'd shot this impressive bull on Marajó Island, in the mouth of the Amazon. While I knew that various European and Asiatic animals had been introduced into Argentina, I hadn't heard of old-world game in any other South American country, and hadn't even dreamed of wild water buffaloes living there.

Mentioning that he'd read a couple of stories I'd written about Argentine shooting, Senhor Machado listed the kinds of Brazilian game and invited me to hunt as his guest. He explained this would be done on large private land holdings not ordinarily open to strangers. His letter also revealed how the buffalo got to the Amazon delta.

About 70 years ago some ranchers there decided to experiment. The Brazilians tried crossing their cattle with tame Asiatic buffaloes to get a hybrid especially suited to the rainy local climate. This plan failed. The cattle and buffaloes are of separate species and could not cross. So the imported buffaloes were abandoned on Marajó Island. Possibly the ranchers didn't realize the tame buffaloes of Asia are physically the same as the wild ones. The Marajó climate suited the buffaloes perfectly; they thrived and multiplied. In a short time they were as wild—and as dangerous—as any in the Asian jungles.

Senhor Machado also noted that if I wanted to make a trip for buffalo, which are hunted with dugout canoes at a season unsuitable for other game, he'd let me have my choice of several elephant rifles, as nearly all the shots are at uncomfortably close range. He mentioned that customs restrictions make it practically impossible for foreigners to bring rifles into his country.

As a final comment, he wrote, "These magnificent animals have given me the most thrilling moments in all my hunting anywhere. If you come to Marajó Island, I believe you may feel the same before the trip is over."

Before I left for Brazil, my friend Donald Hopkins came through New York. Although this great Spokane trophy hunter hasn't been in Asia, his African safaris total more than five years.

"Where do you hit an African buffalo to stop him in his tracks?" I asked Don. "I hear the Brazilian ones are a close-range job. If I shoot one in the heart, he might mess me up before he falls over."

"The only shots I know that will really anchor an African buff," he told me, "are in the brain or well forward in the spine. The spine shot paralyzes him; you finish him later."

In early April, I landed in Rio, and Alberto Machado met me at the airport. As I'd suspected from his letters, he speaks excellent English, so my ignorance of Portuguese was no handicap. His business is manufacturing cattle vaccines, and he soon proved to be one of the best informed and most enthusiastic hunters I've ever known. At his house that evening I met his charming family and some of his friends.

The following night I went ahead to Belem, doubling back northward to the Amazon's mouth in an 1,800-mile flight. When Alberto joined me there a day later, he brought two keen and widely experienced sportsmen from São Paulo who would be our hunting companions. They were Raul Natividade, a civil engineer, and Marcos Keutenedjian, an industrialist.

"We'll have a 40-minute flight to Irval Lobato's ranch in northeastern Marajó," Alberto told me. "The bush airplane we've chartered can take two of us at a time. Do you want to go on the first trip?" I said it made no difference.

It was partly cloudy when we reached the airport. Marcos and Raul, taking off first, went on to our shooting base at the Ribancera ranch. Then the weather turned so bad that Alberto and I couldn't get there until two days later. Having waited for us until that morning, our friends were out on their first hunt when we arrived.

Wandering out from the main ranch house, I found we were in a region different from any I'd seen. On the porch behind the kitchen I met a baby capybara; these largest of the world's rodents are aquatic and look like gigantic brown guinea pigs. Other pets included a baby monkey, a parrot, and a big red macaw. A pen of large turtles waited their turn in the soup kettle, and off to the west, where the houses of the ranch hands were strung out for several hundred yards, I saw some ordinary domestic livestock.

But dominating everything were the flooded marshes. They crowded close to the Ribancera buildings on all sides. Although the name of the ranch means "High Banks," the site of those buildings was hardly two feet above water level.

On the wide front veranda, I found Alberto relaxing in one of the hammocks.

"Marajó Island is about the size of Switzerland," he explained, "and this pantanal country covers most of the eastern half. Through the whole rainy season it is more or less flooded, but in the rest of the year it dries up. The rains begin in January and last until the end of

August. Buffalo hunting is best when the water is deepest, which happens to be right now. Tomorrow you'll see why."

Not much later, a handsome, strongly built man came up the porch steps. A dark-skinned native boy followed him. The man, after a short conversation in Portuguese with Alberto, came over, smiling, to shake hands with me. This was Irval Lobato, the ranch owner, who had been hunting with our friends. After a few polite words in English, he climbed into a hammock and stretched out.

"Raul shot a buffalo," Alberto said. "They're bringing it in now. Let's go down and see it."

Taking cameras, we walked to the bank of a winding channel near some of the ranch-hands' houses. In the brilliant sunshine, we saw the dugout canoes coming in. Depending on their size, they were poled by two to four men, and one of them carried the whole gutted carcass of a buffalo. I wondered how they'd loaded it into the boat, but then Marcos and Raul stepped ashore, and we congratulated Raul on his prize. It was not an exceptionally big-bodied bull, but it carried a head that would ornament any trophy room, with massive horns curving back in beautiful conformation like a pair of giant calipers.

I didn't get the full story of Raul's hunt until after dinner, which featured beefsteak, chicken, pork, and buffalo liver.

"There wasn't much to it," Raul said. "The boys knew where this one was hanging out. They made a drive through the reeds, and he showed up right in front of me. I hit him hard with the first shot, and finished him with no trouble."

"It's a very nice trophy," I said. "Have you measured the horns?"

The question seemed to surprise him.

"We don't pay much attention to horns," he explained. "We go by the buffalo's size and the kind of fight he gives you. Last year, when I was hunting with Alberto, one came out almost on top of us. That bull went right under the boat and upset it. We were lucky to kill him before anybody got hurt. Did Domingos Acatauass show you his leg?"

I shook my head. At Alberto's suggestion, I'd looked up that owner of a Marajó Island ranch on my first day in Belem. Senhor Acatauass told me we'd hunt his ranch if we didn't get good shooting with Irval, but because of language difficulties we'd had little conversation.

"Domingos got in a jam," Raul said. "A buffalo drove its horn through the canoe and into his thigh. He was crippled quite a while."

Before our after-dinner talk ended, one thing was clear: the closer a hunter comes to getting killed, the better the show.

The more I thought about this, the more sense it made, for the water buffalo has one handicap that keeps him from being ranked as one of the world's greatest trophies. The wild and the tame ones look exactly alike. I saw several tame buffaloes in Asia with really enormous horns. Any mounted head could be that of a purchased tame one, so hunting the water buffalo is more important to the genuine sportsman than to the trophy collector.

At sunrise next morning our dugouts started for the buffalo haunts, but not before a difference in viewpoints put me in an embarrassing spot.

"It is your turn, today," Irval told me as he assigned us to our boats. "We are going after the biggest bull I know about."

"Let Alberto take him," I suggested, whereupon Alberto announced that he had no intention of shooting at any buffalo until mine had been bagged.

"There is one good bull where we are going, and he is very dangerous," Irval continued. "You cannot mistake him; one of his horns curves back, and the other turns down. Don't shoot unless you see that, or you might kill a cow."

Only Alberto could get me out of this. I didn't want a trophy with freakish or broken horns, no matter how big or sporting the buffalo might be. On the other hand, I didn't want to seem ungrateful or cowardly. When my ideas were made plain, Marcos became the hunter.

We never did see that bull, possibly because the weather stayed clear. Water buffaloes have keen senses, so they're most easily approached when a pouring rain makes hunters hard to hear and beats down their scent. But I learned something about the flooded country, where the water seemed to average about three feet deep. Occasionally the boatmen poled the dugouts through open channels and small lagoons—and poling must be good exercise, for most of those boatmen were uncommonly muscular. There was also a thin scattering of small islands, just high enough to support heavy stands of jungle, but nearly always the boats were pushing through a great variety of aquatic vegetation. Some of it grows six or eight feet above the surface in dense thickets extending hundreds of yards. Here the buffalo spend the daylight hours.

The hunting technique calls for at least four or five boats, and a dozen boatmen. These ranch hands know the patches the buffaloes frequent, and in circling the tall reeds it's easy to spot where a buffalo has recently gone through. As our party was only interested in big, solitary old bulls—which are invariably shot when the chance offers, regardless of trophy quality—the next question was whether the buffalo was worth following. To find out, one of the veteran boatmen would jump overboard. By feeling around with his bare feet in the animal's hoofprints on the muddy bottom, the man could get a close idea of the buffalo's size while standing in waist-deep water.

If a big, fresh track is found to windward of cover, the man to do the shooting takes his place in the extreme front of the smallest dugout; these are hardly 12 feet long, so normally only one hunter will go. The other boats wait while the hunter's two boatmen pole him quietly around to the thicket's downwind side. The buffalo is unlikely to come out into open water. He wants the shortest route and the most concealment in crossing from one thicket to the next, and this combination dictates where the hunter's boat should be. If it isn't as close as possible to where the bull will appear, the animal may escape unnoticed.

When driving boats fan out to enter the tall reeds, the bull hears and smells them. To keep track of his pursuers, he goes downwind. If the plan works smoothly, the buffalo wades out and finds the waiting hunter only a few yards away. This, of course, is why the buffalo so often charges if he isn't stopped by the first shot. He may even charge before the shot is fired if he thinks he's cornered.

With Marcos in the hunter's boat, we tried an unproductive drive for the bull with the freak horns. Somewhat earlier, Alberto had shot a big capybara, which he left at an outlying ranch house. The natives value them for both meat and hide. Irval used a .22 rifle to pot a couple of lizards four or five feet long. Otherwise, nothing much happened that sunny day, and I had time to marvel at several things.

One was the weather. We were almost on the equator, where the sun packs a real punch, but the temperature on Marajó never climbed above the low 80's while we were there, and the trade wind made the sunniest hours quite comfortable. Another feature was the swarming life around us, varying from caymans to dragonflies. The pantanal country is a paradise for wading birds; we saw huge jabiru storks, and spoonbills, egrets, and herons of many kinds.

Of the myriad kinds of insects, only two wanted to bite. Mud wasps sometimes resented being disturbed. The tiny, vicious red ants were rarely encountered. While we dutifully slept in mosquito-netted beds, there had been more mosquitoes in my hotel room in the hot city of Belem than we ever found on all Marajó.

"Tomorrow we make a long trip," Irval announced at bedtime, "so we must get up early."

That night the weather changed. We needed raincoats when we left the house half an hour before dawn, and used flashlights to find our places in the boats. Pushing off in a new direction, the boatmen kept up their rhythmic poling five hours with hardly a pause, while the storm mixed drizzles with lashing torrents that had me bailing steadily with a big calabash. But it was good hunting weather. The action came quickly when we arrived at the buffalo cover and found a track.

Marcos was still the hunter. Our tactics were planned in Portuguese, and I can only report that my dugout was soon pushing through a hard rain into a thicket of arumá that was often taller than the boatmen. That stuff has big leaves. I couldn't see farther than a couple of feet on either side.

Before long we heard two shots that almost blended into one, and after a short interval there were a couple of other shots, fired hardly 50 yards from us. In another minute we pushed through to find a dead buffalo, lying in a tiny channel that must have been made by the buffaloes themselves. Only one horn tip and a small patch of its side showed above the water. Marcos and his crew were there. While we were all fairly wet by this time, it struck me that Marcos looked drenched to the skin.

I already knew that he has a collection of 1,500 rifles—yes, that's right—in his São Paulo home, from ancient ones to all the modern makes. For this trip, possibly because of his experience in African shooting, he had chosen a beautifully engraved and gold-inlaid elephant rifle, a double-barreled Holland and Holland in .500/.465 caliber. He now told us that when he'd taken his first shot, his wet finger had slipped onto the second trigger. The double recoil had kicked him right out of the boat.

Fortunately, the buffalo was hard hit by the first bullet, and it floundered away 40 yards or so. When Marcos came up, he shook water out of his artillery, climbed back into the dugout, and finished his bull.

After the other boats came, the men cleared up a question that had puzzled me. They towed the bull a few yards, then opened him up and cleaned him below the surface. Now they filled one of the larger dugouts with water, sank it to the bottom, brought the bull back beside it, and rolled him in. Although the carcass would have weighed over a ton on dry land, it was somewhat buoyant. About 10 of those fellows lifted the boat until one side was well above water, and when they had rolled it onto an even keel and bailed it out, we headed for Ribancera.

It was my turn the next day. After an early rain, the morning was sunny. In the middle of it we found a big track on the northern, upwind side of a thicket.

"Load your rifle chamber now," Alberto suggested as the boys began to pole me around to the leeward border of the high growth. I nodded, bolting a cartridge into the barrel of the well-balanced .416 Rigby I'd borrowed in Rio; I normally kept the magazine loaded and the barrel empty. Alberto also carried a bolt-action. His was a .425 Westley Richards. Raul and Marcos both preferred the English double-barreled type.

We were soon out of sight of the other boats. The trip around the eastern edge of the cover was long, so I was glad Irval knew the country well enough to keep the drive from starting too soon. Then, after we began to skirt the southern side, I saw open channels, with few screened places that might tempt the buffalo to come out. Much of the thicket was aninga, with leaves like elephant ears. These are the biggest of the water plants, and some of them must have been very close to 15 feet high.

We were nearing a place that looked fairly good when a snort stopped us. It reminded me of the starting puff of an old-time steam locomotive. An instant later we heard that buffalo sloshing through the water. He was close to the edge, but a trick of the wind had brought him our scent. After he'd moved a short distance to our right, there was silence. Shifting with him, we slipped into some concealing reeds and waited for something to happen. Nothing did.

Alberto's boat was first to show up; for a few minutes he held a position to support mine if trouble developed. Then the other boats arrived. After a short conference, Irval sent two boys into the cover to chase the bull out. This, I decided, was a job I wouldn't want. But they went willingly enough after one of them had turned back to get a little military carbine. Wading hip-deep, they quickly disappeared, a bit to the left of where we thought the buffalo might be.

In a few minutes there was a short outburst of frantic yelling, along with high-powered splashes that only the buffalo could make. After a brief silence we heard more splashing, and just a few quick yelps. Then came a long interval of quiet before the boys came out to report.

They'd found an old, very big and short-tempered bull with part of his left horn broken off. He had started away in the wrong direction, but when they tried to turn him, the buffalo decided to do the driving himself. The boys heard him coming. There was a single one-man tree among the reeds, and one of them had time to climb it, but the boy with the carbine didn't know how to chamber a cartridge, which wouldn't have helped much anyhow. The charging bull chased him under water, gun and all.

This, in the rainy season, is the standard escape method. The buffalo doesn't quite understand it when the man disappears. The natives are hard to see when submerged, and their usual stunt is to swim a few yards under water—if the reeds will let them—and come up with only their eyes and nostrils above the surface. If the bull sees the man at all, he apparently doesn't recognize him, so the animal finally goes away. I was told that a man wearing a shirt is a bad risk; the shirt tends to float.

When I heard about the broken horn, I didn't want this specimen. The boys who'd chased him didn't want him either, so we took time out for lunch. Along with a beefsteak, Irval handed me something that tasted like breast of chicken, only better. Rolled in farina and fried like a veal cutlet, it was a slice from the tail of one of those lizards he'd shot.

In the next couple of hours no other promising tracks were found, so Irval called the boats together. He wanted to know if I'd spend a night away from home base.

"The boys have heard of two big bulls near a ranch called Arraial," he said. "It is too far to hunt from Ribancera, but we could get there from here this afternoon. You might shoot your buffalo tomorrow. I can send a boat back, and it will bring us anything you need this evening, along with some extra food."

I needed almost nothing, but Raul went back in one of the faster dugouts. With Alberto, Irval, and the other boat crews, my boatmen headed west to Arraial, a small place where the native rancher welcomed us before sunset.

After dinner, Irval remarked that the buffaloes have been hunted hard for meat in the past 20 years, and that a lot of calves have been caught and domesticated. The ranchers now use buffalo milk, especially for cheese. He estimated that about 1,000 wild ones were left.

"Have any Americans hunted on Marajó?" I asked.

"Denver Wright of St. Louis was down here several years ago. He had a narrow escape. Do you know him?"

I'd heard of Mr. Wright, who has hunted widely on several continents. To check the details of his adventure I wrote to him after I returned to New York, and his reply told the same story. He wounded a bull on the edge of a thicket. The buffalo took refuge in the cover, and charged when the boat was poled in. Hearing it coming, the boatmen took to the water, but Wright, having decided to try a brain shot, stood waiting his chance. The reeds were so dense he couldn't see the buff. He had to take the shot at no more than four feet, and then—with no time to check results—he jumped under the far side of the boat, which promptly rolled over on him. Hearing the natives yelling, he pulled himself out to find the head of the dead bull resting on the overturned dugout, in the very place from which the fatal shot had been fired.

Soon after Irval told me this story, we bedded down in hammocks that had been hung for us. The rain had started again, and it was still raining at our dawn breakfast.

Our trip to the buffalo cover was short. This thicket turned out to be mostly pirí, a tassel-topped reed much like papyrus, and we'd hardly begun to skirt the edge when the reeds showed where a buffalo had gone through. After their barefooted checkup in two feet of water—a process that always amazed me—the excited boys told us a big bull had made them. But the wind was wrong for a drive.

"The track is red-hot," Alberto whispered. "They'll pole you in to him. Be very quiet."

A moment later I was sitting in the bow of the hunting dugout, and the boatmen were pushing it through the hole the bull had made. A water buffalo is so powerful he can barge through a couple of feet of water with astonishing speed, but my boatmen could pole even faster. This one hadn't started to run yet. In a few minutes we heard him sloshing ahead.

I listened intently. If the splashes stopped, it could mean that the buffalo—in fear of being overtaken—had doubled back to ambush us. Otherwise we'd see him ahead at close range, and he might whirl in desperation and charge. I'd have to knock him down to stay with the first bullet, and I remembered what Don Hopkins had advised.

"Brain or spine," I kept telling myself. "Brain or spine. Hold 14 inches below the withers for a spine shot."

As the splashes grew louder, the tension mounted, and up there in the bow I began to feel very much alone. I couldn't see through the towering reeds, which often brushed my shoulders on both sides. The raindrops smacking down on my wide-brimmed hat ran off in rivulets when I moved my head. Then the hole in the thicket straightened out enough to let me see the buffalo, perhaps 40 feet away.

He was turning left—I soon learned we were getting close to the edge of the reeds—and I forgot about the brain shot. From that angle, the massive horns covered the brain and the neck bone as well. As the boat swept forward, I aimed carefully and squeezed off a shot for the spine. Down he went. The boatmen yelled, with triumph, relief, or both. But I knew the nearly submerged bull wasn't necessarily down for keeps.

When the buffalo's head next appeared above water, I pressed the trigger, and the rifle merely clicked. Much of my shooting has been done with a .30/06, and I hadn't yanked the bolt far enough back to eject the much longer Rigby cartridge case. Things like that can be unhealthy when dealing with dangerous game.

After a few seconds of floundering, the buffalo reared up on his front legs. When the swinging horns exposed his neck, I planted one of those heavy, full-jacketed Rigby bullets in it, then slammed in two others to make sure of the job.

The other boats soon came up, and a grinning bunch of men hacked through the reeds that hid a lagoon. Without stopping to open the bull, they towed him to an island of solid ground and rolled him ashore. I could see I'd be happy with the trophy; those wide-spreading horns weren't exceptionally long, but they were heavy, symmetrical, and unbroken. So out came the cameras.

The light was bad, and the rain spattered our lenses, but we got a few photographs before the boys dressed out the carcass. They salt down the meat to make a product much like our corned beef.

When we returned to Ribancera, I learned that our hunt there was over. Marcos and Raul were packed to leave. The bush pilot came in for them next morning. Irval then took off in his own plane, which

I POSE WITH MY BUFFALO BULL after it is rolled ashore.

he flies to the ranch from his Belem home. Those men were unbeatable hunting companions, and one thing alone had kept our days with them from being ideal. Alberto, my most thoughtful host, had not yet shot a buffalo.

"Don't worry about that," he said when the others had left. "I'll have my chance at Domingos Acatauassú's ranch. The boys can pole me there in four hours when I go. I'll let you know how I make out."

"I hope you get the best head on the island," I said. Only one northbound plane a week left Belem, and I had to catch it. Alberto's letter reached me a couple of weeks later, and it made the whole hunt perfect.

He had bagged three buffaloes. One carried the finest head our party had taken, but that wasn't all. It gave Alberto a hair-raising adventure. I was delighted, for I'd come to understand Marajó Island buffalo hunting—the most dangerous big-game shooting in the whole western hemisphere. The way those Brazilian sportsmen chase their buffaloes, they want to find both excitement and trouble. ❖

DECEMBER 1961

Africa's
Meanest Game
by Fred Bear

FROM LEFT, Dick Mauch, Bill Wright, Wally Johnson, Fred Bear and Walt Johnson Jr..

❖

*T*HE BUFFALO WAS A SOLITARY bull, the native said, and very bad. The man had flagged us down at a small African village on the Save River in Mozambique to tell us his troubles.

First, his people were badly in need of meat. Second, this buffalo had been terrorizing the village, destroying gardens and chasing anyone he came across. He spent his days in thick reeds along the river, and we'd find him there now. Would we kill him?

It wasn't an assignment either Wally Johnson, my white hunter, or I was eager to take on. True, I wanted a buffalo bad enough. I'd made two previous hunts in Africa and taken some good trophies, including an elephant, and there were only two animals I was interested in this time—buffalo and lion. But, if I took them, I wanted to make the kills with a bow, since that's the only way I have hunted for more than 30 years. I also hoped that Bob Halmi and Zoli Vidor, the two New York photographers who were with me, would be able to make a motion picture record of the kills.

I realized I was setting my sights high. To the best of my knowledge, the number of African buffaloes ever killed by a white man with bow and arrow could be counted on the fingers of one hand, and I was sure that photographing such an encounter had not been done more than once or twice. As for the lion I was hoping for, Art Young, the great pioneer archer, had killed one with a bow in the 1920's, but, so far as I knew, it had not been done since. If I succeeded on that hunt, I'd be hanging up an almost unheard of record, and again, the chances of getting movies of the kills would be extremely slim.

Anyway, I wanted a buffalo, but the one the native had told us about didn't sound like the right candidate for what I had in mind. The reeds along the river would almost certainly be too thick for either a bow kill or for the cameras. We knew that at a village three or four miles away a lone buffalo had killed five persons in the past six months, and it had not yet been hunted down. If we went into the reeds and pushed this cantankerous bull around, he might prove every bit as dangerous as that one.

Johnson cocked a quizzical eye in my direction. "Want to have a look?" he asked.

"It won't hurt to look," I agreed cautiously.

Where the river bank dropped down onto wide flats covered with a dense tangle of bamboolike reeds, we came on a makeshift camp where natives were making a potent beer from the sap of palm trees. Wally asked them about the buffalo.

"He is there," one of the men declared, pointing to a spot about 60 yards out in the reeds.

"This bloke is probably full of palm beer," Wally muttered, "but we'll find out."

There's one bad feature about an undertaking of that kind. Once you start, there's not likely to be much chance of backing out. Nevertheless, we started into the reeds. They were 10 feet high and had stems half an inch thick. We could see only a few steps in any direction.

I was carrying a 65-pound hunting bow of my own make and four razorhead arrows, one on the string and three in the bow quiver. I had killed grizzly bears, Alaska browns, an Indian tiger (so far as I know the first taken with a bow in the last 100 years; I told that story, "Tiger With An Arrow," in *OUTDOOR LIFE*, October, 1964), and even an elephant with that same kind of equipment, and I had complete confidence in it. But, at the same time, I knew it was poor buffalo medicine in the spot we were in. There is almost no chance that any arrow, however well placed, is going to drop in its tracks an animal as big and tough as a buffalo, and that was what would have to be done if this bull came for us. In those reeds, the odds were against my even getting a shot.

Johnson was carrying a Winchester Model 70 in .458 Magnum caliber. I had a Browning .375 Magnum along for emergencies. Wally handed my rifle to one of his trackers. "He's a good, steady boy and handy with a gun in a pinch," he said. In a place like that, and considering the close range necessary with a bow, it seemed wise to have two back-up rifles.

Two natives from the beer-making party tagged along with us to show us the buffalo. They said there were openings in the reeds through which we could take pictures, but I didn't think it likely that the bull would walk out in one of those places, and the only openings we found were buffalo trails crisscrossing in every direction.

We had walked only a short distance when we heard the bull jump up and lumber off no more than 20 yards ahead. We picked up his track and followed it, moving cautiously. Several times in the next half an hour we heard him thrashing through the reeds, never far away. "He's circling us," Wally warned.

I was feeling more and more like buffalo bait and liking the situation less and less. Finally, Wally and I held a whispered consultation and agreed the risk was too great. We turned back, walking single file, with the two local natives in the lead, our tracker next, and Wally just ahead of me. Halmi and Vidor, loaded with camera gear, were bringing up the rear.

The only warning the buffalo gave us was a harsh, throaty grunt. It came from a tangle no more than six paces to the left of the trail we were following, and it was enough to lift a man out of his shoes. In the same instant, we heard a pounding of hoofs and a great crashing of reeds. Our bull was coming hell-bent.

Wally said afterward that the bull had charged by sound and had headed for the men in the lead. They panicked. All three vanished in the reeds like groundhogs disappearing down a hole, and my rifle went with them. Then the buffalo came crashing into the trail. That was the first we had seen of him, and he spotted Johnson and me in the same split second we saw him. He swiveled around, only 20 feet away. Wally's .458 bellowed and the bull crumpled and skidded down in a black heap.

Johnson poured in a second shot to make sure. When the bull didn't so much as kick, Wally took three or four wary steps and bent over him. He dropped just 10 feet from us. Johnson had shot from the hip as the bull lowered his head for the toss, and he had made an amazing hit. The 500-grain solid had gone in over the lowered head, breaking the neck.

We had killed our first buffalo on the first morning of the hunt and had had about as close a call as I could remember in all my years of hunting dangerous game. As a bowhunter, I hadn't played much of a hand, but I was entirely satisfied with the outcome. Seeing that maddened bull sledged down with a single shot at 10 feet had been an experience so fantastic that I later found myself wondering whether I hadn't dreamed the whole thing. Had Wally's snap shot missed the spine, one or more of us would almost certainly have been trampled or gored to death.

We learned now why this bull had given the natives a bad time. He had been caught by a hind foot in a poacher's snare and the wire had cut deep. The foot was badly swollen and the walking surface was raw and bleeding. No wonder he was on the prod.

We had left Beira in Mozambique for our camp on the Save on June 1, 1965, having flown by jet direct from Rome to Salisbury in Southern Rhodesia and on to Beira by propeller plane. We were going into an area that is regarded as among the best hunting country remaining in Africa, and our hunt got off to a fast start. We killed the buffalo on June 2.

Our party numbered eight: four bowhunters besides myself, the two cameramen, and Jim Crowe, an outdoors writer from Detroit, who was along as a reporter but did not intend to hunt. The four bowmen, all hunting partners with whom I had made previous trips and all well known in archery circles, were Bill Wright of San Francisco, Dick Mauch from Nebraska, K. Knickerbocker from Virginia, and Bob Munger, a Michigan hardware and sporting-goods dealer and a contributor to *OUTDOOR LIFE*.

Though Zoli Vidor, around 45, was a professional movie photographer, he had had little experience in photographing wildlife. However, he got a complete initiation before this hunt was over. Halmi, a few years younger, had been with me as cameraman on a tiger hunt in India in 1963 and an African safari in 1964.

As for me, I head the Bear Archery Company at Grayling, Michigan, and have put in a lot of time hunting trophy game with a bow the past 12 or 15 years.

Our outfitter was Mozambique Safarilandia, directed by Werner von Alvensleben, formerly a Prussian baron. Bitterly anti-Nazi, he had fled one of Hitler's concentration camps, escaped to Mozambique, and started a career as a white hunter.

I had read and heard enough about Wally Johnson, who was to be my white hunter this time, to know that he was one of the best in the business. An old hand, around 50, he was an ivory hunter in the old days, has held a professional hunter's license in Mozambique for many years, is a dead shot, cool and level-headed in a pinch, and knows African game as well as any man.

To better our chances, and also because we were not all interested in the same trophies—Bill Wright, for example, wanted an elephant— we agreed to disperse the party in separate camps. As a result, I did not see much of my companions, with the exception of Halmi and Vidor. They trailed me faithfully with their cameras wherever I went.

A lot has been written and said about which of Africa's big five— elephant, rhino, buffalo, lion, and leopard—is the most dangerous. Hunters with whom I have discussed it are not in agreement, and I'm not qualified to have any firm opinion. I suspect that, given the right provocation and opportunity, one will try to kill a man about as quickly as another. Certainly, they are equally capable of doing it.

But I will venture one opinion. For meanness, the buffalo takes first place, and everything about him tells you so. The elephant is a mountain of animal, perhaps the most awe-inspiring creature that walks the earth. The rhino is a tank on four legs, and when you look at him you get the feeling nothing can stop him. A lion close up is something to take your breath away, and the leopard is the sinister incarnation of power and fury. But, in my book, none of them can match the buffalo for malignant cussedness. You know the instant you lay eyes on him that he's ready for trouble.

The sweep of his horns, their tremendous boss, the drooping ears, the burly neck, the surly stare, his whole shape and attitude say unmistakably, "Keep your distance. I hate you and all your kind, and if you tangle with me one of us is going to take a one-way walk." He is Africa's black fury, and no other animal I have hunted flies the warning flag so defiantly.

For three or four days after Johnson killed the lame bull, we had no luck, mostly because of my determination to get movies of any hunting we did. We saw plenty of buffaloes, including some good heads. A few times we watched herds of 50 to 100 thunder off across the plains, but we were never able to get close enough for a shot under the right conditions. Lugging camera equipment on such a hunt is a tough chore, and when you add sound gear, as we had, stalking to the close range necessary with a bow becomes almost impossible. We were putting ourselves under severe handicaps.

The buffalo hunting was proving rugged. The country was rough, much of it covered with six-foot brush. It was also broken by dongas, (deep ravines and dry creek beds) heavily timbered and laced with thornbush. By keeping to the open places, we could go almost any-where in the hunting cars, but buffaloes do not spend the day in the open and our actual hunting had to be done on foot. Our hunting cars took an incredible beating, and we fared no better. Rarely a day passed without our having at least two flat tires from thorns or sharp pieces of wood. The thorns were equally rough on us, and many times we had to return to camp to repair damage to our cameras or ourselves.

Wally relied chiefly on two ways of locating buffaloes. One was to ask the natives. Just to stay alive, they have to know the habits and whereabouts of every animal in their area. The other was to watch for the brownish, sparrowlike tick birds that accompany buffalo herds from morning to night.

The buffalo grazes at night, waters early in the morning, and leaves for his bedding ground about daylight. He spends the daytime hours in the shade, usually in thick cover. Morning after morning, while we followed fresh tracks away from the river, we'd see flocks of tick birds searching for the herds. When they dropped down into the brush, we knew where to go. When a herd stampeded and ran in the open, the birds followed them in the sky, waiting for a chance to pick ticks.

When I finally got my chance for a shot, the circumstances were totally unexpected and I had no time even to think about getting pictures. We were bumping across fairly open country in the hunting car when I caught a glimpse of a buffalo disappearing in a thicket. We circled the place and found tracks of two coming out, headed toward a nearby donga.

"Both bulls," Wally decided. "One looks big. We'll send Luiz in on the track to follow them, and we'll drive around on the other side of the donga and be there when they come out."

Luiz was his head tracker, a reliable native who had been with him for years and spoke some English. The two of them had been in more than one tight place together. Wally gave him instructions, he walked into the brush carrying Wally's spare gun, and we rattled off.

We were no more than in position when the two bulls burst out of the bush and ran straight for the car. Wally gunned it to get out of their path but the bigger one wouldn't have it that way. He slued around and charged us.

What followed was as near to a mechanized bullfight as I ever hope to see, and I was both spectator and participant. That buffalo meant business. He made three or four determined passes, turning on a dime, tossing his head, kicking up dust, and grunting like an enraged farm bull. Wally twisted and dodged, shot the hunting car ahead, skidded it to a stop. The ground was rough and I was sticking to my seat like a rider on an outlaw horse, hanging on with both hands. The buffalo missed a lunge by hardly three feet as Wally swerved away. As he galloped beside us, close enough to touch, I found myself looking almost straight down on the burly black head and the curved tips of the wickedest looking pair of horns I had ever seen.

Then he connected. He slammed into the side of the car near the rear wheel, hard enough to knock the car sideways three or four feet, skidded off, and took the spare tire with him. One of our trackers, Juca, was hunkered in the back, holding a camera and rifle. The camera flew in one direction, the gun in another, and Juca in a third. He landed flat on his back, but the buffalo was circling around the rear of the car and didn't see him.

Wally stopped the car, but Juca didn't need rescuing. He was up and running before the bull even knew he was there. In fact, I didn't know he had been thrown out until it was all over.

By that time, I had jumped out and had an arrow on the string. The buffalo must have thought he had won the battle, or else his collision with the car had been more than he bargained for. He circled it and galloped for the brushy donga. As he pounded past me, quartering at 35 yards, I let my arrow go. The razorhead sliced into his rib cage and the shaft went in almost to the feathers. I expected him to wheel and come back, but he kept going. I guess he realized he had hit something bigger and harder than he was.

He left a blood trail a blindfolded man could have followed. We found him dead 300 yards away, with green paint from the car ground into his horns. Those tips I had looked down on were a little more than 40 inches apart and spread 46 inches at their widest sweep. The boss was 12 inches across and very heavy. The head was a trophy to satisfy any hunter.

"That was good shooting, and bloody good luck," Wally told me when the excitement quieted down. In his concern about Juca, he hadn't even known I got an arrow off. Then he added, "He didn't run far, either." I could see he was astonished that an arrow-shot buffalo had died so quickly.

I was an elated bowman. I had taken one of the two trophies I had come for and one that very few bowhunters can claim. I had made a clean, quick kill with a single arrow on an animal about as tough as they come. There was one thing lacking, however. I had no film to show for it. There hadn't been time even to think about the cameras until the action was all over. My license entitled me to a second buffalo. We'd try again and hope for a better break.

The next one we went after got help from a crippled lion, however, and the two of them proved too much for us. We stopped at a village early one morning, and a native told us that buffaloes had been in his garden during the night. He thought we'd find them in tall grass nearby or in the brushy hills beyond.

The grass was too high and thick to hunt on foot, but we drove through it without finding anything. The hills paid off. We saw tick birds, scouted the place, and found the tracks of two good bulls. Wally sent Luiz in with a rifle to push them out, while we went around to the far side. But they evaded us, crossed a stretch of flat country, and took refuge in a thicket.

We circled the place on foot and got within 20 yards of them, close enough to hear them grunt and break brush, but again they gave us the slip. They went into another donga, and again Luiz followed them. Wally and I found a stand in an open place, where it seemed likely they'd come out. Vidor and Halmi set up their cameras behind us. The whole setup looked perfect.

But before long we heard more grunts and then a series of snarls and deep growls that didn't sound as if they were being made by a buffalo. Luiz came flying out of the brush, yelling in his native Changaan, "A lion! A lion that is hurt. She came for me!"

Luiz went on to explain that the lion was a female and had a crippled hind leg that looked as if it had been caught in a snare. Both she and the two bulls had charged him, but he was on a high bank that the buffaloes couldn't climb, and the lion had turned off. "I don't go back in there unless you go too!" Luiz finished.

Wally translated for my benefit. "He sounds as if he means it," he added with a dry grin.

"I don't blame him," I replied. "I'm not going in there either unless you go along—with a gun."

The buffaloes had gone out on the same side where they came in, the tracker said. So far as he knew, the lioness was still in the thicket. We inched in cautiously and found her tracks, but she had cleared out. We gave up on the two bulls, since by that time they were out of sight and headed into country where we could not use the cameras.

We lost three days now because of bad weather and poor light for photography, but filled in part of the time with some lively fishing for tigerfish in a deep pool on the Save near camp. The fish ran up to 10 and 12 pounds, and they had the most wicked-looking teeth I had ever seen in any freshwater fish. We used red-and-white spoons on spinning rods, and the fish struck savagely and fought hard. A small herd of hippos watched us from the middle of the pool, keeping our nerves on edge. We carried rifles as well as rods, both for the hippos and for crocodiles. It was a very strange setting indeed.

I spent two of those days alone in a blind at a water hole with a long-lens camera and made a record of the birds and animals I saw. It added up to an amazing score: 28 wildebeests, 72 impalas, 49 nyala, 105 warthogs, 76 baboons, 28 monkeys, seven zebras, three kudus, a mongoose, three saddlebill storks, and three hornbills. I had never watched a more fascinating wildlife show.

A few days later, at another water hole where I spent a night on a tree platform with Luiz, I chalked up a second high tally: 100 buffaloes, 12 kudus, 131 impalas, 32 warthogs, 132 baboons, 25 monkeys, and four ostriches. It was interesting to me, in view of the opinion I hold about buffaloes, that they were the only animals that barged straight in to the water without any show of caution. All the others approached warily.

The most unusual thing I saw at either water hole was a mock fight between two nyala bulls. The nyala is a medium-size antelope found only in that part of Africa. The bulls weigh up to 250 pounds. This pair never really got down to business, but they circled each other with their tails erect and their manes and the hair along their backs standing straight up, moving like animals in slow motion. They threatened repeatedly to lock horns, but always called it off in the nick of time. The graceful impala bulls also put on a flashy show, but they were more serious about it, crashing their horns and heads together with resounding whacks.

The weather turned good and we went after buffaloes again. We hunted hard for three fruitless days, then, early one morning, we drove to the village where Conjone lived. He is a brother of a native who had been our tracker the year before, and he is a local authority on buffaloes.

Conjone had recently taken a fancy to one of the wives of a chief and, as a consequence, had been jailed for three months. The chief had also burned his crop of sugar cane. But if he was chastened his appearance certainly didn't indicate it. We found him wearing cowboy boots, khaki shorts, an ornately decorated jacket, and a wide-brimmed hat pinned up on one side, Australian style.

Whatever his weakness for women, however, he certainly knew the local buffalo herds, and he was glad to help us since the buffaloes were raiding crops and his people needed meat.

Right now, he said, several bulls were bedded down in tall grass just beyond a small patch of corn that would have been knee high if the buffaloes had not eaten it. He was right, too. We flushed two good bulls out of the grass without getting a shot.

Conjone then climbed on the back of the hunting car and directed us across country to a brushy area where he said we'd find a large herd. We found one lone bull and drove him out of a brushy donga, but he got away.

Conjone insisted the herd was somewhere in the neighborhood. This solitary bull often hung around on its outskirts, he said, and he urged us to have another look. We took his advice, and his wisdom in buffalo ways was proved when we came on a herd of at least 60 in the thick cover of that same creek bottom. They milled around, watching us defiantly, reluctant to leave. Finally we spotted what we had been looking for for two weeks, a good bull and cow by themselves in an open place at the edge of the brush.

I had seen hundreds of buffaloes by that time and could have shot at least half a dozen, but never under the right circumstances for the pictures I wanted. Now, at last, here was an ideal situation. I felt it was almost too good to be true.

There was plenty of cover for the stalk, and I worked to within 45 yards very easily. The bull was standing broadside. When I stepped into the open for the shot, he saw me, threw up his head, and gave me that sullen, truculent buffalo stare. But he made no move.

Halmi was in position behind me. I waited until I heard his camera start, then released my arrow. It drove almost out of sight between the bull's ribs. Both buffaloes wheeled and went crashing into the brush. But there was no doubt in my mind that I had made a kill.

We circled the herd, gave them our scent, and they cleared out. We followed the blood trail 250 yards and found my bull lying dead in a thicket. He was not as good as the first one, but he was a very satisfactory trophy, and at last we had the movie record of the buffalo hunt that I wanted so much.

That kill was the climax of 13 days of some of the hardest hunting I've ever done. The second buffalo had come fairly easy, but I figured that by that time I had earned him a dozen times over. Two of Africa's meanest had bowed to my bow, and I had had as exciting and thrilling a hunt as ever came my way.

The top trophy of all was yet to be taken, a lion, the great cat that to me is the most majestic and desirable animal any man can hunt. No bowman had killed one in more than 40 years. Art Young's stood as the only record of its kind. What sort of luck would I have?

That quest was to lead me into the most hair-raising adventure in all my years of hunting dangerous game. In another story, in a forthcoming issue of *OUTDOOR LIFE*, I'll tell you how I made out. ❖

FEBRUARY 1966

The "LION-MAN"

by W. S. Chadwick

MANY CENTRAL AFRICAN natives—amongst them the Barotse—firmly believe that certain men have the power of changing into lion shape at will; and that to refuse a demand for cattle from these individuals will result in a visit from them in leonine form. The belief is backed by the assertion that when hunting lions the spoor sometimes vanishes, and is replaced by that of a man. They state also that this usually happens when a beast has been killed at a village where one had first been refused to an applicant.

Meeting one day old "Sambara"—a rascally old witch doctor of my acquaintance—I asked his opinion of the matter. As I expected, he gravely assured me that the belief was founded on fact; for without superstition he and his like could not live. I then asked whether he had ever suffered such depredations. He replied that he and his brethren were immune by reason of their own greater "magic."

So I recalled to his memory certain deaths under circumstances different from the account given to the officials, and sundry illegal ceremonies at which he had officiated as high priest. When he appeared sufficiently uncomfortable I suggested that a true explanation of the "lion-man" myth would be of such interest that I might possibly forget these incidents. Under seal of secrecy he at length provided an explanation remarkable alike for its simplicity and ingenuity.

A lion which kills tonight at one kraal will in all probability visit a neighboring village a night or two later. This the witch doctors know as well as anyone else. Therefore, on news of a kill at any village these gentry will send any strange native who happens to be available—and they usually have a few handy under the guise of hospitality—to the village attacked, to ask for the best-looking beast in sight.

Should a refusal result, other well-trained emissaries are sent to visit the likeliest villages, there to await the lion's second foray. When this occurs, the doctor's scout vanishes silently with the dawn, and takes the lion's spoor. Once out of sight he dons a pair of buckskin sandals, with thongs specially fitted to allow of their being worn with the narrow heel part under the toe. Proceeding in these, the wily native leaves a spoor going *towards* the kraal instead of *away* from it. This spoor travels parallel to that of the lion, converging only at intervals to keep the direction.

When the lion spoor definitely turns in a new direction—usually at a few miles from the village—the scout carefully obliterates the sandy tracks for 50 yards or so in the new direction (removing his own at the same time) and then with naked feet strides forward for one or two miles on the lion's original line of march before turning homewards to make his report.

As a result, the hunters from the village follow on the lion spoor for a few miles, only to find it gives place to human spoor. And seeing no tracks in the vicinity to indicate the lion's actual line of retreat, they return to the village to lend further support to the belief such clever trickery has established. Future demands for a beast at such kraals are usually complied with. So the witch-doctor fraternity increases its cattle wealth at the expense of their ignorant neighbors, and such is their loyalty to the clan that the secret is closely kept.

I was rather contemptuous therefore, when old Makengaam—an intelligent induna—confessed himself a convert to the lion-man theory. Yet the tale he told me presented such unusual aspects of leonine behavior, and such a series of coincidences, that his superstition might well be pardoned.

Arriving at his village one morning, I found only two old men and the women there. As the harvest had long been reaped, and the rains were still three months away, it was plain that something unusual had happened. On inquiry I found that a lion had killed a cow the night before, and the men had taken his trail at dawn. I waited to hear the result, and at noon the men returned—unsuccessful.

"Well, Makengaam," I said, "I see you did not get the lion. Why did you give up so soon?"

"Sir, we should never get that lion," the old man answered, "though we should follow him for a month. He is a lion-man.

"Two days ago Kabuku, of Sandara's village, asked me for a cow, and I was a fool not to give it to him. Twice in other villages he has desired a beast and been refused; and each time the lion has killed afterwards. I have long thought he was a lion-man and now I know it. For look you, when we reached the big *vlei* by the Namatetse river, Kabuku's spoor was there, and we saw the lion spoor no more."

"Makengaam," I said, "surely you do not believe that idle tale? You—an induna who has been to the white man's school! It is well enough for herdboys and foolish women, but I thought *you* would laugh at such stories."

"I used to laugh, Sir, but since M'vu was killed I have believed."

"M'vu the induna?" I asked, startled. For a year earlier I had known the chief's cattle induna well. I had not heard that the light-hearted, powerful young man was dead.

"Yes, M'vu. The chief's cattle induna whom you saw the last time you were here. Come and sit in the shade, sir, and I will tell you how he died, and why I now believe in the lion-men."

After we had refreshed ourselves with native beer, the old man began the story and these are his own words as nearly as is possible for me to repeat.

"One afternoon just before the last rains, a traveling Mashukulumbwe named Kasoka called at M'vu's village and asked for food. He had come from far, and said he was going across the Okavango river to visit his son, who was working in the mines—a month's journey beyond the desert. He looked lean and hungry, but his eyes were savage and watchful; and M'vu saw that he lied. For, how could a stranger travel that country of thirst alone, and without food? M'vu asked him this, and he said that he hoped to get a beast in Barotseland and dry out sufficient meat for his journey. This he would pay for on his return, with money he would receive from his son.

"M'vu told him that no Barotse would give him a beast on the word of one whose people had been our enemies, but that food for a few days should be given him. He advised him, too, to turn back to his people; as in the country to the west, a man traveling alone would surely be killed by the Bushmen, or die of thirst. Then he gave him *mwanja* [cassava] meal and milk, and told him he might rest the night there.

"Watching him while he ate, M'vu saw that he ate unwillingly; as a man eats who thinks of other food. Always, too, his eyes wandered to the cattle out on the *vlei*. Also, M'vu saw that from the man's left foot the big toe was missing. When he spoke of this, the man tucked the foot beneath him quickly, and speaking angrily, said that the foot had been in a trap when he was a young man, and the toe being broken, he had cut it off.

"When the cattle came to the kraal he looked long at a young red and white ox, which was very fat. Then he asked M'vu to kill that ox and give him food for his journey. When the induna refused he was very angry, and said: 'You Barotse have many cattle. Yet you refuse meat to those who are hungry! It may be that *N'yambe* (God) will one day punish you, and take your cattle from you! I will not sleep here. I will go to Imoosha's village, where perchance I may find men of a better heart!'

"'Go if you will,' said M'vu. 'But Imoosha's village is far, and the sun is setting. You will arrive there by night.' But the man left, and we knew afterwards that he did not go to Imoosha's.

"That night a lion stampeded the cattle from M'vu's kraal, and the red and white ox was killed. The men drove him off before he had eaten more than a little, and when M'vu said that he would follow the lion at dawn and slay him, the others tried to stay him.

"Old N'yero the counsellor said: 'M'vu, this ox is the one Kasoka desired, and Kasoka would travel by night, when men seek the fires of the village. Certainly Kasoka is a lion-man. It is he who has killed this ox, and no lion. If you follow you will see I have spoken truth; for you will find no lion.'

"'Pish! Am I a babe, to believe such tales?' asked M'vu angrily. 'And if it be true, then I will find this Kasoka and kill him. For I—M'vu— fear neither lions nor lion-men! Neither shall one or the other steal my cattle and live.'

"So at dawn M'vu took the spoor, and because they feared him the others went with him. But they had not gone far when they saw that from the lion's left front paw one toe was missing. They all stopped, and one said to M'vu: 'Truly N'yero was right! Did not Kasoka lack a toe on his left foot? You yourself saw it, M'vu. Let us return, for this is no lion we follow, but a thing of evil!'

"M'vu laughed angrily and said: 'Even if it be true, can we not kill this Kasoka, in lion or in man shape? I will go on.'

"So they went forward again, murmuring and shaking their heads. And when they reached the *mutema* bush by the Luia river the lion spoor disappeared. An assagai [spear] length beyond, Kasoka's spoor came on the path from the right, and went on towards the Luia. Then the men halted and pleaded again with M'vu to return.

"But he said, 'I believe that Kasoka is indeed a lion-man, as you say. Yet if we kill his man's body, his spirit shall have but one shape, and as a lion all men may seek him until that body, too, is destroyed!'

"Then one said: 'You speak wisely, M'vu. And in our father's day this could be done easily enough. But if now we catch Kasoka, he who deals the deathblow must answer to the white man's law.'

"'Are you then fools as well as women?' M'vu asked angrily. 'We will follow Kasoka and tell him that our hearts are sad because we refused him meat for his journey; and that now the lion has killed the ox he desired, he may have the meat.'

"'And that meat he shall have. But—have we then forgotten how to poison jackals? He shall die tonight with a full stomach. Afterwards we will bury him, and because he is a stranger none will seek to know how he died. If any ask, they must be told that he arrived weak from hunger and long travel, and that N'yambe called him.'

"The sun was high overhead when they overtook Kasoka on the great path which goes to the north. When M'vu had asked him why he traveled again towards his country he answered: 'When the night grew dark, M'vu, I thought of your words and saw that they were wise. I said to my heart that the way to my son is too great for my strength, and that I would return home and await his coming. So I turned and traveled the short way through the veldt until I came to the Luia; that by tomorrow at this time I may reach Nanda's village, where I have a brother with whom I may rest.'

"M'vu knew that he lied. But he saw the cunning of his words and said: 'But today is not as yesterday, Kasoka. N'yambe has sent you meat in plenty. It lies at our village. Come back and eat, and rest. Afterwards you may take meat for the journey, and go to Nanda's or to your son—as your heart speaks to you!'

"So presently Kasoka agreed to return with them, and at sunset they reached the village. That night there was feasting and dancing. But in the bowl from which Kasoka drank there was a poison which M'vu had placed there—a poison which has neither taste nor smell.

"In the morning he lay dead, and calling the people to the *khotla* [court-house] M'vu said: 'My people, N'yambe has visited this Kasoka. If he be indeed a lion-man he must live henceforth in lion shape, and there is no law which shall hold our hands against him. But if any man asks, we know naught of lion-men. We know only Kasoka, who died of hunger and weariness, although we fed him well; as all men have seen!'

"So Kasoka was buried beyond the *vlei*, and for two nights the cattle slept safe in the kraal; while the women sang of the courage of M'vu.

"Then on the third night—at first cockcrow—M'vu's cattle broke from the kraal, and with the noise of falling poles and running beasts, came the growling of a lion. When the men seized firebrands and assegais and ran to the kraal, the lion had gone; taking with him a young heifer. Because of the darkness the men could not follow; and while they waited for dawn many whispered that Kasoka had come again to punish his slayer.

"In the morning they found the body of the heifer, and saw that the lion had feasted well. But the spoor beside the dead beast turned their hearts to water; for from the left front foot a toe was missing. From mouth to mouth passed the whisper: 'Kasoka has come again!'

"But M'vu shouted: 'What of it, fools! Did I not say he would come again? Did I not say, too, that as I have destroyed his man-body, so I will destroy his lion-body also? This day Kasoka the lion shall follow Kasoka the man to the abode of spirits! Get your weapons and come.'

"But not a man moved, and N'yero said: 'M'vu, the lion in which a man's spirit lives is not as other lions. In him dwells the strength of the lion, and the cunning of the man also. The spirit of Kasoka knows the slayers of his man-body, and will surely kill those who would drive it forth again. Let him go in peace, and perchance he will trouble us no more?'

"With a sneer, M'vu said: 'Must I ask the chief to give my impi a new name? Must I ask him to call it the impi (regiment) of foolish women? And to name you—N'yero—its induna? For if there be no man amongst you I will follow alone!"

"Then one M'panda answered: 'I will go with you M'vu, although my heart likes it not. There is much in N'yero's words. Yet all men must die, and if you go to death I will go with you, that your spirit may not reproach me.'

"So M'vu and M'panda took the spoor together, and afterwards M'panda told me what no man would have heard had M'vu gone alone. He told me how M'vu died, and how he kept his word to destroy Kasoka.

"They had not walked a great way, and the sun was still newborn, when from under some dark bushes ahead came the thunder of the lion's voice, and his body passed from sight quicker than a man might raise his hand. Following the spoor again, by the time of turning the cattle out (10 A.M.) they had twice seen the lion flee before them without chance to shoot or strike.

"Then a strange thing happened. The lion spoor turned back towards the village, and following in a half-circle they came to some thick *mutema* bush closer to the village than his first hiding place. Within the shadow they heard the low tones of his voice in anger; but, though they shouted, he would not come forth.

"M'panda's heart weakened, and he said 'What lion would turn back when hunted, nearer to the homes of men, save an evil spirit such as this? It may be that he hunts *us,* and not *we* him! Also, we cannot enter there to drive him out!'

"M'vu laughed angrily and said: 'There is one who may enter. An evil spirit feared by both lions and men!' So saying he struck fire and put it to the dry *mutema* bush.

"The lion sprang forth quick as the lightning flash; and roaring with anger came straight at M'vu. He fired and the lion fell; but before a man might draw a deep breath he was up again. M'vu's gun (a Martini) would not open quickly, and M'panda had only assagais. But he hurled one, and it stuck in the lion's side.

"Then they ran for the trees, and turned to look again. The lion stood snarling and watched them while a man might count two; then seized the assagai shaft in his teeth and broke it. As it fell to the ground he dashed away with a roar.

"M'vu got his gun open and placed in it another cartridge, saying 'This shall mean death to him! For lion-man or not, we have seen that he can bleed; and the body which can bleed can also die!'

"As they took the trail again, M'panda said: 'Again I say I like it not. Truly this lion is not as others. Why did he not attack us as we ran? And why, now, does he go more swiftly, as the spoor shows? I fear he carries a plan of evil in his man's heart!'

"But M'vu only walked faster, for as M'panda had said, the lion was now running swiftly. The sun was high overhead when they crossed the great *vlei* of Sibandi's, and M'panda looked back and gave a cry. M'vu looked also, and there from the edge of the forest behind them came the wounded lion; limping yet swift.

"Seeing them looking back, he turned aside snarling, and with shaking lips M'panda said: 'We do not follow a lion M'vu. A devil follows *us.* Who but a devil could follow behind while his spoor still goes on in front?'

"'Bah,' M'vu answered, 'he has turned back on his spoor to track us. That is all. Certain am I that he will fight. But to fight he must come close; and when he comes close I—M'vu—will kill him!'

"So they turned and took the spoor again from the place where the lion had turned aside, and M'panda glanced always behind him as though an enemy followed. The sun was halfway down when they came to a patch of tall grass and the lion rushed swiftly out; straight at M'vu. He fired and hit the lion, so that he staggered. But the devil in him carried him on, and he knocked M'vu down and seized him.

"As the gun fell to the ground and the lion sprang into the grass with M'vu, M'panda threw an assagai but missed. Before he could pick it up the lion was hidden in the grass, and he walked quietly round the patch thinking to make sure the lion was within, and fearing to enter.

"But in an open space at the farther side—at the foot of a tall ant heap—he found the lion and M'vu—dead! With his short stabbing assagai the induna had found the lion's heart at last. But the teeth of the evil one were locked in his throat and his neck was broken. They died in an embrace as close as that of a woman and her lover.

"So, Sir, if you would laugh at my belief, think first of the lion's spoor which vanished, of the missing toe, and of the lion which showed himself so often to lure his pursuers, that he himself might pursue. Think also, how bullet and steel failed to drain his strength until he had slain his enemy. And of his leaving cover when dying, that M'panda might see his revenge!"

It occurred to me that the unfortunate Kasoka had probably told the truth. Coincidence, and an unusual ferocity and cunning, might explain the rest. But I saw in the induna's face a steadfast belief in native tradition, and I remembered another tradition which says that "all white men are fools." So lest I strengthen the latter without weakening the former, I said only: "It may be as you say Makengaam. But at least M'vu proved that lion-men may be destroyed, did he not?"

"That is true, Sir. Kasoka came no more. But the showing cost M'vu his life. It is better to give an ox to a stranger than to lose more—and men's lives, too—in such hunts. And there is always the white man's law. Had M'vu yet lived I dared not have told you this.

"I refused Kabuku because he is of our people, and few Barotse are friends of the evil ones. I shall not refuse him again."

So I expect one day to find Kabuku a large cattle owner, by virtue of a reputation established by an accident which cost two lives, and in which—as far as I could discover—the wily medicine men had no part. ❖

OCTOBER 1932

The Lost Virgin

by Charles Elliott

❖

AT LEAST I KNEW I WAS NOT hopelessly lost. Somewhere within twenty miles was dry land upon which a man could walk without sinking out of sight into bottomless mire.

But pushing a boat through this jungle of brush was like trying to thread the eye of a needle with a two-by-four. To the east lay the open, clear-water run that was the main artery of traffic between Jones Island and Big Water Lake. It split the heart of the Okefenokee Swamp, straddling the Georgia-Florida line. The swamp lay humid and sweltering for 1,000 square miles all around me. I had paddled away from the open, blackwater trail, into a maze of sloughs that had no beginning and no end. The emerald wall had gradually tightened against my boat, bottling me up like a frog in a green-glass jug.

I stopped to rest my arms, aching from paddle strain, and smoke a pipeful of tobacco. The thread of water I had followed in from Minnie Lake had vanished in a lane of grass and lily pads. Each sprig of aquatic vegetation dragged at the boat with gluey fingers. Beyond the bow, the lane was rolled out like the close tufts of a carpet, but I wasn't fooled for an instant. The moment I stepped out of the boat, I knew I'd wallow out of sight and vanish from the eyes of man forever.

Lem Griffis, one of the native swampers, had planned to come along and fish the hidden lakes with me, but that morning he'd had a hurry call into Waycross. Something to do with government land. He hadn't come right out and told me, but he'd hinted that the big swamp was the devil's own tool, its beauty a trap of destruction.

"There are some big 'gator holes," he said, "around the head of

Minnie Island that haven't been fished in years. But I've sure got an uneasy feeling about letting you tackle them alone."

When I insisted, he sketched a crude map as a guide. But he forgot to tell me that the runs, or water trails, were snarled together like a backlashed fishing line, and that each one looked exactly like its twin.

For twenty years I had fished the easily accessible lakes on the chain leading into the heart of the swamp. There was a time when any lure dropped on the water brought a surging crash out of the depths and a bronzeback battle royal through the cypress knees and along the fringes of the lily pads. Although public fishing in the lakes and runs was heavy it remained good, since bass and bream were continuously

funneled into them from the 300,000 acres, or more, of actual lake area making up the Okefenokee. Any diligent, careful fisherman could lure some bass out of the lakes and alligator holes, but few knew about the hidden waters off the beaten track, many of which are as primitive as the day the Big Boss hid them there.

The guides don't give out that information. It's dangerous for a man, inexperienced in the treacheries of the swamp, to travel alone off the recognized water trails. The once-cutover cypress forest is impenetrable in many places. The brush, growing in water from four to ten feet deep, is so interwoven and entwined that walking, swimming, or paddling a boat through it is physically impossible.

Scattered throughout the swamp are wide, deep holes of open water. These are kept clear by the alligators, which in the last few years have increased tremendously under government protection. Fish experts say that alligators feed on the sluggish water creatures, such as turtles and terrapins, and take only an occasional faster gamefish. They must be right. I know that any alligator hole (known locally as a den), when fished with long casts over the lilies and grass, will almost always yield up one or two good bass.

I knocked out my pipe and pushed on into the narrowing grass trail. It drove like a wedge into the phalanx of brush. Every foot I gained was like driving a champagne cork back into the bottle. I was almost ready to give up and back out of the bottleneck when it opened into a run of clean, black water. The walls of brush spread out and I could paddle again. I was so relieved that when a deadly cottonmouth moccasin nearly dropped into the boat off a low, overhanging limb I almost didn't see him in time to pull out of the way. After that I guided the boat more cautiously and a dozen bends of the trail brought me into the neck of a large pond, bordered by a rim of lilies and studded at the edge with cypress knees.

The little lake curved out of sight into the brush. Beyond the distant shore a group of pine trees thrust up their emerald crowns. From long experience I knew this meant dry land. Water around its feet is death to a pine. Nevertheless, the presence of the pines set off an alarm in the back of my brain. According to Lem's crude map, if this was Minnie Island it was on the wrong side of the little lake.

All Ready for Action

I forced myself to relax and look around. From all appearances this was virgin water—typical of many such nooks I had found in the Okefenokee in years gone by. An eight-foot alligator slid off the rim of grass and slowly submerged into the dark depths, leaving a wake that rippled in the moss hanging at the water's edge. The wave disturbed a huge cottonmouth that dropped from sight out of the low branches. I laid my paddle where I could snatch it up and use it as a weapon. Then I clicked my fly rod together and soaked a leader over the stern.

My choice out of the tackle box was a small fly-rod frog with hairy legs. I tied him on and moved cautiously down the left shore of the hidden lake. For the first time the witchery of the place stole over me and I pushed aside all thoughts except those of being in a lost corner of the world, in a spot few eyes had seen. The moment was sufficient unto itself.

I dropped the lure beside a clump of cypress knees and worked it slowly out. I put the second cast into a mirrored corner beside the partially submerged trunk of a tree. The ripples died and I twitched the frog once. The tiny waves curled out and vanished, and I touched it again.

I had tensed my arm to retrieve the floating bit of colored wood and hair when the water erupted violently. Even though I was expecting action, I jumped as if Lem had prodded me with his heavy gig.

The bass erupted in a shower of bright drops and swept the surface of the lake for ten feet with his tail. I gave him line, took it in again, and gave him more. The bite of the hook sent him into an aerial performance that would have done credit to a coldwater smallmouth. Then he bored for the safety of the submerged trunk.

Holding on with every ounce of strain I thought the leader would stand, I turned him back into the middle of the pond. His fourth and final jump almost threw him into the boat. Then he gave up, exhausted, and I slid the net under him. He tipped my mental scales at a good six pounds, so I filed him on the stringer for further reference.

I waited until the lake settled once more to its normal mirrored beauty. Four more casts at the edge of the lily pads brought another explosion. This was a small three-pounder. He went into battle maneuvers that took him completely around the boat. I checked his bid for the safety of the lily patch and, after a breathless five minutes, snapped him on the stringer.

While the water calmed a second time I examined my leader for frayed spots and tested the knot between the line and gut. I worked out the remainder of the flat-padded shoreline and a narrow neck that jutted off the main lake. The shell of a mammoth cypress tree crowded the entrance to the neck. Its base was split by an inverted V that showed the black water in its bowels. I luckily made a perfect cast into the opening of the V and left the frog there, almost out of sight, for a full minute until it became part of the dark surface. I flicked the rod tip to move the frog into the opening, but the lure didn't move toward me.

It disappeared in a silver arc that boiled the surface inside the cypress hull like a bold spring.

The frog was no longer visible so I set the hook—hard. Nothing happened, except the rod held its quivering arc and the line vibrated like the E-string on a violin. For a moment I thought the fish, whatever it was, had wrapped my leader around the bottom of the cypress tree. Then the line began to move with quiet stubbornness toward the middle of the lake. I had my choice of playing out line, or breaking rod or leader, so I played out line.

The critter on the other end of the stiff-backboned bamboo took silk through the straining guides and kept taking it. For a moment a queer feeling welled through me that I had hooked the old boss alligator of the hole. With one hand I turned the boat and paddled awkwardly after the line that plowed inexorably into deep water.

The Real Battle Begins

I had a sudden inspiration. There was another frog plug in my tackle box so, risking the strength of the leader, I set back on the rod with a jerk that would have broken the neck of a tarpon. That did it. The barb bit deep. The fly line straightened suddenly and swept into a curve as the fish plowed out of the inky depths and hit the surface with a crash like a falling tree.

I threw down the paddle and caught the rod in two hands. The chunk of flesh done up in scales was the biggest I had seen since Vernon Phillips came up to his boathouse triumphantly dragging a 14½-pounder behind his boat. My blood pressure shot up a dozen points. I pumped him again and he waltzed across the water, shooting for the crop of lilies and that submerged trunk. I swung on as grimly as I dared, muttering a little prayer that my slender gut would hold— while wishing I had him on the right end of a sailfish rod.

He went down again into the center of the lake, hanging there as though he had anchored himself to the tip of the sunken tree. For three breathless minutes I was not able to budge him. Lem had shown me once how to move a big bass by jarring the rod butt with the heel of my hand. It worked. The finned giant turned loose, raced twice across the lake, and came in, his struggles growing less frantic by the moment.

When he drifted to the surface ten feet away from the starboard side, the hook had torn through his cheek and was hanging by a thread of skin. Cautiously I held on with one hand and picked up the net. He was a record fish in anybody's division and I didn't want to lose him. Catching a glimpse of the net as I slipped it into the water, he made a final lunge. I tried to give him line, but it was too late. The wooden frog tore out of his jaw and whipped against my fishing hat. The mammoth sank slowly out of sight into the dark water.

For a long minute I watched the spot where he had disappeared. I laid my rod across the seat and dug for my pipe, spilling tobacco grains on the floor of the boat. With trembling fingers I stuck a match into the bowl, then turned the boat and slowly paddled to the upper end of the lake.

I knew there was no chance of finding my way out before dark. I wasn't eager for night to trap me between the jungled fringes of a water trail, with venom-loaded moccasins hung on every second bush. Lem knew I was without supplies and would come looking for me within a day or two.

The sun was still more than an hour high when I pulled my boat up on the cypress knees and waded ashore in ankle-deep water. The little island where the pine trees grew was some four feet above the surface of the lake. Here was partial security from the hidden dangers of the darkening swamp.

With my heavy hunting knife I cleared out brush around the pines and gathered heaping armloads of firewood by breaking dead branches off the trees. From the low limbs I pulled a dozen loads of Spanish moss. Shadows had lengthened over the lake when I went back to the boat and pulled in my two fish on the string. The gator was floating a few yards out in the pond, with only his eyes above the surface.

A Difficult Decision

If I left either bass tied to the boat, the gator or a turtle would get him before morning. If I hung him above the water out of reach, he'd spoil. The six-pounder was too large for my meal, so I turned him back to his liquid home. I gutted and skinned the three-pound bass and brought him back to the campsite with my tackle bag, in which I always carry salt and a can of hard-tack. I whittled a three-pronged stick out of the brush, wrapped the fish on it with one of my gut leaders to keep the cooked meat from falling off, and built a campfire there in the heart of the Okefenokee. By the time I had broiled the bass steaks and put my teeth into the delicious meat and the hard-tack, the sun was gone and twilight had cast its purple shadows over the land of trembling earth.

There is no peace on earth like that of being alone in the deep wilderness. With my back against a giant pine, I sat out the last vestige of day and listened to the awakening night life of the drowned wilderness around me. From somewhere out in the swamp I heard the distant call of a barred owl, blended with the soft treble of a raccoon padding along his run. Above the rising symphony of night an alligator boomed and the strident cry of a heron answered. I might have been the first man or the last, alone in a universe at the dawn of the world, or at its end.

My pile of wood was almost gone when I curled up on the pile of moss and went to sleep.

Right Lure for Bronzebacks

Cold, gray daylight had invaded the swamp when I awoke. The damp wind moving through the trees had dewed the bushes at the water's edge. I built a fire on the warm ashes and baked out my moist clothing until the sun came up. Nibbling a piece of leathery biscuit for breakfast, I crawled into my boat just as the first flaming rays touched the tops of the gray cypress.

The surface of the lake was quiet, so I tied on a deep-running bucktail and spinner, tipping the hook with a strip of pork rind. The first two casts got strikes from bluegill bream larger than my hand, but the hook was too large for their mouths. They dragged the streamer under, shook it once or twice, and turned it loose. Then I caught a bream that weighed more than a pound. I turned it back and took off the spinner and bucktail, replacing the rig with a small broken-back plug that was really too heavy for my fly rod.

The selection was a choice one. The third cast brought a walloping strike that I missed, then a bronzeback snagged the plug and came out of the water in a twisting, turning, slashing attack as he tried to disgorge the steel barb. He was in the five-pound class, so I put him on the stringer.

I picked up another five-pounder, then one that went almost four pounds, before I worked back to the cypress tree with the inverted V. For twenty minutes I fished the spot carefully, but the bite of my frog evidently had been too sharp and the old giant wasn't rising to any bait I put into the water.

Reluctantly I left him there and turned down the lake to the maze of runs. By the time I reached the end of the lake I had strung six bass that would read O.K. in anybody's book, so I took my rod apart and permitted myself a last, lingering look at my virgin lake. Then I plowed recklessly into the river of grass, hoping fervently it would lead me to traveled water and Lem's camp.

There were some traces of my previous day's trip. Here and there a bush had been skinned by the heavy boat, or a twig broken. The openings I'd made in the grass had been washed closed again by the flowing water, which, on this side of the swamp, drained into the headwaters of the Suwanee River. That discovery gave me sudden inspiration. There were innumerable runs, but those leading east and west were crossed by slow currents of water. All pliant vegetation leaned toward the south. By traveling with the current from left to right, I knew that eventually I should stumble into the narrow trail that would lead me into Minnie Lake.

I've known the Okefenokee for a long, long time. I have a profound respect for its temperament. And, brother, it's loaded with temperament. One moment it lies in wait, like a coiled moccasin. The next it strikes in sudden fury that rips the open prairie and whiplashes the timber in wind and rain. But never is it more terrible than when it sprawls sinister and brooding—by its very silence building tension and suspense.

At noon the wind died and the sun bored in. Not a leaf quivered. No bird sang or streaked across the unnaturally bright sky. The bream no longer plopped or swirled under the stillness of the trees. The splash of my paddle was unnaturally loud. I paused for a moment, wedged on a cypress knee, and strained my ears against the empty silence.

And then I heard it.

It was like the distant roll of thunder, except there wasn't any sound and it didn't die away. I felt it against my eardrums, in the palms of my hands, against my throat, like a swelling pulse beat of the earth itself. I leaned forward, waiting and listening.

Gongh—gongh—gongh—gongh.

It was the drums—men call it that for lack of a better name—a phenomenon of the vast, flat wastelands of the earth that has no known explanation. The Okefenokee Swamp is the only place I've ever heard it.

Panic—and Retreat

With every creature in the drowned world around me so still, a sudden panic grabbed me amidships. I remembered Lem's troubled warning—the swampers have a grim superstition about the drums.

Sweating, swearing under my breath, I dug the blade of the paddle deep and tried to shove the craft off the knees. When it wouldn't budge, I plowed it around by awkward force and jammed my paddle against a sunken log, shoving until my arms struck bone against the shoulder blades and until my muscles ached.

The next few moments were so swift, so incredible, that they might have been something out of a dream. The boat broke loose with a grinding tear and flew backward as if it had been shot out of a torpedo tube. It crashed against the wall of brush that hemmed me in.

Before I could regain my balance, I was struck behind the shoulder with something that felt like the crack of a whip. I was convinced that nothing but a rusty old cottonmouth could pack a wallop like that. I plunged out of the boat, just as another staggering blow hit me behind the ear.

The bottom of the run was as grassy as a cow pasture. I don't know how long I stayed down. I remember crawling under the water until I bumped into a lot of crooked stems. I wiggled into them and cautiously came up for air. With the back of my hand, I slapped the water out of my eyes. The stern of the bateau was covered with a swarm of storming hornets!

I breathed relief so loud I thought they would hear and come gunning for me in the brush.

The Rugged Way Out

My pounding pump throttled down to normal and I looked around. Open water glimmered beyond the brush wall. Moving carefully, I slid through the branches. The lake looked like the one I had paddled away from only a few hours before, but then all Okefenokee lakes are similar. But it was open and clear of the beastly brush. I dug my knife out of a soaked pocket to clear a path through which I could rescue my bateau from the raging horde. But the warlocks seemed determined to put me down.

Just as I deposited an armload of limbs, I slipped on an underwater root. The knife flew out of my hand and I went down again, completely submerging in the oozy goo. I floundered for air, blowing moss and mud out of my head like a wounded porpoise.

"Gawd-a-mighty!"

Lem and Dan MacMillan crouched in a boat, not thirty feet away, their eyes run out on stems.

I spluttered under my breath.

"In fifty years," Lem gasped between guffaws, "I've seen some strange sights in the swamp, but this beats 'm all."

"We almost potted you fer an old black bear," Dan grinned.

Lem peeled off his clothes and helped me complete the tunnel through the brush. We maneuvered the boat gently from under the paper globe where the hornets lived and hauled it through the snags, into the deep water of Minnie Lake.

"Other than that knot on your head," Lem asked bluntly, "what luck did you have?"

I felt for the string of bass, but somewhere in the confusion it had been torn loose from its moorings and had vanished in the murky water.

"None," I said. "I went to the wrong place."

Lem's gray eyes shot me through, so I described the lake with the pines at its head. He smirked.

"You were too far north. I remember that gator hole. Used to trap coons in there."

I didn't tell him about the fish I'd caught, or the giant I had missed. I didn't want him beating that water with his rod. I've got a date with the bronzeback myself, some spring again. But if you want to try it, let me know. I'll be glad to give you its exact location. There's only one thing. Lord help you if you find it. ❖

MAY 1951

171

FROZEN TERROR

by Ben East

❖

TRAMPING ACROSS THE ROCK-
strewn, snowy beach of Crane
Island with two companions that
bitter-cold winter morning, on his way
to the rough shore ice and the lake-trout

grounds beyond, Lewis Sweet had no warning of what grim fate the next seven days had in store for him, no intimation that before the week was up his name would be on the lips of people and the front pages of newspapers across the whole country. Nor did he guess that he was walking that Lake Michigan beach for the last time on two good feet.

The date was Tuesday, January 22, 1929. There was nothing to hint that the day would be any different from the many others Sweet had spent fishing through the ice for lake trout, there on the submerged reefs off Crane Island.

He'd walk out to his lightproof shanty, kindle a fire of dry cedar in the tiny stove, sit and dangle a wooden decoy in the clear green water beneath the ice, hoping to lure a prowling trout within reach of his heavy seven-tined spear. If he was lucky he'd take four or five good fish by midafternoon. Then he'd go back to shore and drive the thirty miles to his home in the village of Alanson, Mich., in time for supper.

It would be just another day of winter fishing, pleasant but uneventful.

The Crane Island fishing grounds lay west of Waugoshance Point, at the extreme northwest tip of Michigan's mitten-shaped lower peninsula. The point is a long narrow tongue of sand, sparsely wooded, roadless and wild, running out into the lake at the western end of the Straits of Mackinac, with Crane Island marking land's end. Both the island and the point are unpeopled. On the open ice of Lake Michigan, a mile offshore, Sweet and the other fishermen had their darkhouses.

Fishing was slow that morning. It was close to noon before a trout slid into sight under the ice hole where Sweet kept vigil. He maneuvered the wood minnow away and eased his spear noiselessly through the water. Stalking his decoy, the trout moved ahead a foot or two, deliberate and cautious. When it came to rest directly beneath him, eyeing the slow-moving lure with a mixture of hunger and wariness, he drove the spear down with a hard, sure thrust.

The steel handle was only eight or ten feet long, but it was attached to the roof of the shanty by fifty feet of stout line. When Sweet felt the barbed tines jab into the fish he let go the handle and the heavy spear carried the twisting trout swiftly down to the reef thirty feet below.

Wind in the Nor'east

After the fish ceased struggling Sweet hauled it up on the line. When he opened the shanty door and backed out to disengage the trout, he noticed that the wind was rising and the air was full of snow. The day was turning blustery. Have to watch the ice on a day like that. Might break loose alongshore and go adrift. But the wind still blew from the west, onshore. So long as it stayed in that quarter there was no danger.

About an hour after he took the first trout the two men fishing near him quit their shanties and walked across the ice to his.

"We're going in, Lew," one of them hailed. "The wind is hauling around nor'east. It doesn't look good. Better come along."

Sweet stuck his head out the door of his shanty and squinted skyward. "Be all right for a spell, I guess," he said finally. "The ice'll hold unless it blows harder than this. I want one more fish."

He shut the door and they went on, leaving him there alone.

Thirty minutes later Sweet heard the sudden crunch and rumble of breaking ice off to the east. The grinding, groaning noise ran across the field like rolling thunder, and the darkhouse shook as if a distant train had passed.

Sweet had done enough winter fishing there to know the terrible portent of that sound. He flung open the shanty door, grabbed up his ax and the trout he had speared, and raced across the ice for the snow-clouded timber of Crane Island.

Halfway to the beach he saw what he dreaded, an ominous, narrow vein of black, zigzagging across the white field of ice.

When he reached the band of open water it was only ten feet across, but it widened perceptibly while he watched it, wondering whether he dared risk plunging in. Even as he wondered, he knew the chance was too great to take. He was a good swimmer but the water would be numbingly cold, and he had to reckon, too, with the sucking undertow set up by 100,000 tons of ice driving lakeward with the wind. And even if he crossed the few yards of water successfully, he would have little hope of crawling up on the smooth shelf of ice on the far side.

He watched the black channel grow to twenty feet, to ninety. At last, when he could barely see across it through the swirling snowstorm, he turned and walked grimly back to his darkhouse.

A Yawning Black Chasm

He had a stove there, and enough firewood to last through the night. He wanted desperately to take shelter in the shanty but he knew better. His only chance lay in remaining out in the open, watching the ice floe for possible cracks and breaks.

He turned his back resolutely on the darkhouse, moved to the center of the drifting floe, and began building a low wall of snow to break the force of the wind. It was slow work with no tool but his ax, and he hadn't been at it long when he heard a pistol-sharp report rip across the ice. He looked up to see his shanty settling into a yawning black crack. While he watched, the broken-off sheet of ice crunched and ground back against the main floe and the frail darkhouse went to pieces like something built of cardboard.

Half an hour later the two shanties of his companions were swallowed up in the same fashion, one after the other. Whatever happened now, his last hope of shelter was gone. Live or die, he'd have to see it through right in the open on the ice, with nothing between him and the wind save his snow wall. He went on building it.

He knew pretty well what he faced, but there was no way to figure his chances. Unless the ice field grounded on either Hog or Garden Island, at a place where he could get to the beach, some sixty miles of open water lay ahead between him and the west shore of Lake Michigan. There was little chance the floe would hold together that long, with a winter gale churning the lake.

There was little chance, too, that the wind would stay steady in one quarter long enough to drive him straight across. It was blowing due west now but before morning it would likely go back to the northeast. By that time he'd be out in midlake if he were still alive, beyond Beaver and High and the other outlying islands. And there, with a northeast storm behind him, he could drift more than one hundred miles without sighting land.

Sweet resigned himself to the fact that, when buffeted by wind and pounding seas, even a sheet of ice three miles across and two feet thick can stay intact only so long.

In midafternoon hope welled up in him for a little while. His drift carried him down on Waugoshance Light, a lighthouse abandoned and dismantled long before, and it looked for a time as if he would ground against its foot. But currents shifted the direction of the ice field a couple of degrees and he went past only one hundred yards or so away.

Waugoshance was without fuel or food; no more than a broken crib of rock and concrete and a gaunt, windowless shell of rusted steel. But it was a pinpoint of land there in the vast gray lake. It meant escape from the icy water all around, it spelled survival for a few hours at least, and Sweet watched it with hungry eyes as his floe drifted past, almost within reach, and the squat red tower receded slowly in the storm.

By that time, although he had no way of knowing it, the search and rescue resources of an entire state were being marshaled in the hope of snatching him from the lake alive.

The Alarm is Spread

The two men who had fished with him that morning were still on Crane Island when the ice broke away. They had stayed on, concerned and uneasy, watching the weather, waiting for Sweet to come back to the beach. Through the snowstorm they had seen black water offshore when the floe went adrift. They knew Sweet was still out there somewhere on the ice and they lost no more time. They piled into their car and raced for the hamlet of Cross Village, on the high bluffs of Sturgeon Bay ten miles to the south.

There was little the Cross Villagers or anybody else could do at the moment to help, but the word of Sweet's dramatic plight flashed south over the wires to downstate cities and on across the nation, and one of the most intense searches for a lost man in Michigan's history got under way.

The theme was an old one. Puny man pitted against the elements. A flyspeck of humanity out there alone, somewhere in an endless waste of ice and water, snow and gale, staving off death hour after hour—or waiting for it, numb and half frozen, with cold-begotten resignation. None heard the story unmoved. Millions sat at their own firesides that winter night, secure and warm and fed, and pitied and wondered about Lewis Sweet, drifting unsheltered in the bitter darkness.

The fast-falling snow prevented much action for the first twenty-four hours. But the storm blew itself out Wednesday forenoon, and the would-be rescuers went into action.

There was too much ice there in the north end of Lake Michigan for boats. The search had to be made from the air, and on foot along the shore of Waugoshance Point and around Crane Island, south into Sturgeon Bay and on the frozen beaches of the islands farther out.

Coast Guard crews and volunteers joined forces. Men walked the beaches for four days, clambering over rough hummocks of shore ice, watching for tracks, a thread of smoke, a dead fire, any sign at all that Sweet had made land. Other men scanned the ice fields and the outlying islands, Garden and Hog and Hat, from the air. Pilots plotted 2,000 square miles of lake and flew them systematically, one by one, searching for a black dot that would be a man huddled on a drifting floe.

Lewis Sweet, who on Monday of that week had hardly been known to anyone beyond the limits of his home town, was now an object of nation-wide concern. Men bought papers on the streets of cities 1,000 miles from Alanson, to learn what news there might be of the lost fisherman.

Little by little, hour by hour, hope ebbed among the searchers. No man could survive so long on the open ice. The time spun out—a day, then two days, three—and still the planes and foot parties found no trace of Sweet. By Friday night hope was dead. Life could not endure through so many hours of cold and storm without shelter, fire, or food. On Saturday, the last day of the search, those who remained in it looked only for a dark spot on the beach, a frozen body scoured bare of snow by the wind. At dusk the search was reluctantly abandoned.

Nearing the Islands

Folks no longer wondered whether Lewis Sweet would be rescued, or how. Instead they wondered whether his body would be found on some lonely beach when spring came, or whether the place and manner of his dying would never be known.

But Sweet had not died.

Twice more before dark on Tuesday he believed for a little time that he was about to escape the lake. The first time he saw Hat Island looming up through the storm ahead, a timbered dot on a gray sea that smoked with snow. His floe seemed to be bearing directly down on it and he felt confident it would go aground on the shingly beach.

No one lived on Hat. He would find no cabin there. But there was plenty of dry wood for a fire and he had his big trout for food. He'd make out all right until the storm was over and he had no doubt that some way would be found to rescue him when the weather cleared. But even while he tasted in anticipation the immense relief of trading his drifting ice floe for solid ground, he realized that his course would take him clear of the island and he resigned himself once more to a night of drifting.

The next time it was Hog Island, much bigger but also without a house of any kind, that seemed to lie in his path. But again the wind and lake played their tricks and he was carried past, little more than a stone's throw from the beach. As if to tantalize him deliberately, a solitary gull, a holdover from the big flock that bred there in summer, flew out from the ice hummocks heaped along the shore, alighted for a few minutes on his floe, and then soared casually back to the island.

"That was the first time in my life I ever wished for wings!" Sweet told me afterward.

The Storm Plays a Prank

That night was pretty bad. The storm mounted to a raging blizzard. With the winter darkness coming down, the section of ice where Sweet had built his snow shelter broke away from the main field suddenly and without warning. He heard the splintering noise, saw the crack starting to widen in the dusk only a few yards away. He gathered up his fish and his precious ax and ran for a place where the pressure of the wind still held the two masses of ice together, grinding against each other. Even as he reached it the crevice opened ahead of him, but it was only a couple of feet wide and he jumped across to the temporary safety of the bigger floe.

Again he set to work to build a shelter with blocks of snow. When it was finished he lay down behind it to escape the bitter wind. But the cold was numbing, and after a few minutes he got to his feet and raced back and forth across the ice to get his blood going again, with the wind-driven snow cutting his face like a whiplash.

He spent the rest of the night that way—lying briefly behind his snow wall for shelter, then forcing himself to his feet once more to fight off the fatigue and drowsiness that he knew would finish him if he gave in to it.

He was out in the open lake now, and the storm had a chance to vent its full force on the ice field. Before midnight the field broke in two near him again, compelling him to abandon his snow shelter once more in order to stay with the main floe. Again he had the presence of mind to take his ax and the trout along. The same thing happened once more after that, sometime in the small hours of the morning.

Toward daybreak the cold grew even more intense. And now the storm played a cruel prank. The wind hauled around to the southwest, reversing the drift of the ice field and sending it back almost the way it had come, toward the distant north shore of Lake Michigan. In the darkness, however, Sweet was not immediately aware of the shift.

The huge floe—still some two miles across—went aground an hour before daybreak, without warning. There was a sudden crunching thunder of sound, and directly ahead of Sweet the edge of the ice rose out of the water, curled back upon itself like the nose of a giant toboggan, and came crashing down in an avalanche of two-ton blocks! The entire field shuddered and shook and seemed about to splinter into fragments, and Sweet ran for his life, away from the spot where it was thundering aground.

It took the field five or ten minutes to lose its momentum and come to rest. When the splintering, grinding noise finally subsided, Sweet went cautiously back to learn what had happened. He had no idea where he was or what obstacle the floe had encountered.

To his astonishment, he found that he had brought up at the foot of White Shoals Light, one of the loneliest lighthouses in Lake Michigan, rising from a concrete crib bedded on a submerged reef, more than a dozen miles from the nearest land. The floe, crashing against the heavy crib, had buckled and been sheared and piled up until it finally stopped moving.

Sweet was close to temporary safety at last. Just twenty-two feet away, up the vertical concrete face of the crib, lay shelter and fuel, food and survival. Only twenty-two feet, four times his own height. But it might as well have been twenty-two miles. For the entire crib above the waterline was incased in ice a foot thick, formed by freezing spray, and the steel ladder bedded in the concrete wall showed only as a bulge on the smooth, sheer face of the ice.

Sweet knew the ladder had to be there. He located it in the gray light of that stormy winter morning and went to work with his ax. He chopped away the ice as high as he could reach, standing on the floe, freeing the rungs one at a time. Then he stepped up on the first one, hung on with one hand, and went on chopping with the other, chipping and worrying at the flinty sheath that enclosed the rest of the ladder.

Three hours from the time he cut the first chip of ice away he was within three rungs of the top. Three steps, less than a yard—and he knew he wasn't going to make it.

His feet were wooden stumps on which he could no longer trust his weight. His hands had long since lost all feeling. They were so badly frozen that he had to look to make sure his fingers were hooked around a rung, and he could no longer keep a grip on the ax. He dropped it half a dozen times, clambering awkwardly down after it, mounting wearily up the rungs again. The first couple of times it wasn't so bad, but the climb got more and more difficult. The next time he dropped the ax he wouldn't be able to come back up the ladder. He took a few short, ineffectual strokes and the ax went clattering to the ice below. He climbed stiffly down and huddled on a block of ice to rest.

It's hard to give up and die of cold and hunger with food and warmth only twenty-odd feet overhead. Sweet didn't like the idea. In fact, he said afterward, he didn't even admit the possibility. There had to be some way to the top of that ice-coated crib, and he was bound he'd find it.

Hunched there on his block of ice, out of sight of land, with ice and water all around and the wind driving snow into his clothing at every buttonhole, the idea came to him. He could build a ramp of ice blocks up to the top of the crib!

The material lay waiting, piled up when the edge of the floe shattered against the base of the light. Some of the blocks were more than ten men could have moved but some were small enough for Sweet to lift. He went to work.

Three hours later he finished the job and dragged himself, more dead than alive, over the icy, treacherous lip of the crib.

Any man in normal surroundings and his right mind would have regarded Lewis Sweet's situation at that moment as pretty desperate. White Shoals Light had been closed weeks before, at the end of the navigation season. Sweet was on a deserted concrete island 100 feet square, in midlake, with frozen hands and feet, in the midst of a January blizzard—and no other living soul had the faintest inkling where he was or that he was alive. It wasn't exactly a rosy outlook, but in his fifty-odd years he had never known a more triumphant and happy minute!

The lighthouse crew had left the doors unlocked when they departed for the winter, save for a heavy screen that posed no barrier to a man with an ax. Inside the light, after his hours on the ice and his ordeal at the foot of the crib, the lost man found paradise.

In Sight—Out of Reach

Bacon, rice, dried fruit, flour, tea, and other supplies were there in abundance. There were three small kerosene stoves and plenty of fuel for them. There were matches. There was everything a man needed to live for days or weeks, or maybe until spring!

At the moment Sweet was too worn out to eat. He wanted only to rest and sleep. He cut the shoes off his frozen feet, thawed his hands and feet as best he could over one of the oil stoves, and fell into the nearest bed.

He slept nearly twenty-four hours. When he awakened Thursday morning he cooked the first meal he'd had since eating breakfast at home forty-eight hours before. It put new life into him, and he sat down to take careful stock of his situation.

The weather had cleared and he could see the timbered shore of the lake both to the north and south, beckoning, taunting him, a dozen miles away. Off to the southeast he could even see the low shape of Crane Island, where he had gone adrift. But between him and the land, in any direction, lay those miles of water all but covered over with fields of drifting ice.

From the tower of the light Lake Michigan was a curious patchwork of color. It looked like a vast white field veined and netted with gray-green. That network of darker color showed where constantly shifting channels separated the ice fields. Unless and until there came a still, cold night to close all that open water, Sweet must remain a prisoner here on his tiny concrete island.

At noon on Thursday, sitting beside his oil fire opening bloody blisters on his feet, Sweet heard the thrumming roar of a plane outside.

He knew it instinctively for a rescue craft sent out to search for him, and he bounded up on his crippled feet and rushed to a window.

But the windows were covered with heavy screen to protect them from wind and weather. No chance to wave or signal there. The door opening out on the crib, by which he had gained entrance to the light, was two or three flights below the living quarters. No time to get down there. There was a nearer exit in the lens room at the top of the tower, one flight up. He made for the stairs.

The pilot of the plane had gone out of his way to have a look at White Shoals on what he realized was a very slim chance. He didn't really hope to find any trace of the lost man there and he saw no reason to linger. He tipped his plane in a steep bank and roared once around the light, a couple of hundred feet above the lake. Then, seeing nothing but a jungle of ice and snow piled the length of the reef, he leveled off and headed for his home field for a fresh supply of gas to carry him out on another flight. He must have felt pretty bad about it when he heard the story afterward.

While the pilot made that one swift circle Lewis Sweet was hobbling up the flight of iron stairs as fast as his swollen, painful feet would carry him. But he was too late. When he reached the lens room and stepped out through the door the plane was far out over the lake, disappearing swiftly in the south.

Most men would have lost heart then and there but Sweet had been through too much to give up at that point. Back in the living quarters he sat down and went stoically on with the job of first aid to his feet.

"It doesn't hurt to freeze, " he told me with a dry grin months later, "but it sure hurts to thaw out! "

Before the day was over another plane, or the same one on a return flight, roared over White Shoals. But the pilot didn't bother to circle that time and Sweet didn't even make the stairs. He watched helplessly from a screened window while the plane winged on, became a speck in the sky, and vanished.

Sweet was convinced then that if he got back to shore he'd have to do so on his own. It was plain that nobody guessed his whereabouts, or even considered the empty lighthouse a possibility.

After dark that night he tried to signal the distant mainland. There was no way for him to put the powerful beam of the light in operation, or he would almost certainly have attracted attention at that season. But he rigged a crude flare, a ball of oil-soaked waste on a length of wire, and went out on the balcony of the lens room and swung it back and forth, hoping its feeble red spark might be seen by someone on shore.

Twenty miles away, at the south end of Sturgeon Bay, he could see the friendly lights of Cross Village winking from their high bluff. How they must have mocked him!

On Friday morning he hung out signals on the chance that another plane might pass. But no one came near the light that day, and the hours went by uneventfully. Fresh blisters kept swelling up on his feet and he opened and drained them as fast as they appeared. He cooked and ate three good meals, and at nightfall he climbed back to the lens room, went outside in the bitter wind, and swung his oil-rag beacon again for a long time. He did that twice more in the course of the night, but nothing came of it.

The Last Gambling Chance

The lake still held him a prisoner Saturday. That night, however, the wind fell, the night was starlit and still and very cold. When he awoke on Sunday morning there was no open water in sight. The leads and channels were covered with new ice as far as he could see, and his knowledge of the lake told him it was ice that would bear a man's weight.

Whether he would encounter open water before he reached shore there was no way to guess. Nor did it matter greatly. Sweet knew his time was running out. His feet were in terrible shape and he was sure the search for him had been given up by this time. This was his only chance and he'd have to gamble on it. In another day or two he wouldn't be able to travel. If he didn't get away from White Shoals today he'd never leave it alive.

How he was to cross the miles of ice on his crippled feet he wasn't sure. He'd have to take that as it came, one mile at a time.

His feet were too swollen for shoes, but he had found plenty of heavy woolen socks in the lighthouse. He pulled on three or four pairs, and contrived to get into the heavy rubbers he had worn over his shoes when he was blown out into the lake on Tuesday.

When he climbed painfully down from the crib that crisp Sunday morning and started his slow trek over the ice toward Crane Island he took two items along, his ax and the frozen trout he had speared five days before. If he succeeded in reaching shore they meant fire and food. They had become symbols of his fierce, steadfast determination to stay alive. So long as he kept them with him he was able to believe he would not freeze or starve.

Now an odd thing happened, one of those ironic quirks that seem to be Destiny's special delight at such times.

At the very hour when Sweet was climbing down from the lighthouse and moving off across the ice that morning, three of us were setting out from the headquarters of Wilderness State Park, on Big Stone Bay on the south shore of the Straits ten miles east of Crane Island, to have a final look for his body.

Floyd Brunson, superintendent of the park, George Laway, a fisherman living on Big Stone, and I had decided on one more last hope search along the ice-fringed beach of Waugoshance Point.

We carried no binoculars that morning. We left them behind deliberately to eliminate useless weight, certain we would have no need for them. Had we had a pair along as we snowshoed to the shore and searched around the ice hummocks on the sandy beach, and had we trained the glasses a single time toward White Shoals Light—a far-off gray sliver rising out of the frozen lake—we could not possibly have failed to pick up the tiny black figure of a man, crawling at snail's pace over the ice.

Had we spotted him by nightfall, we could have had him in a hospital, where by that time he so urgently needed to be and where he was fated to spend the next ten weeks while surgeons amputated all his fingers and toes and his frozen hands and feet slowly healed.

But the hospital was still two days away. Toward noon Brunson and Laway and I trudged back from our fruitless errand, never suspecting how close we had come to a dramatic rescue of the man who had been sought for five days in the greatest mass search that lonely country had ever seen.

Lewis Sweet crept on over the ice all that day. His progress was slow. Inside the heavy socks he could feel fresh blisters swelling on his feet. They puffed up until he literally rolled on them as he walked. Again and again he went ahead a few steps, sat down and rested, got up and drove himself doggedly on. At times he crawled on all fours.

Still Seven Miles to Go

He detoured around places where the new ice looked unsafe. Late in the afternoon he passed the end of Crane Island, at about the spot where he had gone adrift. Land was within reach at last and night was coming on, but he did not go ashore. He had set his sights on Cross Village as the nearest place where he would find humans, and he knew he could make better time on the open ice than along the rocky beach of Sturgeon Bay.

Late that day, Sweet believed afterward, his mind faltered for the first time. He seemed to be getting delirious, and found it hard to keep his course. At dark he stumbled into a deserted shanty on the shore of the bay, where fishermen sometimes spent a night. He was still seven miles short of his goal.

The shanty meant shelter for the night and in it he found firewood and a rusty stove, but no supplies except coffee and a can of frozen milk. He was still carrying his trout but he was too weak and ill now to thaw and cook it. With great effort he succeeded in making coffee. It braced him and he lay down on the bunk to sleep.

Before morning he was violently ill with cramps and nausea, perhaps from lack of food or from the frozen milk he had used with the coffee. At daybreak he tried to drive himself on toward Cross Village but he was too sick to stand. He lay helpless in the shanty all day Monday and through Monday night, eating nothing.

Tuesday morning he summoned the little strength remaining to him and started south once more, hobbling and crawling over the rough ice of Sturgeon Bay. It was quite a walk but he made it. Near noon of that day, almost a week to the hour from the time the wind had set him adrift on his ice floe, he stumbled up the steep bluff at Cross Village and called to a passing Indian for a hand.

Alone and unaided, Lewis Sweet had come home from the lake! When the Indian ran to him he put down two things he was carrying—a battered ax that had been dulled against the iron ladder of White Shoals Light, and a big lake trout frozen hard as granite. ◆

JANUARY 1951

MAD WOLF

by C. Blackburn Miller

❖

OUR RED-HEADED TEAMSTER, Jesus, was the first to see the mad wolf. He had been freighting supplies back to the ranch from Comstock.

"*Senor*," he said, his dark face pallid with fright, "I come from Comstock. I have the letters, the beans, and the bacon. I open the range gate, and lead the horses through. They stop. I go back to close the gate. The horses they start to walk on quick. I call 'whoa,' but they go faster. Then, *senor*, I look back and a *lobo*, what you call the timber wolf, he trot at me. His eyes are green. His tongue is a foot long. The wolf, senor, is loco—what you call mad. I run quicky for the wagon, *senor*. The horses trot, the wolf trot, and I, senor, I run. I get in over the back of wagon, and take my rifle from under the seat. I look back, and the wolf is gone."

Overcome with superstitious dread, Jesus had lashed the horses into a run, and had covered the eight miles between the range gate and the ranch house at a gallop. There was nothing odd about his story. Many animals go mad in the heat of a Texas summer. The little spotted hydrophobia skunk is a constant peril to those sleeping in the open.

Realizing the danger to man and beast from this animal, apparently made fearless by rabies, I sent Manuel to ride fence on the north pasture the following morning, and told him to watch for the mad wolf. Manuel was a good shot, and I was anxious to have this mad beast removed from the range.

That evening I heard Manuel's spurs clanking over the sun-baked soil, as he carried his saddle from the corral to the shed. Then he came to where I was sitting in the shadow of the thatched veranda.

Squatting down in the moonlight, he rolled a corn-husk cigarette, took a puff, then told me what he'd seen.

He had dismounted from his horse, and was inspecting a weak wire in the fence. He looked around suddenly, and saw a gaunt, gray timber wolf trotting toward him. The beast's eyes had a greenish glare, and foam dripped from the open jaws. Manuel, thoroughly frightened, had run to his horse, mounted, and dragged his carbine from its scabbard. He shot three times at the wolf, but missed because of his horse's nervousness. The wolf had run in, and slashed at the horse's leg. The horse saved itself by leaping aside, nearly unseating Manuel. Then, swerving under the wire, the wolf had disappeared down a gully. Manuel said he followed it on foot until he lost the track on the rocks.

I was annoyed at Manuel's failure, and told him so.

When Ramorez brought up the horses at dawn, he said a pinto mare was missing. After the men had saddled up and left, I threw a saddle on a roan, shoved my .250/3000 Savage in the scabbard, and set out with Ramorez. We picked up the mare's trail where she had left the saddle bunch, and within a mile we found her in an arroyo—hamstrung, and her throat torn. Wolf tracks were plentiful, but careful inspection showed they had been made by one wolf. We followed them a short distance, but lost them.

Sending Ramorez back to the ranch for steel traps, a pair of old gloves, and some wire, I rode to the crest of a knoll, dismounted, and scanned the range with binoculars. A gray fox stole from the shelter of some brush, crossed an opening, and disappeared into a den in the rocks. Far down on the Lagoona flats, two range bulls were pushing each other about. There was no other sign of life.

In an hour, Ramorez returned, carrying the traps. Smearing them in the blood of the dead mare, I concealed the traps about the carcass, and swept away all trace of our presence with a green branch.

Days passed. The traps remained undisturbed, nor was there any sign of the mad wolf. I decided he had succumbed to rabies. I had read that dogs afflicted with the malady did not long survive, but I'd never studied a wild animal afflicted with it.

Jesus kept pigs in a large pen back of his jacal, or adobe hut. They were his wife's special charge, and the pets of his numerous children. The moon was high in the sky one night when there came an ago-nized squeal from the inclosure. Jesus rushed out, rifle in hand. Two young sows lay kicking on the ground; the rest were being herded about by a gaunt, ghostly-gray shape. Jesus recognized the mad wolf, and, with trembling fingers, pulled the trigger. He missed the wolf, but laid out a prime young porker. He again threw the gun to his shoulder, but the wolf leaped the fence, and escaped into the darkness.

This episode filled the Mexicans with terror, and, as a result, the children were kept huddled within the jacals day and night. The Mexicans knew that a mad wolf possessed no fear, and that the merest scratch from his fangs meant death. I shared their dread, for coyotes, or even our own dogs, if bitten by this mad beast, might inflict injuries, the results of which I dared not contemplate. The wolf's caution puzzled me. Any ordinary animal, afflicted with rabies, could be tracked down easily and shot, but this beast com-bined cunning with its madness.

A week went by, then Ramorez found a white-face heifer that had been pulled down and killed within a mile of the ranch. I hired a passing trapper to set his snares over the entire range. I rode the line with him frequently. We found the tracks of the big wolf many times, where he had circled warily, sniffing at the baits, but we failed to catch him.

Aroused by the wolf's cunning, and my offer of a large reward for its capture, the trapper rode away one morning with a grim look on his face. He reappeared in a week with three large hounds, all exception-al trailers, and possessing, according to him, the ability to whip their weight in wildcats. I resolved to put them to the test the following day, and see what they could do.

The stars were paling before dawn when we rode out of the ranch inclosure. Fortune favored us, for we struck the big wolf's trail in a dry wash and followed it from the ravine through a thick growth of cactus. The youngest dog collided with a cactus plant, and we aban-doned the pursuit temporarily to pick thorns from him. We then cir-cled the cactus area at a gallop, only to find that the wolf had dou-bled back and reentered the wash.

The dogs were far ahead of us now, giving tongue on the hot trail. We spurred forward as fast as the loose shale would permit, but the going was hazardous. Suddenly the baying turned to a deep-throated barking, and then there was a strangled howl. As we rounded a bend, we saw the lank body of a hound stretched out, his back broken, and his throat badly torn. The other two dogs continued the chase, but it was soon over. The bodies of the dogs were found lying across the trail. One was dead, the other so mangled that it had to be killed.

The rage and the grief of the trapper over the loss of his dogs was intense. He asked permission to continue his trapping, resolving to use poison baits. I finally consented, but the mad wolf refused to go near the baits. In fact, he seemed to have disappeared again, and I deluded myself into believing he had died.

Then, on a cool night in early September, I walked out on the veranda for a final look at the weather before retiring. The moon was clear, and shadows of the China trees were etched in black on the pale ground. Faint, but sweet, from the Mexican quarters came the strumming of a guitar, and from the bluffs echoed the high-pitched, blaring challenge of a range bull.

Suddenly I became aware of a vague shape in the shadow of a tree, which gradually assumed the form of a crouching dog.

I was about to dismiss it as an optical illusion, and had looked toward the distant corral, when out of the corner of my eye I detected a slight movement in the shadow. Again focusing my eyes on the blackness, I saw the outline of an animal distinctly. Its head was sunk between its shoulders, and I heard a deep-throated snarl. Suddenly I realized I was in the presence of the mad wolf at last. I was unarmed. My gun hung in its holster inside the door. There wasn't even a chair with which to defend myself should the mad brute rush. As I hesitated, I saw the wolf move forward stealthily.

There was but one move for me—a backward leap toward the door. If I missed—well, I couldn't afford to miss. I sprang backward, collided with the angle of the wall, caromed off, and fell inside the door, slamming it shut as I toppled over. Gaining my feet, I ripped my revolver from its holster, and went to the window. The wolf was gone.

This encounter affected my nerves more than I cared to admit. I insisted that the ranch hands carry rifles when riding range, and doubled the reward on the wolf's head. The only sign of him, however, was two yearling colts found hamstrung in the north pasture.

It was the end of September when Sid Hawkins came over from the Pecos country in a chuck wagon to look at a bunch of cattle. He brought with him a dog named Mescal, whose ancestry was questionable, but in whom the bulldog strain predominated. Covered with scars, he was the reputed victor in a hundred fights, and looked it. Homely though he was, he possessed a winning personality, and during the evening we became friends.

Chuck Reynolds, the range boss, had an idea with which Sid agreed, though I was skeptical. It was Chuck's plan to hunt down the mad wolf, and let Mescal dispatch him. Skeptical though I was, we rode out at dawn, Reynolds on his big bay horse surrounded by a motley collection of Mexican dogs, Sid Hawkins astride his white broncho, carrying Mescal across the saddle in front of him, while I brought up the rear with Ramorez.

A herder, running a flock of goats to the south of the Lagoona flats, had reported seeing wolf tracks, so we rode toward this section of the range. As we emerged from the gloomy walls of Gunshot Canyon, the sun was shining dazzlingly over the plain. A mile from the flats, we crossed a wolf's trail. It was fresh enough to excite the dogs, and, after some discussion, we urged them on.

For the first hour, the dogs made sorry work of it. Finally, a yellow, bandy-legged bitch, working well out in front, gave tongue, and dashed away to the right. The pack followed, a jostling group of red, yellow, and black bodies, their hysterical yelping echoing back in ear-splitting discord.

Mescal apparently held the pack in contempt, for, soothed by the easy motion of the horse, he closed his eyes, and snored as we followed the other dogs. Twice the wily wolf circled around us, and once, if we had looked back, I think we should have seen him. The scent grew warmer, and the pace increased. We loped over a level plain to a thick growth of mesquite that fringed a winding arroyo. Up this gully dashed the pack, and soon shrill barking told us the wolf had been brought to bay.

The noise of the pack aroused Mescal, and, with deep-throated growls, he announced his desire to join the fray. Hawkins lowered him to the ground, and we followed the broad-shouldered brute as he waddled toward the scene. Parting a screen of mesquite, we entered an opening, and there, with his hindquarters protected by a jutting shoulder of rock, stood the largest wolf I have ever seen. His head was sunk low between his shoulders, his eyes were green slits, and, behind wrinkled lips, his fangs were bared in a snarl of rage. From his jaws dripped shreds of white foam.

I expected him to charge the pack, but he held his ground. I yelled at Hawkins to call Mescal back, so we could shoot the wolf, but it was too late. Mescal had shouldered his way through the frightened pack, and was waddling across the open space toward the waiting wolf.

There were no preliminaries on the part of the dog, nor was there wisdom in his attack. He merely flung himself headlong at his gaunt antagonist. There was a lightning chop of the wolf's jaws, and Mescal was flung to one side, a ripped shoulder streaming blood.

We slipped our rifles from their scabbards, but Mescal had closed in, and fastened on the wolf's neck. I couldn't tell how vital a grip he had, as a wolf's heavy ruff offers great protection. It was impossible to shoot, with the battling brutes obscured in a curtain of dust, and the danger of hitting Mescal too great to risk. The cowardly pack refused to aid, merely barking their encouragement.

Twice the wolf reared, and I could see his fangs snapping at the dog. Mescal was red with his own blood, but he hung on grimly. A few more minutes, and out from the encircling dust curtain hurtled a body. It struck some rocks, rolled over, and lay motionless. It was what was left of Mescal. As the dust subsided, Hawkins threw his gun up, but the wolf was gone.

We buried Mescal there, and raised a cairn of stones to mark a warrior's last resting place. Hawkins was silent as we rode homeward, but, when we swung from our saddles at the ranch house, he asked if he might stay a while at the Lazy T.

The victory over Mescal spurred the mad wolf to more depredations. It marked the beginning of a reign of terror on the range. Two flocks were stampeded, and many sheep killed. One of the herders was severely bitten, and had to be sent to the hospital at San Antonio. Two of my favorite colts were slain, and still the killer ranged unchecked. Hawkins rode the pastures night and day, but the mad wolf avoided Mescal's avenger with astute cunning.

A mass drive, in which every one on the ranch participated, proved futile. A few coyotes were killed, and that was all. The presence of the wolf affected our nerves, and the Mexicans were convinced that the brute was endowed with supernatural powers.

Then the end came unexpectedly. Two weeks had dragged by. The lines on Hawkins's face had deepened, and there was a set look about his mouth. There had been a light rain the night before, and the wind had shifted, bringing a biting norther which numbed exposed fingers.

"I'm riding over to Castle Canyon," said Hawkins. "Want to come along?" I accepted the invitation, and saddled up a broncho, although there was work at the ranch that needed my attention.

After following the south road for about five miles, we turned off and watered the horses at the Sink, disturbing a flock of mallards feeding there. I asked Hawkins why he had chosen Castle Canyon, and he replied that he just had a hunch. Pressed for details, he lapsed into silence.

Castle Canyon has steep cliffs on either side, and the water-worn walls resemble towers and turrets of medieval castles. It is several miles long, and, starting at California Creek, gradually ascends to a level plain. We forded the creek, and Hawkins explained his plan. He was to ride back of the bluffs, and take his stand at the other end of the canyon. I was to continue through it, making as much noise as possible to drive the wolf out, if he was there, and Hawkins was sure that he was.

I allowed Hawkins an hour to make the detour, and then, taking my rifle from its scabbard, spurred my horse between the towering walls. My yells came crashing back to me from the cliffs. I could easily imagine how, in the old days a band of marauding Comanches might have given vent to their feelings as they rode through this canyon, and what a hair-raising effect the echo must have had on a listener.

Halfway up, I thought I saw a gray shape slide from behind a rock and disappear, but I couldn't be sure. Fox squirrels, disturbed by my war whoops, scrambled frantically up the canyon walls. The height of the walls began to diminish, and in a few hundred yards were but rocky knobs on the plain. As I rode out of the canyon, I heard a yell from Hawkins. Running off to one side was the wolf.

Riding to the left to head him back, I saw Hawkins shake out his rope, and realized his plan. The wolf altered his course, and made a bee line for a thick growth of cactus half a mile away. Sid's white horse leaped forward, and was soon running hard. The rider was trailing his loop. Fifty yards separated the wolf from his pursuer, when I saw Hawkins stand in his stirrups, and twirl his rope. Fearing the wolf might dodge beneath his horse, he was going to make an Arizona throw—the full extent of the rope. Hawkins kept that rope spinning, awaiting his opportunity.

The wolf looked back over his shoulder once, then unleashed a fresh burst of speed. The protecting cactus was close now. The rope snaked out, and the loop settled about the killer's neck. As the horse suddenly checked his stride, the rope tautened, and the great, gaunt body of the wolf described a flying arc in the air. Wrenching his horse around, Hawkins spurred him to a mad run, and dragged the strangled wolf a quarter of a mile before he paused to survey what was left of his vengeance.

"And that," he said, as I rode up, "squares old Mescal." ❖

JUNE 1937

193

Outlaws of
BALD MOUNTAIN

by Wes Jasper, as told to Eric Collier

*T*HE OWNER OF THE RISKE Creek Trading Post, Becher by name, English by birth, waggled his graying head and said, "Sorry, young fellow, but the Indians down at the ranch still owe me for supplies they wasted trying to corral those outlaw horses on Bald Mountain. Nigh a month they camped out there, chasing billy-be-cussed out of that wild herd. Never got a one of them within hollering distance of a trap gate. I want cash on the counter before I outfit any more wild-horse chasers."

Well, no man could rightly say I had no cash, for I was gripping the dime in my pocket as I listened to Becher's ultimatum. It was an American dime, a survivor of the small stake I had when I migrated from the state of Washington to central British Columbia in 1911. Two years of hard times since then had sent all my other dimes rolling, but I was 10 cents short of being broke.

Down the short corridor behind me, in the sitting room of the trading post, two chairs bumped square to the floor and I heard two heavy sighs. My partners, Bill Owens and Ezra Knapp, also late of Washington State, were the sole occupants of the room at the moment, and I knew their chairs were drawn up close to the corridor so they could hear what was transpiring in the store. We'd flipped my dime to determine who'd hit the trader up for the credit our venture required.

Now I eased my dime out of its sanctuary, flipped it idly, then dropped it back. The trader glanced at the lone coin and yawned. Then he opened the lid of a massive gold watch that probably came with him from England 20 years earlier. Without looking at its hands, he returned it to the pocket with the suggestive comment, "Well, time's rolling."

But I ignored the hint. I still had a couple of cards up my sleeve—a king and a possible ace. I played the king first.

"That herd's not ranging on Bald Mountain any more," I remarked. "They crossed the main fork of Riske Creek and are over in the Red Rock country east of here."

The trader's face showed interest. "You don't say."

I pressed the attack. "We saw the stallion night before last at Red Rock. It's the Bald Mountain stud sure enough. Bay with a blaze face, three stocking feet, weighs close to 1,300 pounds. Got around 30 head of mares and colts in his harem. I reckon at least six of the mares have had their tails docked one time or another."

"Branded, eh?" muttered the trader, palming his chin.

I nodded. "As I see things, that band has been chased by so many outfits the past couple of years they've been worried plumb off their old range and have traded the mountain for the Red Rock country. Now if the right men with the right sort of saddle horses built the right kind of a corral trap in just the right place—"

"Bald Mountain, Red Rock, or Old Nick's back yard" interjected the storekeeper, "I'll risk no more hard cash on that wild herd."

Then I played my ace. "That stallion's stolen himself a percheron mare that'll weigh close to 1,600. She's iron gray, has a roached mane and harness marks. Now who hereabouts," I asked innocently, "has lost just such a mare as that?"

The trader hunched forward in his chair. His eyelids twitched. "The Pearl mare! That stud's got my Pearl mare?"

"If that wasn't your Pearl mare," I replied, "it must have been her twin sister."

The trader sighed. "She disappeared last spring. We turned her loose on the range in June along with a couple of geldings. Come haying time we couldn't find hair nor hide of her, although we did locate the geldings."

"You couldn't find her," I informed him, "because that Bald Mountain stallion came down in the night, whipped the stuffing out of the geldings, and herded the Pearl mare back to his harem." I leaned closer across the counter and added, "You've posted a $25 reward for the return of that mare, and I reckon there are at least five more in the bunch belonging to ranchers hereabouts with a $15 or $20 reward out for them. Now if me and Bill and Ezra can corral that whole outfit, you get your mare back, we collect over $100 in reward money on the other branded stock, and the unbranded ones are likely to fetch $30 or $40 apiece after we break them. All we're lacking is grub, hay, oats, rope for hackamores—"

"How much cash have you three got among you?" the trader cut in.

I showed my dime.

The trader groaned. "Never met a wild-horse chaser yet with more than 25¢ to his name." Then, with a lift of the shoulders and a wince, "All right. I'll outfit you. But only on account of that Pearl mare. Outpull any other horse of her weight in the Chilcotin, that mare will."

He flipped open a ledger and picked up a pencil. "I'll stake you to $70 worth of grub, hay, and oats. Not a nickel's worth more."

There was a sudden scraping of chairs in the sitting room, then the jingle of spurs in the corridor. My two partners ambled up to the counter, wide grins on their faces. Both had a slightly bow-legged gait. Either one would hoist aboard the meanest bucking horse in the land.

On that December day in 1913 the horse was the key to commerce in British Columbia's Chilcotin region. Every pound of freight destined for the ranchers and fur traders had to be hauled in by teams of horses from Ashcroft, about 200 miles to the south. A man was judged by the quality of the horse he rode or the animals that pulled his freight wagon. Any horse sound of wind and limb was sure of ultimate sale, and if cash was lacking to close the deal, cattle or raw furs did as well. Few rail or wire fences cluttered the land, save those encircling hay meadows. The thousands of acres of unfenced bunch grass were free to all with stock to crop it.

There was many a clean-limbed horse without brand competing with cattle for that grass. Shy as fawns, with the speed and endurance of steeplechasers, these wild horses evaded capture with more cunning than any other creature that shared the wilds with them. They grazed the open range at night, watered at some near-by lake at dawn, and by sunup were deep in the heart of the forest, hidden from the eyes of man.

Rival stallions battled viciously and sometimes fatally for possession of the mares, and in the spring it was customary for a wild stallion to make sweeping forays by night to nose out the tracks of new mares to add to his harem. Thus the studs collected a good many gentle, branded mares that ranchers were pasturing on open range.

With rewards for branded horses and a good market for any others that could be halter-broken, the chasing of wild horses could be profitable. A few buckaroos made a living at it.

Seven miles east of the trading post (which still straddles the roadside) Bald Mountain thrusts high above the remainder of the land. Its westerly slopes stare down at the Chilcotin River. To the south and east of the mountain is open range sloping away to Fraser River. The north slopes of Bald Mountain are covered with endless miles of dense jackpine and fir. It was in that heavy timber that the outlaw horses of the mountain found sanctuary when chased by riders.

The stallion himself led the band in flight, and that stud could dodge the wings of artfully devised trap corrals the way a trap-shy wolf turns off from the scent of steel. Indians, breeds, and whites, all had pitted their wits and their horses against the stallion. But the trader at Riske Creek perhaps voiced the opinion of all when he stated, "The horse has never yet been saddled that'll run that bunch of outlaws into a corral."

Maybe it was the challenge as much as the money that persuaded me and my two partners to tackle the job. Though we had few other wordly possessions, each of us owned top-notch saddle horses. In the past we'd outwitted more than one band of wild horses and closed the trap gate on their tails. Now we were ready to try the wildest and fleetest band of all.

January snow was deep on the range when we pitched our small tent in a thin belt of timber near Red Rock. The timeless rock is still there, but today the wild horses are gone—mostly shot by bounty hunters when in 1924 the government decided that the horses must be killed to save grass for cattle. Close to 5,000 head were shot for bounty. Some old-timers will tell you that the best saddle stock in the Chilcotin was wiped out in this slaughter, and I sometimes think those old-timers are right.

There was definite purpose in our waiting for winter before setting up camp at the rock. The subzero cold that chilled us in bed at night would also sap the wind and strength of the wild horses. As the snow deepened and winter dragged on, the wild ones would lose about as much energy pawing for dry grass as they gained by eating it. They'd gradually weaken, while our own saddle horses ate oats in a lean-to of poles that sheltered them from the knife of the arctic wind.

For four days we tracked the wild band. We saw where they bedded in timber by day, located and memorized each acre of range where they pawed for feed at night. But seven days were spent before we caught sight of them.

We were in the saddle by daylight that morning. We had no thermometer, but the sting of the wind against our faces told us it was a little below zero. Six inches of fresh snow had fallen overnight, raising the overall depth well above our horses' knees. We traveled single file, taking turns at breaking trail to even the strain on our mounts.

Suddenly Bill Owens, in the lead, halted us with a tense "Whoa." Bill was wearing a dilapidated sombrero, his face and ears almost hidden by a black silk handkerchief. Now he pushed the handkerchief back from his eyes and stared into the east. "On top of that ridge," he blurted. "Horses." Knapp and I rode up beside him, our eyes fixed on the horses on the ridge.

The wind stabbed at my face, watering my eyes. The collar of my sheepskin coat was white with my own frosted breath. The horses on the ridge were pawing monotonously at the snow a dozen or so yards from the edge of a stand of jackpines. Bunched as they were, it was impossible to make an accurate tally, but I judged there were 25 to 30.

Suddenly one of the animals broke away from the herd, trotted toward us a few yards and stood with neck and tail arched, ears pointed in our direction. The animal was close to a mile away, but in this clear, crackling-cold air we could see him distinctly. We even heard him snort as he looked us over with hostile curiosity.

"Bay with a blaze face," I said for all of us. "It's the stallion."

We sat there feasting our eyes on that magnificent horse. Then he whistled, shrill and clear. The mares and colts stopped pawing. The stallion took a few stiff steps toward us then paused, right front hoof pawing the snow.

"They won't stay there much longer," I surmised. "That stud's thinking about hitting the timber right now."

The words had barely left my mouth when the stud wheeled back to the mares and led them at a stiff trot into the timber.

"Let's give them time to calm down," I suggested, "then we can circle around them and come in from the north. I want to see what they do when they're chased."

Backtracking out of sight, we found just the right sort of a pitchy tree, pried loose some of its bark, and kindled a roaring fire. What we needed to know first was where to build the corral. Like deer, wild horses have their favorite escape routes. Before starting work on the trap corral, which would have long wing fences forming a V leading into it, we had to learn how the outlaws of Bald Mountain would behave when the chase began in earnest. Now was the chance to do it.

Back in our saddles, we headed north through thickening timber for a mile, then turned east. Now Red Rock was due west of us, the deep gash of the Fraser River some 15 miles to the south. If we were able to move in behind the outlaws, cutting them away from the tangle of boulder-littered forest to the north, we'd have a chance to push them out on the open range. One thing was certain: if the outlaws were corraled, it would be out on that open range, not in the forest.

We circled north through deep timber to get beyond the wild bunch, then spread out half a mile apart and headed south toward the open range. With good luck and hard riding, we'd flush the stud and his harem out ahead of us.

Bill Owens, on my left, jumped the herd. I heard his whoop in the distance, then his shout, "They're swinging north, coming your way!"

"Head them off," I shouted to Baldy. And Baldy, nine years old, weighing 1,200 pounds, grabbed at the bit and hurtled forward through the snow.

We met the wild ones head-on in second-growth pine where I could see only a few feet ahead. One second I had all of the second growth to myself, the next I was engulfed in a tide of neighing, galloping horses that swung my own plunging horse off course and pressed him into the north. "Head 'em, Baldy," I roared.

Two wild-eyed colts fell away behind. Then a mare sheered sharply off on my right, unable to match Baldy's yard-gulping strides. From up ahead and out of the north, Bill's cries suddenly added to the tumult. The mass of horseflesh ahead of me veered east.

Bill Owens pivoted his horse due east, forcing the outlaws to make still another shift in course, this time straight south.

I turned Baldy west for 100 yards then cut south again, outflanking any attempt the wild band might make to turn west and follow the shelter of the timber.

As they broke out of the woods into the open, Bill and I were but 100 yards from the tails of the stragglers. That's where we pulled our own sweating horses to a stop. A few seconds later Knapp trotted out of the woods.

"If it never happens again," grinned Bill "that's one time they were outrun and outsmarted."

I watched the wild horses spill out across the open. There was no need to chase them now. This morning had proved that, given the right sort of a break, we could at least push them into open country. Now, by tracking along behind, we'd find the spot for the corral.

At a slow walk we trailed along in the tracks. The band held to the open prairie for a mile and then cut east toward a strip of mature pine. Their tracks followed this fringe of timber until it petered out at the shoreline of a lake, then crossed the ice and melted into another isolated hedge of timber on the other side.

There was little need of crossing the ice ourselves. Bill accurately summed the situation up when he thumbed to the timber behind us and said, "It's a natural."

"If we ever get to crowd them this way again," grunted Knapp.

The main corral could be built where the timber petered out at the lake and the funnel-shaped wings leading into it run back to the far end of the jackpine. If ever we put the band this way again they'd be into those wings before they knew they were there.

It took a week to cut the necessary timber, snake it into position, and throw up the corral and wings. The main trap had walls seven feet high, its logs the heaviest we could handle. We gave the corral a drop gate, reckoning that no other gate could be closed quick enough.

January was half spent by the time the job was completed. Almost 30 inches of snow now covered the range. Our hay and oats were dwindling, with slim chance of our getting more. The moon was full and the outlaws pawed for their feed on the range by its light, trailing far back into the thickest timber at dawn.

We lost four precious days trying to cut in on them from the north and herd them south for the open range. Each time the stallion defeated us. Twisting, dodging, at times almost doubling back in his tracks, he led the band to safety through an area of boulder-strewn gulches where it was impossible for a rider to follow faster than a slow trot.

Crouched over the flames of the campfire at the end of the fifth day of fruitless effort, Bill said meaningly "If something'd happen to that stud ..."

I laughed. "Yes, the mares and colts would be easy to trap without the stallion to lead them. Reckon you could line the sights of your .30/30 on an animal like that and squeeze the trigger, Bill?"

Bill studied a moment then shook his head. "I'd travel afoot first."

I looked at Knapp. "Ezra?"

The reply was prompt. "Never shot a good horse yet and don't contemplate starting now."

"Neither do I," I agreed.

Bill had been toying with his rope. He flicked one end at the flames and said, "How about a snare?"

"Could try one," I replied with little enthusiasm. I'd snared wild horses before, but only on well-used runways. The outlaws of Bald Mountain seldom followed the same trail twice when chased, so setting a snare for the stallion would be like fishing with an unbaited hook. Still, we could always try.

Next morning Bill and I went about the job of placing the snare in a pocket of young pine straddling a rock-littered ridge along which the stallion sometimes led his harem when we were following in their tracks. Ezra Knapp had remained in camp to re-shoe an animal. We hung the loop of the snare between two pines, camouflaged it with limbs, and made a wide sweep to locate the band's tracks. We finally jumped them two miles east of the snare and headed them west.

The combination of deep snow and January cold was sapping the strength of the mares. The stallion seemed strong as ever, but he had to slow his pace to enable his harem to keep up.

We clung to their tracks, shooting off at a tangent now and then to hold them in the direction of the snare. They reached the foot of the ridge and spilled along its crest, heads aimed arrow straight for the fringe of brush which concealed the snare. We were a scant 50 yards behind the stragglers when the leaders plunged into the brush.

We heard a quick scream of fright as an animal hit the snare, glimpsed it rearing on its hind legs as the noose tightened on its neck. Then it was down in the snow, four legs flailing the air. We jumped from our saddles and moved cautiously forward. But the stud had beaten us again; the animal quivering in the snow was an old sorrel mare.

I worked my hand along her neck, loosened the neck loop, and slipped a noose over the mare's nose. She heaved to her feet, made a desperate bid for freedom, then turned snorting to face us.

"Branded, by heck!" Bill said, pointing to the animal's right shoulder.

I studied the brand and finally traced its outline beneath the shaggy hair. "One of Durrel's mares," I decided. Harry Durrel, who ranched a few miles west of the trading post, had offered a $15 reward for the return of this mare when she first disappeared.

"Fifteen bucks," I said, snubbing the mare to a tree. "We're back in the chips again."

"Sure," grunted Bill. "Five bucks apiece."

I took a peek at the sun and muttered, "Just about noon." We both carried lunches and a feeding of grain for our horses behind the saddles, and now I suggested, "How about you leading the mare back to camp and leaving your grain with me?"

"What's on your mind?" Bill asked.

"Those mares are weakening." I said and having trouble keeping up to the stud. What I aim to do is stoke up Baldy with both rations of oats right now and then take up the tracks again—before the wild bunch has a chance to rest. You and Ezra can ride out from camp and perch yourselves somewhere on that slope west of the corral, where you can see the wild ones if I crowd them out of the timber."

"You push 'em into the open," mocked Bill "and we'll haze them into the trap."

Half a mile beyond the snare the wild horses again swung north. They were trotting now instead of traveling at a lope. I moved steadily along behind and by 2 o'clock I had the band in sight. I figured I was about three miles due north of the corral with three hours of daylight left in the sky. The outlaws had been under steady pressure from behind for six hours, and the pace was beginning to tell. But given a night's rest they'd again be capable of running five or six miles without breaking stride. Now was the time to call on Baldy for the run that could turn the band out on the open range.

Baldy surged into a hard run as if he knew my plan, and we were soon on the heels of the mares and colts. They picked up speed, pulling away a little, but it was a speed that couldn't last. One by one they broke gait and sheered off into the east.

Baldy pounded up beside the leaders, a cluster of young mares hugging the heels of the stallion. I swung my quirt once, and my big gelding responded with a burst of speed that swerved the stallion into the east. Then I drove Baldy forward again, and the wild stud, outrun and almost winded, wheeled to the south. There he joined the remainder of the band, the mares and colts that had broken away unable to maintain the pace.

I held Baldy back to let the renegades draw away from me and sort themselves out. When they were again traveling in a solid mass I moved in on their heels, thwarting the stallion's attempts to veer east or west.

They were only a few yards ahead of me when we pounded out of the trees into open range. Without slackening speed I stared out over the prairie, trying to get my bearings. We were coming out on a ridge, its crest showing a dirty gray where the wind had almost swept it clean of snow. Beyond the ridge, maybe a mile and a half to the southwest was the fringe of timber hiding the wings of the corral. My eyes raked the slopes west of that timber, searching the crests for sight of my partners. Where were Bill and Ezra?

The stallion galloped steadily to the south, taking advantage of the shallow snow on the ridge. Did Baldy have enough speed left to turn the band off the ridge and into the wings of the corral ? There was only one way to find out.

"Come on, Baldy!" The gelding lengthened his stride, giving what I knew was the last run left in him. Mares began breaking away on my right, their flying feet almost blinding me with snow. A dozen lengths ahead raced the bay stallion, ears flat against his skull, nostrils dilated. Born in the wilderness, belonging to the wilderness, he was making a final desperate bid to remain free.

But now Baldy's nose was even with the outlaw's flank, inching along his girth. Then we were neck and neck. I flicked at the plunging stud with my quirt, turning him into the southwest, straight for the timber and the trap.

Something warned the stud of the trap. Maybe it was the marks in the snow left behind when we snaked out the logs. It's possible that he saw the wing fence in the timber, even though it was 300 yards ahead. Perhaps it was some wild instinct that told him of the danger. Anyway, he abruptly went up on both hind legs, wheeling so fast that the mass of mares and colts engulfed him. Then he was galloping away from the trap with his harem following. Baldy had nothing left to match the stud's new burst of speed. Inch by inch the band drew away from me, heading into the west.

They were starting up the slope when a single rider flung over its crest at full gallop, plunging down the sidehill to head off the wild band.

"Bill!" I yelped.

Bill, whooping and waving on a fresh horse, forced the stallion south again, almost parallel to the wings of the corral.

But escape was blocked there now. Off the rise to the south came Ezra Knapp, his rawboned chestnut gelding raising a cloud of snow. The outlaws were forced down to the floor of the valley and into the jaws of the trap.

Baldy had caught his breath enough to flank the herd. With my rope snaking out at their rumps, I crowded them through the trees, down the V of the wings and into the corral. The stallion threw himself at the high log walls, fell back, then tried again. He stood on his hind legs, pawing the air, squealing with frustration.

Too late, the stud charged back to the opening by which he'd entered. I was already tripping the catch on the heavy gate. It banged down, sealing the trap shut.

Suddenly we were men of property, with rewards to collect and unbranded horses to tame and sell. We could swagger a little when next we walked into Becher's store. ❖

JULY 1957

Last of the MOUNTAIN MEN

by Frank C. Hibben

MANY OF MY FRIENDS HAD told me not to see the old man at all. "He's bushed and he's dangerous," they said. "He talks to imaginary dogs, and he sees people that aren't there."

I went out to the ranch near Silver City, New Mexico, nevertheless, and found Ben Lilly, who was then about eighty years old. The pale blue of his eyes, as we shook hands, disturbed me. They were calm blue eyes, with all of the sadness of a man who had lived a lonely life. It was the blue eyes you noticed first and the round and wrinkled face afterward. His white hair had not been cut for many months and hung down over his gnarled ears and forehead like a forkful of hay. His cheeks were pink and he seemed to radiate latent energy. If Lilly was as sick as I had been told, his appearance gave no indication of it.

But I felt uncomfortable in his presence. His placid look had an air of inquiry about it, as though he constantly expected me to say something.

"Lions, young man? I expect it's panthers you mean. I've killed a heap of them." It was obvious that Lilly wasn't talking to me, for he never again glanced in my direction, nor even seemed to sense my presence at all. He went right on talking, ignoring my questions and making no effort to stay close to me or make sure that I had heard. We simply started walking from the spot where I had first met him and kept on walking. We were gone three days.

I had not come to see Ben Lilly on any casual visit. There was a compelling purpose in my questions, for I had undertaken a study of the American cougar, or mountain lion. This old lion-and-bear hunter was the first from whom I hoped to learn much.

Range Was Shrinking

A career is doing what you want to do and then finding someone to pay you for it. I was fortunate enough to do just that. In 1933 I was offered a position hunting mountain lions. A group called the Southwestern Conservation League, centered at Albuquerque, New Mexico, professed great interest in these most colorful of American animals, about which there was little or no knowledge, and concern that they were becoming greatly reduced in numbers.

Mountain lions, which formerly ranged all of North America from Canada southward, were now to be found in only small fragments of their former range, for the most part in the rugged mountains of our Western states. Lions still existed in the rank fastnesses of the everglades of Florida and in the comparatively untouched wilderness of central Mexico. It was only in such wild spots that I might yet find enough cougars to get a comprehensive story of their life and habits.

The Southwestern Conservation League furnished me a car, a horse, and a horse trailer. My pockets bulged with letters of introduction to the various professional lion hunters of the Southwest with whom I might hunt to gain the information desired. My instructions were comprehensive and flexible. "Find out all you can about lions," was all I was told. The project was to take twelve months.

Actually, I must confess, the enthusiasm with which I prepared my equipment and started forth on the quest was not due entirely to the zeal to learn. The hunting fever had seized me, fanning my efforts to a pitch of anticipation. The cry of hunting hounds was ringing in my ears as I started out. In the ensuing months, on some hundreds of lion trails with the most famous hunters in the business, I came to know the cougar for what he is—one of the most fascinating and interesting animals in our whole repertory.

But as I asked my first questions and sought a place to begin, the answer was always the same: "If you want information about lions, go to Ben Lilly. He is the dean of lion hunters." Ranchers, forest rangers, seasoned hunters all said: "Ask Mr. Lilly, he knows more than anyone else."

A Tenacious Tracker

In telling me about him, they recounted stories of how he left money in banks all over Texas and New Mexico and never kept any accounting of it. He wrote checks on scraps of wrapping paper or a fragment of bone. Ranchers told me how "Mr. Lilly," as they called him, even behind his back, slept and ate with his dogs and followed the track of a lion or bear with the tenacity of a terrier. And he had made a living all over the West hunting animals for stockmen who wished to be rid of troublesome predators.

But as I started out that morning by the side of the old hunter, I wondered if I was not too late. Before we had gone a few hundred yards it seemed obvious that a young cowboy of whom I had asked directions in Silver City was right: Ben Lilly was "as nutty as a fruit cake."

He talked quietly as we walked along. He recited the events and painted the scenes of his past—which must have been full of the baying of hounds and the excitement of the chase—with complete lack of emotion. Although he spoke of panthers and bears by the hundred, the story which he wove with his words was the story of himself, certainly one of the most remarkable lives that has ever been lived.

About fifty years before, Ben had had a wife and three children back in Louisiana. There he had killed his first bear with a pocketknife, and with the blood had acquired a lust for killing. You could scarcely believe, as you looked into his gentle blue eyes, that he had killed several thousand bears and several hundred mountain lions—far more than any other living hunter. Ben was a marvelous shot. He could shoot a lion through the paw in the top of a pine tree and then drill it through the heart as it fell end over end through the branches to the ground.

When his wife, to whom he referred as a "daughter of Gomorrah," thrust a rifle into his hand on a Louisiana morning many years ago, she told him that if he must hunt and shoot, he could at least go out and kill a hawk that was bothering her chickens. Ben didn't come back from his wife's errand for almost three years. His explanation was that "the hawk just kept going."

An Inner Urge

During that time he scoured the Louisiana canebrakes alone, hunting he knew not what. Each bear that he killed seemed only to make him avid to track down and kill another. It was as though he had an inner urge to discover the fullness of life—which is never full.

As Ben Lilly talked and walked, he revealed more than once that he regarded himself as a wild animal. Certainly he showed far more feeling for several of the individual lions he had killed than for any human being he mentioned. He spoke several times of "my friend, Narrowneck"—a lion he had killed in the Mogollon Mountains of Arizona many years before. He also told of a litter of lion kittens which he had fostered after he had killed their mother. He fed them on milk and cared for them the best he could, only to kill them too when they were grown.

Policeman of the Wild

"Panthers don't get along with us," he said in half explanation. Lilly, it seemed, regarded himself as a policeman of the wild, a self-appointed leavener of nature. Bears and lions were endowed with a capacity to wreak evil. Several times he referred to panthers as the "Cains" of the animal world. They couldn't help that, but evil they were and so should be destroyed.

During a pause in his recital, as we stopped for breath on a little ledge high above the river, I asked him if he thought that all bears and mountain lions should be killed. He didn't answer my question for three hours, nor give any indication that he had heard me in all that time.

"A man has to be accepted into the family," he said irrelevantly. "You can't live with them and you can't hunt them if you aren't a member." Apparently Ben Lilly meant, as I gathered from his later remarks, that he regarded himself as a full-fledged member of the wildlife community. He professed quite simply to speaking the language which the animals understood.

He recounted how he had addressed a bear which was brought to bay on a rock. Just before he drove his hunting knife, tied to a long pole, into the bear's side, Lilly addressed his victim in a court-room manner: "You are condemned, you black devil. I kill you in the name of the law." And, so he said, the bear answered: "I cannot escape and I die."

This verbal exchange with animals, dying and otherwise, punctuated Ben Lilly's account many times. I had the distinct feeling that he talked with them more easily than with men, and that if I had been one of his lion dogs I'd have learned even more.

It goes without saying that his ideal was the wild. The ways of people and of towns he understood practically not at all. Most of his life he had spent on the trail, always by himself except for his dogs. After three days with him I was convinced that he could talk with animals. I am not certain of the contrary even now.

As we climbed the rocky trails above the lowlands, striking ever farther back into the brushy hills, I wondered where we were going. I had made no preparations for an extended trip; I supposed we were just going for a walk. I hadn't brought with me so much as a bag of lunch.

Lilly, in spite of his age and seeming feebleness, climbed steadily, talking as he climbed. The farther we got away from the scattered ranches, the wilder the country became, the more he seemed to fit with his surroundings. Where I had first met him, with his back against an adobe wall, he had appeared to be a broken and dying old hunter who had been on his last chase. Now, as we paced along a cow trail between the piñon and juniper hills, he seemed to suck new life from the odor of the woods.

In His Element

The farther we went, the lighter was his step. He swung his head from side to side as he moved among the trees, as though taking the wind in animal fashion, and his pale-blue eyes read at a glance every detail of the trail. This was his element; he was indeed a part of it. Every bird that flitted past, every ground squirrel, seemed to know him and to recognize him as a creature of the wild. I was the outsider.

But fortunately the old man seemed unaware of my presence, although he kept up a steady run of talk. I had the feeling that he usually talked out loud to himself when he was in the field. It also began to dawn on me that Ben Lilly hadn't the slightest intention of returning to his ranch home near Silver City, and that I was on the trail with him certainly for the day, and probably for the night that would follow. A shiver of apprehension spread over me in spite of the hot sun.

Ben Lilly was describing, with gory detail, a grizzly-bear hunt in the state of Coahuila, Mexico: "Old Man Sanborn set me on him. They was grizzlies, four of them, and I tracked them down by myself and killed them. They was desert bears, light-colored with a stripe down their back; but desert or mountain, they didn't get away. I killed the four of them, brought their skins back to Sanborn. Skins don't matter, it's the meat that counts."

X-ray Vision

Fascinated by these bits of philosophy that Lilly wove into his discourse, I almost forgot my apprehensions at being alone with him and so far away from my base. He told me, for instance, that he could see the interiors of animals and men through their skins. Indeed, those penetrating blue eyes might have X-ray vision.

But more than once, Lilly implied that if you kept only the skins of animals you didn't have anything at all. Apparently their hides, and the clothes of men, were simply shabby coverings to conceal what was beneath. A really perceptive person could penetrate this exterior disguise. Why keep the skin of an animal he had hunted down, any more than we would want the clothes of a dead man? Of the thousands of animals that Ben Lilly had killed he had never kept a single skin for himself.

Although he spoke about people much less than he did about lions, it became apparent that his opinion of most humans was very low. He felt rather sorry for them, being confined in houses and in towns where the air was "rancid." The few people he knew in New Mexico, he said, "never took their place."

Advantages of Solitude

It was many hours before I realized what he meant: that they did not take their legitimate place in the scheme of wild things. They didn't fit with the birds and the squirrels. They were not a part of the community. Here was this old man, more lonely, more peculiar than anyone I'd ever met, feeling sorry for me and for other humans because we had not been accepted into the wild community.

Ben Lilly pointed out that there were so many buzzing distractions in a town that a man could never find himself, as he could in the solitude of the woods and mountains. There with the animals, amid the trees and ledges, the soul of a person can develop. Only in such surroundings can a man learn enough to become a member of the community. It became obvious as the afternoon wore on that Lilly and I were traveling, as fast as our legs could carry us and the roughness of the trail would permit, from my community into his.

By late afternoon we had covered eight or ten miles of the rugged, dry terrain of the foothills. The old hunter seemed to be showing his infirmity for the first time since we started. His breath came in whistling gasps and his talk dwindled to a few disconnected sentences.

He was in the midst of a potent bit of philosophy that would have done credit to Thoreau, when he stooped forward at a little bend in the trail with a quick movement as though he had found a valuable coin among the pine needles. He pointed a weather-beaten hand at an indistinct track or depression which he seemed to see—pointing more to assure himself than to mark out anything for me to look at.

"He's here again," he muttered beneath his breath, and started off diagonally away from the trail with a new burst of energy. He half ran, always bending forward and with both hands extended as though his finger tips were sensitive to what he hoped to see. He apparently was following a trail which only he could make out, though I could see no tracks imprinted in the debris on the forest floor. From time to time he pushed his battered old black sombrero back on his head and wiped his ruddy-brown forehead with one sleeve. After each of these momentary halts he started off again, sure of himself for a few yards, then hesitating once more.

I had seen dogs trail this way when the track was difficult, but Lilly didn't appear to be looking at any particular place on the ground in front of him. It seemed as though some sixth sense was guiding him more unerringly than the scenting ability of a keen-nosed hunting dog.

A Bizarre Performance

From his peculiar actions, I judged that we were following a bear or a panther, but we had no hounds with which to track down the scent and we had no gun to shoot the animal if we caught up with him. I had heard marvelous stories of Ben Lilly, but never in my wildest expectations did I visualize a grizzled old man who followed a lion track on pine needles unaided by any dog.

The whole process seemed so bizarre, so out of keeping with reality, that when Ben Lilly paused again, as though in doubt as to which way to go, I ventured one of my rare questions: "What are we after, Mr. Lilly?" Those penetrating blue eyes seemed to bore through me with an almost hostile air, as though he had suddenly become aware of my alien presence in his hunting territory. Every time I looked into those eyes they astounded me. Their mildness was deceiving. The placid expression which they habitually wore concealed an inner man which few if any knew. Tenacity, stubborness, lust for the kill—all these properties were there, but invisible.

Following Phantom Trail

Now, in those far-off hills with the shadows of the afternoon slanting long across the trees on the slope where we stood, the eyes looked almost frightening. I had the fleeting thought that the next time the old man turned his back I would slip away and make my way back to town somehow. Ben Lilly was a madman and was following a phantom lion track into unknown places.

In those seconds when his eyes bored into me as if I was the hunted, Ben Lilly seemed to recall who I was and why I had come. "It's him. He lives here," he answered enigmatically—and turned once more to resume the track.

I fell in behind him and followed step for step. When he swung his head, with his shaggy white hair bulging from beneath his old hat, I swung my head too. When he dropped to one knee to examine the ground I looked there also. If I were to learn the lore of the wild, here was a wild man who could teach me.

In this manner, then, we traveled across one mountain slope after another, through a low saddle and down into a brushy canyon ringed by ledges of reddish stone. In the gathering twilight we came to where a side gully cut precipitously through, in a shadowy black scar filled with brush and tangled bushes. Lilly, shuffling along the bare rock on the edge of this little side canyon, threw back his head so that the sun showed a ruddy red upon his cheeks and the tip of his nose. As I looked at him from the side, he appeared like an old Dutch burgher, full of the joy of living, who had perhaps taken too much ale.

But Ben Lilly, in spite of the jovial outlines of his fascinating face, was not radiating good humor, at least to the things of the wild. He was still half-crouched forward, swinging his head from side to side to take the wind. He was sniffing like a dog scenting a covey of quail. He uttered a single grunt of satisfaction, as if to say, "I thought so all the time!"

He dropped down below the little ledge of rocks and ran back and forth for a few steps in the brushy gully beneath. It was so dark among the bushes that I doubted whether even he could discern any tracks, no matter how plain they might be. In a moment Ben Lilly was pulling something from beneath a big cedar. It was the leg of a deer, attached by a ragged strip of skin to the rest of the carcass. Next, from beneath the leaves, he uncovered the head of the deer—a buck with stubby horns that were in velvet.

A Lion Kill

Now, coming near in the gloom, I could make out the long sweeps and scrapes of some mighty paw that had gathered up this leafy debris to cover the dead deer. Its stomach was eaten clear away, with portions of the bowels and viscera torn and bloody. This close, I too could smell the stench which Ben Lilly's keen nostrils had caught on the ledge above.

This was a lion kill. It was the first one I had seen, but there could be no doubt of what it was, for there were the cougar's tooth marks and the gashes made by its raking claws on the buck's neck and shoulder. I had heard that lions cover their meat after they have eaten a meal, and the old man had followed some dim trail to this very carcass.

The old panther hunter had whipped out a big clasp knife and was pulling off the sticks and leaves that adhered to the haunch of venison which he held in his hand. With the gleaming knife he trimmed the torn and putrid skin and dried blood from the top of the leg. He sniffed critically at the clean surface which he had laid bare. Again he gave that inarticulate grunt of satisfaction and swung the deer leg to his shoulder. It was almost dark as we climbed out of the brushy little gully and started up a hogback toward the main ridge that towered high above us.

Remarkable Tracking

The old man seemed vastly pleased with himself and resumed a running line of talk, only part of which I could hear as I climbed behind him. "He always goes through that saddle," Lilly was saying as we topped out over the ridge. "Panthers always go the same way."

I didn't realize what a remarkable piece of lion tracking I had witnessed, however, until I too had tried my own hand at it, not once but many times. It also did not occur to me until much later just how strange and peculiar the whole day had been. We had started off without any preparation or supplies. We had headed for an unknown destination which we had never reached. We had followed a phantom lion track which I never saw. We had a haunch of venison without firing a shot or without even carrying a gun. On this whole fantastic hunt I had been with a white-haired old man who, everybody told me, was mad. I certainly had entered a world which few have ever seen.

Scattered clouds obscured the southwestern stars as we dropped down over the main ridge. I could see the old man—looking like a hunchback with the deer leg on his shoulder—outlined for a moment against the twilight arc of the sky. Only by his running talk could I keep track of him in the darkness after that; yet he seemed on familiar ground, and despite his age he went as fast as he had in the full daylight.

At Mouth of Cave

He dropped down below an outcropping ledge on the slope of the ridge, and I heard the haunch of venison hit the leaves as he threw it down. While I stood, wondering where we were, he scraped together a few leaves and sticks and struck a match. By the light of the tiny flame that benign face of his was again brought into relief, and the sight reassured me; pitch blackness and a madman are an awesome combination.

The little fire leaped up through the dry branches that the old man heaped upon it, and I saw that we were at the mouth of a shallow cave. As the flames grew higher and brightened, I made out an old pair of gray trousers hung on a ledge at the rear. The stump of a blackened and wax-spattered candle was mounted on a projection above my head. There were two or three old bags that seemed to contain food, and a couple of flour sacks piled one on top of the other. Ben Lilly had been here before.

At that moment he was pulling a battered skillet from under the leaves at the back of the cave. With clean strokes he whittled slabs of venison from the deer leg by the fire. In a few moments there came the smell of roasting meat and the cheerful campfire warmth reflected from rocky walls.

Hearty Appetite

We ate in silence—slices of venison, and thin oatmeal. There was no sugar, no cream, no leavener but a handful of dirty salt, but the meal tasted delicious.

I was amazed at the amount that Lilly could eat. Chunk after chunk of venison disappeared through his scraggly beard. Without saying so, he seemed to be enjoying himself immensely. I had the distinct feeling that I was the excuse for his going on this excursion which took him away from the civilization he so obviously hated.

Bed of Leaves

Supper done, Ben Lilly simply lay back in the dried leaves by the edge of the fire and was soon snoring contentedly. There was nothing for me to do but follow his example. I was surprised at how comfortable I felt.

The next morning, when I awakened, the old hunter was hunched over the fire as before, cooking more venison in the bent skillet. He voiced no word of greeting; he simply shoved the old skillet toward me for my share of the meat. Before I could eat, however, I had to have water, not only to wash the wood smoke out of my eyes, but for a long drink, for we had had none since the afternoon before. I started off down the ridge toward the canyon below and did not come back for an hour.

When I returned, Lilly was seated in the leaves with his back against the rocky ledge, reading a small and battered Bible which I had not seen before. I ate my breakfast in silence. The old man did not look up, but continued reading half aloud.

Day of Worship

That whole day we sat there in the leaves by the ledge. Ben Lilly never looked at me in all that time, as far as I can remember. He kept on reading, mumbling an occasional passage to himself as if he derived huge satisfaction from mouthing the words. From time to time he turned the dog's-eared pages with an ostentatious flourish.

As before, I hesitated to question him—especially now when he seemed so absorbed in the Bible. As the hours wore on, I fidgeted beside the dead fire. Again I debated taking the back trail and leaving Lilly to his solitude and to his Bible. I had stood up and paced back and forth for the tenth time when the old man, without looking up and seemingly as part of the verse he was reading, said sternly, "Sit down, young man; it's Sunday."

Now, we had started out on this memorable trip on a Friday. So unless, like Alice, of Wonderland fame, I had somehow lost a day, Ben Lilly was mistaken and it was only Saturday. But I didn't argue the point. The ranchers had told me that even as a young man he would neither hunt nor travel on a Sunday; so whenever his dogs treed a lion or a bear that day, they had to keep the beast there until Monday morning.

Lilly passed his Sunday and my Saturday in almost complete withdrawal. I heartily wished he would read his Bible to me, for in that case I might have joined him spiritually. As the day wore on I gained at least a small measure of that utter satisfaction with solitude that was a hallmark of Ben Lilly. There was not a single distracting sight or sound in this wild spot. None of the world's troubles seemed to reach this far. There is no doubt that the aged hunter had found an inner peace which few achieve.

Next morning we arose with the dawn. It was cold and a few cloud wisps showed against the rising sun. Ben Lilly was talkative again. As we prepared our breakfast of venison and oatmeal, he told stories of bear hunts and lion chases all over the West. He spoke of being lured from range to range, from state to state, by tales of bigger and more numerous bruins and panthers. He had hired out to many ranchers to hunt down predators in their sections. Apparently he had made a good deal of money in his life, but had spent very little. It was never the pay that attracted him, however; it was ever the lure of the hunt.

Step Less Certain

We came down out of the low mountains by a different ridge. Even with the path slanting ever downward, Lilly seemed more faltering than he had been on the trip to the cave. He stumbled frequently and shuffled his feet and his knees would hardly bend.

As for his mental processes, if he were mad he was mad in a fixed direction. His every thought was of hunting and the wild. It was all he knew, but he knew that more thoroughly, more intimately than any other man I have ever had the good fortune to meet.

As we paused in the shade of a tree on a rocky point, the old man told me confidentially that he had written two books. I told him I would be very much complimented if he would let me read them, admitting that I too wrote on occasion. He reached into his pocket for his Bible and, opening it, withdrew a piece of brown wrapping paper. Written in a bold hand on the wrinkled scrap was a single line: "Panthers is uncommon cautious." That was all. Ben Lilly returned the folded bit to its place beneath the cover of his Bible with the air of one who had let me see a great treasure. Then, without further comment, he started along the trail.

His Last Hunt

Upon reaching the ranch late that afternoon, we shook hands and parted. Lilly seemed hardly to see me as he turned away. His blue eyes were misty and had a far-away stare as though he saw clear through me to the Great Beyond.

He was not very distant from the hunting grounds where all of us go; for two years later, in the poorhouse on Silver Creek, Ben Lilly, the great hunter, died. He was alone at the end, misunderstood by the humans around him. The wilderness was his world, the wild things must have marked his passing.

As far as I know, the hunt which I took with Ben Lilly was his last. It was one I shall never forget. We tracked down no game and we fired no shot, but I learned more about lions than on any subsequent hunt. Certainly it was on those three days with a half-mad old hunter that I caught the spirit of the chase. I was infected with a little of the energy and single-mindedness that had brought Ben Lilly through a lifetime of tracking to the end of the trail. ❖

MAY 1948

1911: A Record GRIZZLY FIGHT

by James Bryce

THE SHEER violence and shared unpredictability of all bear attacks create their own compulsion within sportsmen. Who among us does not find his eyes speeding over the words as the horrific action plays itself out—even as the brain constantly reminds the reader that "this could be me." This story remains arguably the classic of the genre.

The writing is dated and largely dispassionate, but as one incredible fact piles upon another, the reader's eyes flash across the page ever faster until, with relief, the clinical final paragraph is reached.
—*The Editor, 1998*

Of the many battles in the Yukon between man and grizzly, there was probably never one more dreadful—or closer to the death as far as the man was concerned—than that which James M. Christie, now residing in Winnipeg, Manitoba, fought with one of that savage species at the headwaters of the Stewart River over two years ago. The terrific battle, the eight-mile tramp back to camp with his cheeks torn from ear to mouth, his lower jaw fractured in two places and lying against his breast, his scalp thrown back like a cap, right cheek-bone fractured, right arm broken in several places and covered with ugly wounds of more or less serious nature, while weakened and almost dead from loss of blood—these are things which Mr. Christie can look back to now with wonder that he survived them. And his heroic fight with death at the home of J. E. Ferrell, at Lansing Post, his trip to the Jubilee hospital from Dawson to Victoria, and his final recovery all bear evidence of the wonderful vitality of the man, gained in the healthy outdoor life of a trapper in the northern wilds.

Mr. Christie left Carman for the North in the summer of 1898 and prospected along the Stewart River for a time, taking to trapping when the winter set in and learning the lore of the Northland like a book. At times he acted as guide for government parties, on one occasion meeting Agnes Deans Cameron's party far up the waters of the Mackenzie and on another occasion making a geological survey across the unknown land from Dawson to Edmonton. At this time he met George Chrisfield, and they grubstaked and started north for the Rogue River, where they set up camp about 350 miles east of Dawson in the heart of the wilderness.

During the years up North, Christie had learned many things about the silent places, but his experience with Bruin had inclined him to look upon him as an animal not to be feared. This was the view he held about the grizzly when about the middle of October he struck out over the light snow along the Rogue River to look up trapping possibilities. Before leaving camp he told Chrisfield, his partner, that he would be gone several days, and that if he did not return for a short period he was not to worry about him.

The first day out he shot a moose, and hid it in a ground cache, intending to call for it later. The next day he discovered a small lot of martens and other furs, and concluded that he would move camp and gather them in. He then started for the home camp, and on the way back made a detour to visit the cache where he had left the moose carcass a few days before. On reaching the place, he found the brush which he had piled upon it to keep the ravens off pulled away and the meat all gone. Numerous wolf tracks were visible, and the huge track of a grizzly led from the spot straight across the river.

Christie started on the trail after Mr. Bruin, knowing from previous experience that the marauder would not be very far away. A few timber wolves were on the trail and he fired at one but missed. This, according to the trapper, was the means later of saving his life, as he noticed after missing the wolf that his rifle, which he had packed for some time through the scrub without using it, had the sights improperly adjusted. He stopped at once and fixed them and then proceeded on his way.

Continuing across the river and up the bank on the other side for a distance of 200 yards, he struck into the thick scrub but had not gone more than 20 feet when he heard the unmistakable grunt of an angry bear, and the animal loomed up shaggy and terrible through the scrub not more than 30 feet ahead of him, coming straight toward him. It was the work of a second to swing the rifle upon the oncoming monster and pull the trigger.

The bullet, which was a softnose .303, ranged the length of the animal's body, hitting him in the shoulder, but it did not stop his rush. Before the desperate trapper could fire another shot the beast was upon him with jaws wide open and spouting blood. Christie, however, managed to get in another shot, which struck the bear on the forehead but failed to stop him. The hunter then jumped aside but unluckily became entangled in the scrub and fell with the bear on top of him. Then ensued a terrible fight.

The savage brute succeeded in closing its jaws on the hunter's head, and more through instinct than design, the latter managed to wedge his arm between and to free his head, but not before the bear had broken Christie's jaw in two places, and almost ripped the entire scalp from his head. Christie's arm, too, with which he had saved his head, was crushed and broken in two places, and the animal then sank his teeth in his victim's legs, but Christie, with his arms free, fought desperately and the wounds which the bear had sustained began to take effect. Finally he dropped dead within three feet of the desperately wounded man.

The fight was over. It had not lasted more than a minute, but in that time the grizzly had done terrible damage.

When Christie arose from the fray and prepared to return to the camp eight miles away, he could see only out of one eye and even that was continually filling with blood. His lower jaw was hanging upon his breast, one arm was hanging loose by his side and he could hardly use his legs on account of the terrible pain from his wounds. He realized that his partner would not look for him for some days and concluded that he simply must get back to camp or fall prey to the wolves in the wilderness.

He stopped the flow of blood as best he could, fastening the torn scalp with a handkerchief and placing his coat over his head to keep the cold out. Then came the fight to reach camp.

"I'll never forget that tramp," said Christie, "and the hours of pain and misery which I experienced. The pain and loss of blood weakened me so that at times I staggered and reeled like a drunken man. I finally decided to make a detour of half a mile in order to reach a prospector's cabin which lay on the route to our camp. This cabin, by the way, had been built seven years before by four prospectors, two of whom were Winnipeggers, namely, Jack Patterson and Jack Baker, the former being the son of old Lieutenant Governor Patterson of Manitoba. There I decided to go and die if none came for me, and yet I hoped that my partner would come thither in search of me. However, on arriving there, I managed to write a note with my left hand, and decided to battle along to camp before my wounds stiffened.

"How I ever reached there will always be a mystery to me. However, I did manage to do so, and now almost blind, weak and bleeding from many wounds, and dragging my legs, which had become stiffened from my wounds, I staggered to the door.

"I must have swooned away, for on awaking I found Chrisfield working over me, he having followed the track of blood which I left back to the camp. He made me as comfortable as he could for the night and the next morning my whole body was stiff. We both realized that the only chance left of saving my life was to get me to a trading post called Lansing, about 50 miles away, and accordingly Chrisfield secured two dog teams and some Indian mushers, and, making one of the toboggans as comfortable as possible, placed me upon it. So the lonely procession started out over rough country and unbroken trails, every jolt or jar causing me excruciating agony.

"The snow was too deep to make good sledding, and the rough journey started some of my wounds bleeding again, even the bliss of unconsciousness being denied to me. So I lay hour after hour, waiting and praying sometimes for death to come and put an end to my sufferings.

"Lansing was reached at last. It was a stockade and a few buildings kept by a personal friend of mine named Ferrell. With the help of Mrs. Ferrell they washed my wounds with antiseptic solutions, stitched them up and set the broken bones as best they could.

"There I lay between life and death for two months, and after I had recovered sufficiently we started on the 250-mile tramp to Dawson and thence to Victoria, where at the Victoria hospital, under the care of Dr. O. M. Jones, I underwent several operations and had my jaw fixed properly, as it would not allow me to masticate my food."

Mr. Christie, who has spent over 12 years in the North, has crossed the country from the Bering Sea to Edmonton over land with dog teams and snowshoes most of the way and has had many adventures during his sojourn in the West. He has prospected and hunted over a vast territory, and has had many experiences, but the most exciting and terrible was that in which he tackled a grizzly on the headwaters of the Stewart River. Unable longer to stand the northern climate on account of his hardships, Mr. Christie returned to Manitoba a short time ago and is now employed in the civil service of this province. ❖

APRIL 1911